CRITCS RAVE ABOUT
RONALD L. SMITH'S WORK:

"Lively . . .
Thoroughly entertaining . . .
Perceptively rendered."
—*Booklist* (about *The Stars of Stand-up Comedy*)

"Excellent, a Must-Purchase"
—*Library Journal* (about *Encyclopedia of Comedy*)

"Sincere, funny and richly human."
—*Kirkus* (about *Cosby*)

"Impossible to put down. . . ."
—*Los Angeles Times* (about *The Stars of Stand-up Comedy*)

"Compulsively readable . . .
Informative and often amusing . . .
Delightful and enlightening."
—*Chicago Tribune* (about *Comedy on Record*)

"Smith's unpretentious style is refreshing and
readable, pointed & insightful. . . .
[he] has done a lot of research and it shows."
—*PSA*, Penn State University (about *Poe in the Media*)

Other Books by
Ronald L. Smith

Who's Who in Comedy
The Bedside Book of Celebrity Quizes
The Stars of Stand-up
Comedy on Record
The Cosby Book
Johnny Carson
Let Peas Be with You
Poe in the Media
Sexual Humor
The Stooge Fans' I.Q. Test
Sweethearts of '60s TV
Comic Support
Who'd Say That
Murder in the Skin Trade

THE FIGHT FOR TONIGHT

Ronald L. Smith

A division of Shapolsky Publishers, Inc.

The Fight for Tonight

S.P.I. BOOKS
A division of Shapolsky Publishers, Inc.

Copyright © 1993 by Ronald L. Smith

ISBN 1-56171-212-4

For any additional information, contact:

S.P.I. BOOKS/Shapolsky Publishers, Inc.
136 West 22nd Street
New York, NY 10011
212/633-2022 / FAX 212/633-2123

Printed in Canada

1 3 5 7 9 10 8 6 4 2

CONTENTS

INTRODUCTION

The late night talk shows have seen tragedy and drama, from the death of the man originally slated to host *The Tonight Show*, to the on-air demise of a guest on *The Dick Cavett Show*, to the bizarre kidnap-extortion plot against Johnny Carson.

The late night talk shows have seen feuds and insults, from Jack Paar attacking Steve Allen, to Johnny Carson battling Joan Rivers, to Arsenio Hall trying to "kick ass" with Jay Leno.

Most of all, the late night talk shows have given viewers hours of comedy and entertainment, from the stunts of Ernie Kovacs (yes, at one time a regular NBC late night host!) to the Top Ten lists of David Letterman.

All the brightest moments and darkest secrets of late night TV are in *The Fight for Tonight*, written by America's "King of Comedy Books," Ronald L. Smith, author of a dozen volumes including the Literary Guild-selected biography *Cosby* and the authoritative reference books *The Stars of Stand-Up*, *Comedy on Record* and *Who's Who in Comedy*.

In the course of the past decade, there have been few comedians in late-night who have not been interviewed, chronicled or photographed by Ronald L. Smith. In addition to his books, and his own national comedy magazine, Smith's interviews and photos of comedians have appeared in

People, US, Penthouse, TV Guide and many other publications.

Sometimes Smith has shared the jokes with famous talk show hosts. In one of his guest spots with Steve Allen, Ron got the honor of hearing Steve's "warning bell" go off in response to a Smith quip.

Once Ron mentioned to David Letterman that his fiancée Suzanne Barraza had been a guest during one of Dave's stints on *The $10,000 Pyramid.* "Tell her I'm sorry!" Dave said. "You're right," Ron answered, "she lost." Dave shot back, "They *all* lost with me!"

Smith counts among his favorite show biz moments the time Dick Cavett showed him some magic tricks, including the secret of how to magically keep a wooden cane suspended against his palm.

And there was the time he finished an interview with Joan Rivers and the two left the hotel together: "Heads turned. It was amazing to see the way people recognized her and smiled. Since I was with her, I had the vicarious thrill of being a celebrity — for a moment. I could see how a star would love it. And hate it."

The Fight for Tonight offers insights into the comedy and tragedy of late night television's fierce competition. It's the complete story from the early days of Jerry Lester to the reign of Jay Leno. Like late night TV, this book will entertain you. And it will keep you up all night!

THE
FIGHT
FOR
TONIGHT

CHAPTER ONE:

THE FIRST YEARS: CREESH, CASH AND A CRASH

A dream.

A sudden death.

A wiseguy who wanted a mink coat for his wife.

A busty blonde.

That's how the fight for *The Tonight Show* began.

The dream belonged to NBC executive Sylvester "Pat" Weaver.

He had brainstormed with producer Max Leibman to create *The Admiral Broadway Revue*. Retitled *Your Show of Shows*, it became a huge hit, one of the greatest achievements in early TV history.

Turning his attention from prime time to earlier in the day's schedule, Weaver then envisioned a television show that would mirror the average American's busy morning. It would be a show of news, information and chat.

Some thought Weaver was nuts. At the time, many affiliates did not start their broadcast day till the afternoon or evening, and critics felt that nobody would have time to watch TV as they were rushing to get ready for work.

But on January 14, 1952, *The Today Show* premiered with Dave Garroway as host. Within four months, Weaver had smoothed the show into a success. It was another step in the maturing of television, then known as "the idiot box." Weaver believed "television will make adults out of children," and had begun to prove it.

Ready to completely fill America's waking hours, Weaver now turned his attention from early morning to late night. He wanted something similar to his concept to his *Saturday Night Live*-styled show, *Your Show of Shows*, the one that began as a television version of a Broadway revue.

"It should have the glitter and excitement of Broadway," he theorized, "but the backstage ambience of a party."

He decided to call his late night show *Broadway Open House*.

In a memo, Weaver declared that he wanted to see "a zany, light-hearted show on every night... for people in the mood for staying up."

NBC executives kicked it around.

"Late night?" one of them said at a meeting. "At that hour, people are either sleeping or fucking."

"Most people aren't that lucky," another replied.

"So let's do something for most people," Weaver said. "Look what's on TV if you want to watch it."

There was a lot of nothing. Maybe a sermon, a rendition of "The Star Spangled Banner" and some old movie with Richard Barthelmess in it. And ten channels of static.

NBC's executives began to warm up to the idea.

So did the affiliates, who loved the chance of replacing their dead air or creaky movie re-runs with a money-making program of fresh songs and comedy.

The big question was who should preside over the late night *Broadway Open House*.

One of the early contenders in the fight was veteran nightclub comedian Jan Murray. He was quick with ad-libs, good-looking and capable of keeping a show going. He was also being offered a quiz show called *Songs for Sale* by the rival CBS network.

Jan's agent figured that a late-night TV program was risky business. *Songs for Sale* seemed far more solid, a quiz show that would be simultaneously heard on both television and radio. "I was intrigued by the idea of doing the late-night show," Murray recalls, "I really wanted to do that one. I even did an audition. What they wanted was a party. At a party, you tell anecdotes and top each other with stories. That was my strength. My act included a lot of stories and anecdotes, not just jokes."

Ultimately the young comedian listened to his agent's advice. And he listened to NBC say, "Good luck at CBS. We wish we could've done business with you."

Pat Weaver was not exactly crushed by the loss of Jan Murray. Weaver's notion of comedy was more bombastic; more like the wild man Sid Caesar, who played dozens of characters and brawled through zany sketches on *Your Show of Shows.*

Weaver's sense of the ridiculous seemed to run in the family. Brother Winstead Weaver was a cornball comedian who sang on Spike Jones records and went by the name "Doodles."

Even more far out than "Doodles" Weaver was a guy named "Creesh" Hornsby.

Hornsby was the "wild and crazy" man of his day, a cross between Steve Martin and Pee-Wee Herman. He had a penchant for put-on humor and odd slapstick stunts.

Writer Virginia MacPherson called Hornsby "Hollywood's Newest Rage" in a United Press article on him that ran in March of 1950. Describing his nightclub act, she said "his weird antics" included magic, piano playing, squirting customers with dry ice and shouting "Creesh!" as he magically pulled brassieres out of women's blouses or cranked up a machine on stage that spewed potato chips.

His local TV show in California had a kind of *Pee-Wee's Playhouse* set. There was a lot of thrift-shop garbage strewn around and in moments of hysteria Hornsby would start talking to a large prop grandfather's clock — which would talk back.

Bob Hope was a fan of the wild comedian, calling him "a bright new talent, a guy who is going to have a big future." NBC signed him up to a five-year contract.

He and Pat Weaver were about to fulfill a late-night TV dream.

The May 15, 1950, issue of *Life* magazine devoted a few pages of photos to the crazy new comic, including shots of him wearing a football helmet and literally swinging (via trapeze) from the ceiling of a nightclub. In another photo he put a magnifying TV screen over his face (in case anyone couldn't see his grimaces from the back of the room) and waved a rubber alligator.

Everything seemed a target for Creesh Hornsby. Even death. He got big laughs when he sang the morbid suicide song "Gloomy Sunday" with a megaphone over his head for a tomb-like echo.

Hornsby was "the craziest thing turned loose around Hollywood in many a moon," Virginia MacPherson declared. She added, "He's only 26. Gosh only knows what he'll think up when he's been around longer."

Given a job old pros in the business had been fighting for, Creesh offered his gratitude to Weaver and NBC. He brought his wife and three kids to New York with him. With all the excitement of hosting a new late night TV show, Hornsby might have expected to feel butterflies inside, but what he was feeling was something different.

Variety headlined it: "Don 'Creesh' Hornsby Dies of Polio Attack on Eve of TV Preem."

It was May 22, 1950.

The premiere of the show was postponed a week, to May 29.

Then the battle to save the nightly show began.

There was no way to find a new permanent host

so quickly. Weaver and NBC threw a bunch of guest stars into the night. The chat show team of "Tex and Jinx" was quickly booked. The mild-mannered stand-up comic and actor Wally Cox was pushed out on stage for a few days. Martin and Lewis were brought in as hosts, with Jerry pulling a "Creesh" Hornsby stunt and trying to break the "unbreakable glass" being touted by one of the show's sponsors.

Agents and comedians fought for the chance to get in a word with Pat Weaver or David Sarnoff, who was the head of RCA, the company that owned NBC at the time. The fight to become the new host produced immediate bitterness and confusion.

Some executives wanted Martin and Lewis, but the hot comedy team was already over-extended with nightclub deals and appearances on *The Colgate Comedy Hour.* Some big-money men figured Martin and Lewis were worth pursuing at any cost, a high-energy act that could easily play off guest stars and ad-lib fresh material five nights a week. Others argued for little Wally Cox, an acquired taste perhaps, but stable, quiet and easily tolerable night after night.

Meanwhile the only regulars the show had were band leader Milton DeLugg, and the announcer, Wayne Howell.

While agents hurriedly pushed their clients at Pat Weaver, the exec tried to ignore the hype and think of someone who he knew in his gut would be right.

He wanted a comedian he felt could think on his feet, produce the kind of unpredictable corn that was the style of a Creesh Hornsby or Jerry Lewis, and yet have enough smarts and panache to go "on with the show" no matter what.

Jerry Lester was a top-banana comic with ten years of experience. Born in Chicago on February 16, 1910, he had attended Northwestern University and studied ballet with Marcel Berger and voice with

Alexander Nakutin. He was a smart guy. But he was also down-to-earth, and soon developed a comedy act that led to a summer replacement series for Bob Hope on radio in 1940.

The 40's were a good time for Jerry. He recalled: "It was the period of the big bands, big nightclubs, and big columnists like Winchell, Sullivan, Lyons, Earl Wilson... showgirls and millionaire big spenders and gangsters like Al Capone who threw waiters $100 tips. My show played the Capital, The Roxy and the famous Hollywood Restaurant. I got about $7500 a week then, which was big money... I worked The Latin Quarter. It was run by Lou Walters, the father of Barbara Walters... Opening night I slipped and hit my head on the piano, but was so hyped up, I didn't notice, till someone called out 'Jerry your head is bleeding.' I put my hand up, it came away red, I showed it to the audience and said, 'What else can I give you?'"

Pat Weaver enjoyed Lester's antics but was especially impressed with Lester as a master of ceremonies at The Latin Quarter. That clinched him as the man to host *Broadway Open House*.

To Jerry Lester, it was all just a joke. He recalled that at the time he was enjoying the good life of a prosperous nightclub comic. He was living in "an apartment at 40 Central Park South, the ritziest spot in town, ten rooms on the 12th floor... " Sure, he was hearing the rumors about late night TV, but Lester was too busy hitting the late night hot spots in New York to spend time watching some ghosty picture on a tube at that hour.

He remembered hearing something about Creesh Hornsby: "The guy died a week before the first announced show was to go on the air. There was a panic." But the panic didn't concern him. Until now.

"One day my wife Alice began badgering me to buy her a mink coat. I asked, 'How much is it?' She said, 'Forty-five hundred.' At that moment, Pat Weaver called on the phone... he wanted me, he said the fellow that was to go on had died. I said, 'Why didn't you tell him not to?'"

"Pat asked how much would I charge to go on for a week. I turned to Alice and said, 'How much is that coat? Forty-five hundred?' I said, 'Pat, I'll go on for three nights only, at $1,500 a night.'"

Substituting on Tuesdays and Thursdays was little Morey Amsterdam, a man with an almost inexhaustible supply of memorized jokes.

Jerry Lester was a big name at the time and critics began to stay up late to watch. As Weaver predicted, Lester had staying power. He attracted some top names and word of mouth began to build.

Lester, who was very much in the style of the successful top-banana comics of the day like Milton Berle and Red Skelton, loaded up his show with the zaniest of antics. The staid *New York Times* reported that Lester's show was "a concoction of music, talk, dance and noise which has a peculiar fascination for a viewer whose resistance is low after a night of watching television."

Jerry's "you hadda be there" style was best described by Broadway columnist Earl Wilson, who loved Jerry's bit as a man with a broken leg playing golf:

"Carefully gripping his imaginary golf club, making sure he had the right hold on the thin air, he drew back, started his swing, kept swinging — and then rolled over on the floor in a heap... This silly piece of business got one of the biggest laughs I'd ever heard a comedian get.

"But the next piece of nonsense got even a bigger roar. Jerry began to juggle five rubber balls. We were all surprised that he was that good. Now he held out still another ball which he was going to add to the bunch he kept bouncing. All of us wondered whether he would be able to handle this extra ball too.

"Jerry finally bounced the extra ball on the floor while we looked on in suspense. It hit the floor with a thick, dull thud — and flattened out until it looked like a cookie. It was a handful of putty that Jerry had shaped to look like a ball. They were howling with laughter when Jerry, with feigned anger, said, 'All right, who threw that matzo ball in here?'"

Lester liked oddball ideas and quirky people. He gave a staff writer's job to a man who walked in with no credentials but the notion that he could probably write funny stuff. The man had come to the interview barefoot. Another strange man around the set was a featured dancer named Ray Malone. He seemed to be able to perform as if his feet were gliding on air. Jerry sniffed the air outside Malone's dressing room and began to realize that what was making the dancer fly was a good supply of marijuana.

The idea of two hosts for a nightly show may have been good in theory, but the friction of one host trying to top the other began to spark. There was anger and jealousy over which guest stars would go on with Jerry or with Morey. There was the tension of coming up with fresh material every night.

Lester, the more physical comic of the two, didn't have to rely on good gags. He could be corny and crazy instead. He could also be pretty crafty. He adopted a clubhouse atmosphere for his show. The people in the audience weren't just a crowd. They were friends and co-conspirators.

When Jerry went to a commercial, that was a cue for his crowd to shout, "Stop, Look and Listen!" His audience became his "bean bag club" and an appropriate "Bean Bag Song" became a feature as he and the crowd swapped choruses. Arsenio Hall, David Letterman and many others would adopt this early late-night idea of making the audience feel like part of a very special gang.

In November of 1950, Morey Amsterdam left *Broadway Open House*, and the feuding and fighting began anew. Once again, comedians and agents besieged Pat Weaver and the NBC talent scouts. There were plenty of would-be deals being thrown around as hungry stars insisted, "I'll host all five nights. And you can pay me just what Jerry gets for three. Is that a bargain or what?"

Various pretenders came and went on the nights Morey had filled, but NBC had what they wanted in Jerry Lester. They were hoping to get him every night of the week.

Jerry had the capacity to not only cavort and carry on, he was a good host who let other comics come on and get laughs, too. Of course, Jerry was a strong personality and rarely had a problem with guests eclipsing him. That is, until he brought in a busty blonde for a walk-on.

It was more like a bounce-on.

Her name was Virginia Ruth Egnor. She tried to make a name for herself by changing it to "Jennie Lewis," but the name wasn't nearly as interesting as her body. A writer on Jerry's show, Lew Meltzer, just called her "Dagmar," and the clubhouse audience and the crowd at home called her fantastic. She didn't give her age or her weight, but all her interviewers were told she had a 39-inch bust. As if they couldn't guess.

She recalls her first night on the show: "All I had to do was bring a sexy evening gown, so I got out my royal blue velvet with the white ermine on top and got right over to the studio. There was no script or anything. They said, 'You just sit there and act dumb.'"

Dagmar was a throwback to burlesque, just a visual joke, a living prop for the comic's double-takes and wisecracks. Before hooking up with Lester, she'd worked on stage with Olsen and Johnson.

Time magazine reported in July of 1951, that she made a lot of money for "breathing... Dagmar sat on a high stool in a low-cut dress and just breathed. Somehow, televiewers liked to look at her. They clamored for more Dagmar."

Eventually she was given a bit more to do. She recited malaprops. "Please don't smoke," she once said, "I'm anemic to it."

Sometimes she'd stand there and read some serious poetry while everyone ogled her. She'd say something and get topped. But the top-heavy Dagmar was soon laughing all the way to the bank. She became the highest-paid person on the show, with the exception of Jerry Lester. "If this is what you get for being dumb," she remarked, "I love it."

Jerry Lester didn't love it. Soon he and Dagmar began to fight for the spotlight. It didn't seem fair to Jerry. He had to jump around and joke. All Dagmar had to do was stand there. If her jokes were corny or stupid, who cared? Only a few stuffy critics complained that this new-fangled television invention had become nothing but a boob tube.

Dagmar huffed that she was just *"acting* dumb. It takes a little talent to do that, you know... I'm a comedienne and not just a hillbilly from [Huntington] West Virginia." She insisted she was a big star. In fact, she was getting bigger every way possible. In *Time,* she said, "My bust is 40 inches." A year later she told the *Daily News* she was "a size 42. When I first came to New York to model blouses, I said I was 39. Man, how I was cheatin' myself."

She said, "I sat for a whole year on a stool with Lester," and now she wanted more. She wanted to move on to theater, to films, and she wanted to give the audience more of herself on television. She got the cover of *Life* magazine in 1951 and her salary zoomed to high the newly formed "Salary Stabilization Board" in Washington, D.C. demanded an investigation of her (along with baseball star Stan Musial.)

The feud between Jerry and Dagmar sizzled on, until finally Jerry had a brainstorm. If he had created some kind of monster by bringing the blonde creature on stage and dubbing her "Dagmar," well, why not simply create another one? One with less of a competitive brain?

Jerry went on the look out for another blonde and found Barbara Nichols, whom he christened "Agathon."

It would be Agathon vs Dagmar, the battle of the blonde Amazons.

Unfortunately for Jerry Lester, there could be no battle without a battlefield. The unthinkable was happening: the ratings were going down.

The early days of television were marked by frantic comics who burned out quickly. Red Buttons was a notorious example. Ed Wynn fretted that he was using up decades of funny business in just a few weeks. He was soon gone. Abbott and Costello's TV show lasted just two years. Even the acknowledged greats would not be spared. *Your Show of Shows*, for example, was off the air after four frantic years.

It hadn't taken very long before the public lost its fascination with Jerry Lester and his brand of antics. *Broadway Open House* had been a flash. Now it was being panned.

Lester was gone by May of 1951, confident that he could walk into something a lot bigger and better.

Dagmar, on the other hand, could not get any bigger and could not get any better. Decades later, she admitted, "I was the biggest thing in the country in 1950." She'd run out of luck afterward: "Everything's happened to me. I've been married twice — I think — been robbed twice, had a fire in my house... I tried out for a couple of commercials but they told me my name was too big." So was everything else: "There's still enough for everyone", she argued.

In 1971 a writer from *Look* magazine tracked her down to her small home in Connecticut. She said, "I wasn't bitter when *Broadway Open House* went off, but I missed it. People keep asking me when I'm coming back. Will you please tell them I'm ready now? And please don't go yet. Stay a while. It's very lonely here."

Jack E. Leonard, the rumbling, mumbling insult comic from the nightclub world was brought in to replace Jerry Lester, but it was too late. On August 24, 1951, *Broadway Open House* a show with some meteoric success, came crashing back down to earth.

Broadway Open House has often been considered, despite its different name, the first *Tonight Show*. But when it left the air, NBC gave up on late night entertainment. *The Tonight Show* would not premiere for three years!

CHAPTER TWO

THE STRUGGLES OF
STEVE AND JACK

Pat Weaver couldn't fight for his late night show; there were so many other wars going on at NBC that he had to put this one on the back burner. He had to fight to retain his power, and that meant pitching prime time ideas and specials.

"It was like a real fight," one executive from that era recalls "In a boxing match, a fighter can win a few rounds and even have the other guy on the ropes. But if he doesn't have that staying power, in the end he gets knocked out. Pat was managing that kind of a fighter with that *Broadway Open House* show.

"So, he had one fighter down. But he still had a winner with *The Today Show* and he had lots of other things going on. So what's a smart manager like Weaver going to do? Demand a re-match? Not right away. You get back on a winning streak with sure things. And then when you convince everyone you're still a winner, then you get your re-match and you learn from your mistakes and you're ready to become champion of the world."

NBC relinquished its late night show to local affiliates. Ironically, ABC's flagship station in New York jumped at the chance to generate a late night show that could go national. They began producing a local show hosted by comedian Louis Nye.

Jerry Lester made some appearances on *The Colgate Comedy Hour* and *Sound-Off Time*. Still under contract to NBC, in June of 1952 he was given a program called *Saturday Night Dance Parade*.

Jack Gould of *The New York Times* reviewed the premiere, noting, "Until this week Mr. Lester reportedly was receiving $3,000 a week while doing nothing more arduous than sitting at home... NBC's judgment in deciding that it would get more for its money by putting Mr. Lester on the air is open to challenge. His return... was as trying and painful a pretense at humor as has been seen this year. Mr. Lester apparently fancies himself as the life of the party who can put together a couple of old jokes and play the Palace. On Saturday he dug out of the files the one about the dumb musician who thought Paganini stood for 'Page Nine.' What's more, he made a production of it. Come on, Congress, get on with that TV investigation!

"Between lulls, Mr. Lester grimaces, gestures, smirks, screams, runs around, falls down, gets up, stands, sings, frowns, leers and sticks his tongue out. Jerry should be enough of a performer by now to face facts. He desperately needs material and, more desperately, stern discipline and direction."

The direction for *The Tonight Show* was, at this point, still aimless. Pat Weaver was waiting for the right time, and the right host.

And waiting to make the move into the big time were Steve Allen and Jack Paar.

In 1950, Steve Allen was slowly making a name for himself in late night entertainment. He was the midnight man at KNX, the CBS radio station in Los Angeles. He had been developing a hip *Tonight Show* formula even then, improvising gags and inviting guests in for some amusing chatter between the songs.

One guest asked, "Steve, do they get this show in Pasadena?"

Steve answered, "They hear it but they don't get it."

Steve was born into a show business family. His parents were the vaudeville team of Montrose and Allen. After Steve's father died, Belle Montrose continued to tour the vaudeville circuit, leaving her young son with relatives. It was a lonely and stressful life for him.

The shy young man moved to Phoenix when his asthma began to act up. He attended Drake University on a journalism scholarship and returned to Phoenix where he briefly attended Arizona State Teachers College. He dropped out and joined KOY radio, where he remained, his asthma preventing him from completing Army service.

In 1943 he teamed with Wendell Noble for a California radio show called *Smile Time* and then went out on his own. He was hired as a disc jockey, not as a comedian, but developed a subtle style of in-joke humor that attracted attention. Under the station manager's nose and just past his ears, Steve Allen by the cleverness of his work and the geniality of his personality turned a mundane music show into something exciting and new.

Steve brought in a live studio audience. When a guest failed to show up or there was nothing interesting on the hit parade, Steve would plunge into the audience and conduct ad-libbed interviews. He also began to spend time creating sketches and routines.

In the opinion of many, what was going out over KNX in Los Angeles was actually the pioneering audio version of *The Tonight Show*, far closer to the format popularized by Carson, Letterman and the rest than the show Jerry Lester presided over, *Broadway Open House*.

Big stars began to show up on Steve's show, whether it was Jackie Gleason joking around or Al Jolson offering songs. When Frankie Laine turned up one night, he and Steve got into an argument about song writing. Steve pointed out that thousands of people had at least one good song in them but the cliquish music business made it impossible for the average person to break in.

Steve said it was easy to write songs but impossible to get them published.

Laine disagreed and, as the talk heated up, Steve boasted that he could knock out a song a day: 365 of them. In fact, he then declared that he could probably do 365 in one week! Laine leaped at this crazy disc jockey's remark and was ready to bet a thousand dollars that Steve couldn't come up with fifty songs a day for a week.

This was the first famously "outrageous stunt" of Steve's career, and all of Los Angeles paid attention. Steve stationed himself in the window of a huge Hollywood music store and began knocking out the tunes.

"I'm best known for comedy," Steve once told the author, "but my real gift is music." He proved it way back then by winning the bet with Frankie Laine and putting his name on 365 songs.

He would later enter the *Guinness World Book of Records* as the most prolific song writer of all time. He's authored musicals (from a version of *Alice in Wonderland* to shows on Sophie Tucker and Fatty Arbuckle) as well as several pop standards including "Gravy Waltz," "Picnic" and "This Could Be the Start of Something Big."

But even then, it was the comedy that made Steve's reputation. The songs were secondary to the stunt. Steve pulled more stunts on the show and pulled laughs out of nowhere, as evidenced by this ad-libbed interview with a model named Sue England:

Steve: Sue England? That's what we should have done years ago. What do you do, Sue?

Sue: Oh... modeling.

Steve: You do look familiar. Have I seen you on

any shirt labels or anything... you never know when you're going to run into people, do you? When *were* you run into last?

Sue: I don't know how to answer that!

Steve: I hardly knew how to ask it. And I am sorry that I did. Do you model for an agency, Sue?

Sue: No, I model shoes for the manufacturer.

Steve: Well, he's wasting the rest of you, I'll tell you that. I'm explaining to the folks at home that Miss England is an attractive lady. She is wearing some very unusual green shoes. She seems to have *three* of them here! Oh, no, your legs were crossed. I see... What about the dress, where did you get that?

Sue: My fiancé gave it to me.

Steve: Nuts... and the blouse?

Sue: It's all one piece.

Steve: Well, I hope it stays that way. Those are very pretty shoes. They're a vivid green. What shade of green would you call that?

Sue: Kelly.

Steve: It looks more like pool table to me. It fits very well around the cue ball, too. Now, the color of the skirt, what would you call that?

Sue: Well, it's a drab green.

Steve: Grab, did you say? Oh, drab.

Sue: Olive drab.

Steve: Well, olive pretty drab, myself...

At a time when radio hosts delivered formula introductions and all byplay between the guests and the master of ceremonies was carefully scripted, Allen's style of stream-of-conscious puns, whimsy and silliness was something very new.

His late night series was such a success he was given a prime-time radio slot and, in November of 1950, a ticket to New York, then "television city." Steve tested video with quiz show hosting *(Songs for Sale)*, filling in for Arthur Godfrey and other CBS stars, and ultimately starring on his own *Steve Allen*

Show. It was a daytime show. Oddly, Steve was a pioneer here, too. It seemed that most late night hosts (including Paar, Carson, Griffin, Cavett and Letterman) would start out with a daytime program.

The Steve Allen Show premiered on July 30, 1951, and was seen at noon five days a week. *Time* magazine was already impressed: "He is getting a lot of laughs, good reviews, $2000 a week for playing one of the simplest (and most difficult) roles: that of the natural, nice guy who occasionally comes out with a funny crack."

But, like most late night hosts who followed, Steve couldn't generate a big daytime audience. The critics loved him but the ratings were disappointing. Steve became one of the panelists on the quiz show *What's My Line?* He soon became the stand-out, coming up with funny ad-libs and creating the catch phrase "Is it bigger than a breadbox?"

He would be asking questions like that until NBC asked a question of its own: "Why not host a new late night talk show?"

Around the same time, another man was beginning to get some attention as a potential talk show host.

Jack Paar was born in Canton, Ohio and raised in Jackson, Michigan. While Steve Allen battled asthma in childhood, Paar suffered through tuberculosis, conquering it and toughening his body with athletics, becoming a formidable wrestler on the high school team. Possessing both shyness and ambition, Paar found the perfect outlet on local radio, where he could derive fame from a comfortably unseen position. He moved on to stations in Pittsburgh and Cleveland. Like Steve Allen, he married early and divorced, finding a lasting relationship with his second marriage.

It was during World War II that Paar developed his skills as a stand-up comedian. He began as an mc for Special Services shows and between the acts sharpened his material. While Bob Hope and the other comics were gentle in their gags about Army life, since Paar was closer to the soldiers his digs were stronger and more accurate:

"The captain himself is censoring the mail again this week — so let's cut down on the big words... The USO girls were supposed to do the 'Dance of the 'Virgins' for you, but they went to the Officers' Club last night and broke their contract.'"

From the stage, Paar began to feel a sense of power. While his shyness and sensitivity would remain at the core of his personality, the tough shell of a confident wiseguy began to form.

One night a show he was hosting was being held up for the arrival of a Navy bigshot. As the enlisted men squirmed in their seats, Paar fumed. Finally, the commodore arrived with a shapely girl on his arm.

"You wouldn't think one man and a broad would hold up five thousand men," Paar said.

For gags like that, he was threatened with a court-martial.

Word began to spread about the brash comedian and he got some write-ups in the press. Sidney Carroll covered him in an issue of *Esquire*, and that was the springboard for his post-Army career. As he recalls, "This was interesting, because none of the people from whom I received these offers had ever seen me perform." But they had read *Esquire*.

Jack moved to Hollywood and became the wise-cracking mc of *Variety Time*, a quickie movie from RKO that was just an excuse for the studio to recycle some old comedy shorts from Edgar Kennedy and Leon Errol, and use up some musical numbers spliced out of recent films. Paar's quietly glib style was already in place as he glided through the opening monologue:

"Hello. I'm your master of ceremonies for the next hour. I've been in Hollywood for some time, but this is my first appearance on the screen.

"You know Hollywood, one day you're putting your footprints in cement, the next day you're back mixing it.

"I'd like to tell you folks a little bit about what it's like to have a movie contract here in Hollywood. You come out here, and it can change you all around. First they part your hair on the left side, then they part it on the right side. They found that I look best with the part running from ear to ear.

"It looks sort of nice, except when you talk to me you find yourself whispering in my nose.

"When I first signed a contract they thought of me as the second Jimmy Stewart. There's only one thing wrong, they're not through using the *first* Jimmy Stewart.

"As a matter of fact, I can't understand why they don't use me in pictures, really. Because I've got the normal amount of teeth. 32. Four on top, 28 on the bottom. I know it looks like I have 34 but the two in back are Chiclets. Anyhow, my name's Jack Paar, you all know who you are, so let's get on with the show... "

Jack Benny, impressed by Paar's World War II performances, not his movies, took an interest. While Steve Allen and Johnny Carson were still toiling on local radio, Paar was about to get a big chance in front of a national audience. Benny recalled that Paar was "bright and brash... I persuaded NBC to take him as my summer replacement in radio in 1947. He was wonderful."

In New York Paar met up with a funnyman named Allen. *Fred* Allen. Paar told the radio star, "You are my god!" Fred dourly answered, "There are five thousand churches in New York, and you have to be an atheist."

The names of Fred Allen and Jack Benny had become linked through their famous mock feud on radio. The young upstart Jack Paar proved to be more than their equal. He could start feuds with practically everyone! He jeered at his staff, "Writers are the cheapest commodity in the business. I can buy and sell you guys."

Paar was earning $750 a week. The writers earned a fraction of that, but they all walked out on him. Jack couldn't understand it. After all, he had been anointed as the new comedy genius by Jack Benny, and he had rubbed elbows with Fred Allen.

According to one of Jack Benny's writers, Benny soon got a good idea of just how Paar really felt. Paar had been interviewed by *Time* magazine, "and in this article Paar was quoted as saying... as near as I can recall... 'I intend to bring a much needed fresh approach to radio humor. I don't want to do any "old hat" comedy of the type that's being done by Fred Allen and Jack Benny.'

"A few days after this appeared in print, Benny received a letter from Fred Allen. Jack opened the envelope, and it contained nothing but the page from *Time* magazine with Jack Paar's quote underlined and a note scribbled by Fred across the page saying, 'Dear Jack, I'm so happy that you told me not to make any ad-libs at the expense of this nice kid. F.A.'"

Paar claimed to have been misquoted and Jack Benny forgave him.

Paar struggled on, his feuding and fighting style not helping him get bookings. His movie career continued to sputter with a few minor parts in forgettable films. One of his few highlights was the chance to work in a Marilyn Monroe movie, but true to form, he was only impressed with himself. He came away huffing in disgust, especially annoyed that he had to waste time doing some cuddly publicity photos with her.

Despite his lack of success, Paar always considered himself a better comic than a most anyone else out there. In fact, he truly detested some of the old-timers. Of Groucho Marx he recalled, "He bored me." Conversation with Groucho was just "a tiresome monologue, consisting mostly of puns... he was neither known for his wit nor his kindness."

Paar was back East in the early 50's, still looking for that big television break. CBS seemed the network most interested in him, but if he'd asked around, he would've heard some bad things about the place.

Steve Allen, for instance, was not happy with CBS. Steve had been aggravated to see *Songs for Sale* and then *The Steve Allen Show* taken away from him amid network scheduling chess games. He was restless with *What's My Line?* and his local radio show. He was more than willing to leave CBS.

Over at NBC, the local New York affiliate, an executive was looking for a way of snagging some extra money with a late night show. The company that brewed Knickerbocker Beer was sponsoring Louis Nye's show at ABC, and with the proper inducement, they might be willing to put their money behind NBC instead.

An NBC executive, Ted Cott, was a big Steve Allen fan. He brewed the deal: NBC + Steve Allen + Knickerbocker Beer = a brand-new late night TV show.

CHAPTER THREE

THE START OF
SOMETHING BIG

In July of 1953, Steve began his late night show, abetted by announcer Gene Rayburn, Bobby Byrne and his orchestra and the singing duo of Steve Lawrence and Eydie Gorme.

After a year, the ratings for NBC's local affiliate had confirmed that Steve Allen was a hit. Watching with avid attention were Pat Weaver and a new young television programmer, Mort Werner. They knew the time was right for Steve to go national.

On September 27, 1954, *The Tonight Show*, hosted by Steve Allen, premiered. As for the regulars, the main change was in the band. Skitch Henderson was now conducting the orchestra, which included a trumpet player named Doc Severinsen.

With the show now on coast to coast, Steve discovered how much he had to fight just to keep control over *Tonight*.

Some executives, jockeying for position at NBC, began to complain about the show and offer ideas for "creative improvements." One exec, working with a favorite agent, tried to kick Steve Lawrence and Eydie Gorme off the show, convinced that his choices were much better. Another exec, impressed with the announcing of Gene Rayburn, felt the show would be better if Rayburn hosted lengthy news segments and the comic "fluff" was cut down.

Each time one of these Machiavellian plots surfaced, Steve had to deal with it, this in addition to his own pressures as the host and main creative force on the show. Sometimes he was able to quash a scheme on his own. Other times he had to carefully find an ally, or go to the top and Pat Weaver, to keep the ruinous distractions from destroying his show.

It got pretty crazy backstage at *The Tonight Show*, and the more it did, the crazier it got in the spotlight. Steve let off steam with a variety of wild stunts, sometimes veering into a "the hell with it" attitude that was outrageously "un-show biz" for its time.

In an age of rigidly programmed and carefully scripted entertainment, a time when even quiz show contestants were rehearsed so that hosts could come up with "spontaneous" ad-libs, here was Steve Allen bringing his cameras outside the studio, hailing a cab, throwing a salami in the back seat and shouting, "Grand Central Station, and step on it!"

He jumped into a tub full of Jell-O. He festooned himself with tea bags and dove into a huge cup of hot water. He had the camera scan the street below and focus on passersby, while he ad-libbed hilarious comments about who they might be and where they might be going.

Steve developed a cult that savored every offbeat off-the-cuff remark. Gags that other comics might sweat to create and then proudly present in a monologue were quickly thought of and discarded in an aside by Steve Allen. One night when someone handed him a guest's new record album, he held up the disc and said "Look, a licorice pizza." Not long after, a fan opened a chain of record stores called Licorice Pizza.

Cultists even made catch phrases out of nonsense words. One night Steve opened the monologue by cackling, "Schmock! Schmock!" Nobody knew what it meant, but it sounded funny. It became a way for cultists to identify themselves to each other, the mating call of the late night Steverino fan.

For the record, "Schmock! Schmock!" was exactly what it seemed to be: a way to get the Yiddish word "schmuck" past the censors. It was a line in a joke Steve had heard backstage one night. The phrase appealed to his sense of the ridiculous so much that he spontaneously began using it.

It was the story about a pair of middle-aged Jews from the garment district, Sol Pearlman and his partner, Joel, who were enjoying the sunshine of Miami Beach.

"You know what I'd like," Joel said, fingering a tall glass of vodka and Cel-ray, "I'd like to go on a Safari!"

"Don't be a schmuck," his partner Sol said. "What do you know from such a thing? Your toupee will fall off. You're too old! You're five feet tall and completely out of shape! You've been supervising the people making the gabardine for the past two decades! Don't be a schmuck!"

But Joel wanted a moment of glory, he wanted some excitement for his dull, safe life. And so he had his head fitted for a pith helmet (bought retail, no less), took a plane to Africa, bought a big gun he could barely lift, hired a guide and a dozen natives to carry the supplies and began a leisurely jaunt across the rugged terrain of sand and rocks.

"Tell me when there's a lion," Joel told the guide, "And I'll give him such a blast with this gun, he'll be dead. Or worse! Hah, I'll show my partner, Sol! He thinks I'm a schmuck? Wait till I bring back a big game trophy!"

Joel didn't have long to wait. On the second day out, a giant lion appeared from behind some rocks, roaring and snarling. The natives began running. The guide shouted, "There's the lion! Shoot it! Shoot it!"

As the lion raced toward him, Joel looked the beast in the eye, and fainted.

The lion raced right past the prostrate garment

worker and continued to chase the fleeing members of his safari.

When Joel woke up, he was alone, lost, his men long gone. "And I thought I was going to silence my partner, Sol," Joel grumbled. "He called me a schmuck, that wiseguy. Well, I'll get him back, yet!"

Joel trudged for days and days across the scorched plains without food or water. Finally he collapsed. As his partner had predicted, he'd even lost his toupee. The sun was burning down on his bald head. He squinted up and saw a pair of vultures circling above him.

They swooped down onto his shoulders.

And then they croaked, "Schmuck! Schmuck!"

And... when Steve happened to do that vulture cry on the air that night, he created an instant catch phrase. There would be many more. There were even catch noises. To cover the awkwardness when he might have to cough, Steve kept a siren whistle on his desk. As he coughed, he grabbed the siren whistle in his fist and give it a whizzing blow. Now whenever he coughed and then gave out with the whistle-wheeze, it seemed just part of his deliberately disruptive zaniness.

Also on the desk was a slap-bell, the kind used by hotel clerks. Whenever things got too wild, Steve would slam down and give a few rings to bring things back to order. Some considered it a great achievement to get "belled" during an appearance with Steve.

The gags moved fast and furious, and often Steve ad-libbed lines that even surprised himself. That was the origin of his chuckling "heh-heh" laugh that became an imitated trademark. Sometimes he'd give that chuckle for no apparent reason as he was about to answer or ask a question. He admits, "What I am laughing at is usually a double meaning that has suddenly occurred to me."

He adds, "I have the habit of digressing for an ad-lib and sometimes I have to consciously stop it so that it doesn't distract from the conversation itself." He can put on the skids, but not without an inward chuckle.

Steve developed favorite recurring bits, from routines as a nonsensical sports broadcaster to announcements from a late night pitchman (the ancestor of Johnny Carson's Art Fern), to deliberately angry readings from the "Letters to the Editor" page of New York's *Daily News*.

He routinely made random phone calls, often coming up with the kind of comedy no writer could think up. Once he called up an audience member's mother, only to have the woman insist she didn't know anybody named Art Goldstein. She did admit, "I have a son *Arthur* Goldstein... "

Allen's regulars, Don Knotts, Louis Nye and Tom Poston, were most prominent in "Man in the Street" interview segments, with Steve as straight man. In a variation on Fred Allen's radio segment ‹Allen's Alley,› Steve confronted his guests with an improbable question of the day.

Don Knotts, then a struggling stand-up comic with a few nervous spoonerism routines, always played a nervous type.

Steve: Good evening, sir. What is your name?

Don: (twitching and trembling) K.B. Morrison.

Steve: And what do you do for a living, Mr. Morrison?

Don: I'm a munitions and bomb-disposal expert.

Steve: I see. By the way, what do the initials K.B. stand for?

Don: Ka Boom!

Louis Nye was a regular playing the fey and minty Gordon Hathaway, simpering ad-executive. In a typical segment, Steve wanted to know, "What makes you laugh?" Gordon was ready with an answer.

Louis: Hi ho, Steverino... my sense of humor is different from other people's. I've found that I just don't laugh at the same things everybody else laughs at.

Steve: What does everybody else laugh at?

Louis: At me...

Tom Poston was not as quotable as Don Knotts or Louis Nye, but may have been the funniest of the lot. He simply played a literal lamebrain who not only couldn't answer a question, he couldn't remember his own name.

There were other members of Steve Allen's comedy "gang." One of Steve's writers, Bill Dana, soon created a sensational new character, a little fellow who would come in and announce... "My name... Jose Jimenez." The comedy interviews between Steve Allen and Bill's Jose character had nothing to do with Hispanic dialect. The gags were a hip new form of video vaudeville:

Steve: Congratulations on your tremendous feat.

Bill: Thank you, but they're only size eight.

Steve: How come you stayed under water for 84 days?

Bill: I didn't want to come up before the submarine...

Steve: Tell me, did you begin to hate your friends during that time?

Bill: One time. During the third riot.

Steve: As an executive officer, you had a specific assignment?

Bill: No, I had the Atlantic assignment.

Steve: In those 84 days that you were submerged, did you have any mechanical troubles?

Bill: Only with the ballast valve, the one that lets you go up.

Steve: How long did you have that problem?

Bill: 83 days.

Another favorite in Steve's interview spots was

loopy Dayton Allen, a goofy cross between Ed Wynn and Steve Martin, a man prone to wildly ridiculous observations ending with a cry of "Whoooyyyy not!"

In one typically silly routine, Steve interviewed Dayton the criminologist.

Steve: What makes a criminal tick?

Dayton: A criminal tic? I don't know about criminal tics. I seen some gangster cockroaches and very mean fleas, but never a criminal tic!

Steve: What is your advice for dealing with criminals?

Dayton: The only way to combat criminals is by not voting for them... The man who kills his entire family would probably some day commit a serious crime!

In the 70's Johnny Carson would often book wacky experts, like Dr. Stillman, the advocate of a water diet. One of Steve's favorites was advice-giving Professor Voss. On one show, Voss sat in a tub of water with chunks of ice floating in it. He declared, "The first thing you must do when you get up in the morning is drink four quarts of water!"

In the 90's David Letterman would favor anarchistic "network time killers" like segments from movies and plays mechanically recited by stagehands. Steve favored real, and really strange, people, like a man who monotonously sang songs without veering from the single note he had mastered, an A.

The mythology over so many years is that Steve's wit is always gentle and his sense of humor mild. It's true that he avoids gratuitous profanity. He also has the ability to quickly tuck an ad-lib from tongue safely into cheek if he thinks it might hurt someone's feeling. But Steve has always been capable of biting satire and this was especially evident during his years on *The Tonight Show*.

It was not Dennis Miller or David Letterman but Steve Allen who conducted "The National Jerk Test."

Among the top questions for determining if a viewer is a true jerk, Steve wanted to know:

1. Have you ever thrown a roll of toilet paper at a football game?

2. Have you ever honked at the driver in front of you within five seconds after a traffic light turns green?

3. Do you cheer wildly when someone merely mentions your home city or state in a theater, TV or radio studio?

4. Have you ever sought free advice from a doctor or lawyer at a party?

5. Have you ever boasted of fictitious sexual exploits?

6. Have you ever boasted of real-life sexual exploits?

7. When you leave the table in a restaurant to go to the toilet, do you feel obliged to say, "I gotta go shake hands with my best friend," or anything else of an allegedly witty nature?

8. Have you ever spent more than 30 seconds telling someone else how drunk or high you had gotten on the previous evening?

9. Do people occasionally suggest to you that you talk too loud?

10. For men: Do you wear white socks with dark clothes, in the absence of a foot infection?

For women: If you weigh over 170 pounds do you ever wear tight slacks?

The repressive 50's was a time when Lucille Ball could not say she was "pregnant" on her sitcom. Many of Steve's ad-libs were pretty risky for the time. He was talking about religion one night, beginning, "Jesus was looking for a fig." Then he mused, "One would wonder why he didn't know where it was, considering all he had going for him."

While Steve was always prone to mutter "all seriousness aside," and ad-lib light and funny material,

He was the talk show pioneer who wasn't afraid to bring controversial and intellectual guests to late night. While he gave many comics a break and sat behind the piano to accompany a variety of jazz and pop vocalists, Steve also made a point of booking writers, poets and artists. He brought on Ben Hecht, Carl Sandburg and Salvador Dali. One evening might feature Zsa Zsa Gabor and Woody Herman and the following night, a panel discussion of the narcotics epidemic, complete with doctors and junkies.

For the first time, there was such a thing as the "late night junkie," the person who needed that "fix" of laughs and songs before bedtime. Steve was really the first host to develop a cult following, becoming a nightly habit for people who had tuned in to his wavelength and become addicted to his fascinatingly quick mind and his genius for being compelling whether in a serious or silly mode.

Steve has always been known for humility. Lenny Bruce publicly stated that in all of show business there was nobody as good and as moral as Steve Allen. But even Steve could not be immune when the adulation for him as the hit *Tonight Show* yielded offers for movies, record albums and autographs.

Watching from the sidelines, or at least from the orchestra, was band leader Skitch Henderson. He complained to writer Robert Metz that Steve "took on the aura of a star within a few months," and was sometimes imperious with the staff. Henderson insisted that Steve, not trained in the art of reading and writing music, owed a great deal to him for orchestrating his simple melodies for the *Tonight Show* band to play. He also declared that Steve was taking credit for little play-ons and bits of incidental music generated by Henderson and the band and copyrighting them under his own name.

Once Steve had second thoughts about a publicity photo of himself that the show's publicist was sending out. He brought the man into his office and insisted that all the photos be recalled. The publicist tried to explain that asking for the photos back from the various newspaper and magazine editors would look suspicious, and that some editors might deliberately use the photo instead.

Steve disagreed. He dictated a long letter that was duly sent out to the editors, and felt vindicated when he began receiving piles of envelopes containing the offending unflattering photo.

It was no surprise when the publicist left the show. The friction between a star and his lackeys was common, and within the pressure of a five-night grind, it was surprising that more staff members didn't find themselves out on the street.

Staff members were getting annoyed at another tall talk show host in town, Jack Paar, who in 1954 began to host *The Morning Show* for CBS. Compared to Jack, Steve wasn't *that* bad. And he certainly wasn't the cold-eyed dictator that Ed Sullivan was. Sullivan ruled his show and was ruthless in demanding that staff and guests conform to his standards of dress and deportment. The most famous example was when Sullivan ordered his cameramen to train their cameras on Elvis Presley from the *waist up only.*

While a guy like Lenny Bruce could perform on Steve's show, and Allen became known for allowing a wide range of iconoclastic comedy on *The Tonight Show*, Sullivan terrorized comedians by sitting, stone-faced, as they went over their monologues, checking every line for possible offenses.

After going through the wringer for an appearance on *The Ed Sullivan Show*, it wasn't surprising to find big stars happy to relax and say, sing or do whatever they wanted in a guest spot across town on *The Tonight Show.*

The feud between Ed Sullivan and Steve Allen

smoldered, flaming each time a guest chose to do both shows. Sullivan, the uncrowned king of television with the most powerful and top-rated show in prime time, roared out his decree: "If you do my show, you don't do *The Tonight Show!*" Sullivan was known for a fist-shaking threat of "You'll never work in show business again!" and being able to back it up.

It was war, and before long all the trappings of battle began to appear, including covert operations, sabotage and clandestine meetings. Booking agents had to have the skills of secret agents as they tried to grab off guests flying into New York and coerce and entice big stars to make a choice between Ed or Steve.

Ed fumed every time a big name (big enough to be impervious to his blacklist threats) turned up on *The Tonight Show*, especially since the program was "paying scale."

Originally NBC planned on budgeting a fixed sum per broadcast. If it was $1,000, then $500 would be for the main guest, $250 for the second, and $150 and $100 for the third and fourth. Realizing the battles and ill feeling this would produce, "scale" was set up so that everyone would get the same price. When the show began, it was $265.

Of course, some of the people booking *The Tonight Show* would conveniently augment that "scale" price with incentives, like first-class hotels, meals and other sundries that could add up to thousands of dollars.

When it came to hundreds of thousands of dollars, Ed Sullivan was making them. He was doing it mostly be his booking prowess. He had no other talent. He told no jokes, sang no songs, played no piano and couldn't ad-lib a straight line. Steve Allen could do all of those things, and he was beginning to book top guests, too.

Sullivan couldn't believe how popular *The Tonight Show* was becoming. Back in the late 50's, late night television was not exactly prestigious. It was on the fringe of prime time; there were millions of people who lamely muttered "Oh, I can't stay up that late." And now they were staying up for Steve.

Sullivan had to wonder what would happen if Steve chose to invade prime time!

Steve recalls now, "Sullivan had about ten times as large an audience... in the early evening you could have thirty million people looking at you. Also, the money was about five times more than I was being paid because it was prime time."

What was so great about *The Tonight Show?* As Steve points out, "in those days none of us connected with *The Tonight Show* thought it was a big deal at all. It's amazing. It seems a big deal now. It's now part of the national psychological furniture."

But back then? Steve didn't really have to think twice about his decision.

Steve decided to go up against Ed Sullivan, head to head.

CHAPTER FOUR

THIS COULD BE THE START
OF SOMETHING BAD

The spies filtered the news back to NBC: Steve Allen was seriously thinking of leaving *The Tonight Show*. It wasn't long before contingency plans were being drawn up. There were a lot of famous names on the "wish list" for a new host. There were also the names of-up-and coming performers who would work cheap.

There was everybody from NBC's quick-witted star Groucho Marx to that fellow from CBS's early-morning program, Jack Paar.

NBC knew one thing: there was more to "late night" than anybody had thought possible. Out of a dead hour in the night, a new star had appeared, and now this star was demanding — and getting — unheard-of concessions!

NBC was afraid of losing Steve Allen and gave him his prime-time show opposite Ed Sullivan. The network worked out a compromise that allowed him to cut back his nightly chores. Starting in September of 1956, Steve would only appear on *The Tonight Show* three nights a week. And... the show would be cut down to an hour a night!

Meanwhile, network bigshots were seen all over town at posh nightclubs. They didn't even have to use their expense accounts. Managers and agents invited them to eat big meals and drink all they could drink as they watched their clients, top-banana comics and suave singers auditioning in live performance for the job of taking over *The Tonight Show* on Monday and Tuesday nights. Gifts flowed in as stars and their publicists tried to influence the NBC execs. One recent Academy Award winner took a flock of execs out for a lavish party and declared it would be easy to rally friends around for a talk show/party on television every night.

NBC considered all the outsiders, the nightclub comics and movie stars, and decided that these types didn't know "the business." Television, once disparaged as the "idiot box," was now an important industry of its own. *The Tonight Show* job would go to someone with respect for the medium and a real broadcasting background.

It came down to a pair of men who had begun in radio and were now deemed the best of the up and coming, ambitious new talent on television: Ernie Kovacs and Jack Paar.

Jack had been imitating some of Steve Allen's format on *The Morning Show*. The program included some chat and comedy sketches. Paar wasn't much for character comedy but he could play himself. In this sketch he played a wiseguy debunking used car salesman Louis Nye:

Nye: I spotted you the minute you walked on the lot. I said, now there's my kind of people.

Paar: He means "Hello Sucker... "

Nye: I've got just the car in mind for you friend. It's big and roomy and comfortable. I hate to see it go; I use it myself.

Paar: As an office.

Nye: Here it is, friend. If you like it, I advise you to strike now while the iron is hot.

Paar: It just came out of the soldering shop.

Nye: Yes sir, it's a real honey!

Paar: A real honey. If you look underneath, you can see it dripping from the crankcase.

Nye: This car has many extras.

Paar: The former owner left a box of Kleenex in the glove compartment...

Nye: It has a souped-up motor.

Paar: It was made by Campbell's.

Nye: This car can go 80 miles per hour.

Paar: If you push it out a 12th-story window at the Dixie Hotel.

Nye: ...notice the puncture-proof tires.

Paar: They're filled with cement.

Nye: And just look at her low-slung lines.

Paar: The springs are busted.

Nye: She's got low mileage.

Paar: The speedometer's busted.

Nye: She's quiet.

Paar: The horn is busted.

Nye: And I'm going to sell it to you cheap.

Paar: He's busted, too...

Nye: This car is a real bargain, friend. But if you want to think it over, that's ok with me. Just give me a buzz. The number to call is...

Paar: Dial M for Murder!

NBC executives agreed that Paar was glib, had a certain amount of charm, and could also work well in ad-lib situations.

Jack Paar as the new host of *The Tonight Show*?

Well, no.

No, because that other guy, Ernie Kovacs, had perfected his mix of blackouts, visual comedy and jokes. He shared Steve Allen's taste for zany counter-cultural comedy. He could think on his feet and knock everyone off theirs with his "anything goes" attitude.

And so Kovacs and his announcer Bill Wendell (later the announcer for *Late Night with David Letterman*) took over the first two nights of *The Tonight Show* week, starting October 1, 1956

Kovacs had his own cult and they loved his off-beat comedy style, which included quick bits like this:

"Believe it or not! The wife of Paul H. Fletcher

died in 1846. Her husband Paul passed away from grief seventy-four years later!"

It wasn't David Letterman but Ernie Kovacs who pulled the following irreverent sight gag: he introduced an NBC executive with great pomp and respect. As soon as the executive appeared on the stage... the man fell right through it with a tremendous crash.

Rather than lessening Steve's burden, the competition from Ernie seemed to aggravate it. Steve was battling Sullivan in prime time, and now he had to make sure that his three nights of *The Tonight Show* were as good as, or better than, Kovacs the Hungarian wild man.

The fight for the right to be considered late night's zaniest comedian had boiled down to these two contestants a short time earlier, and neither had forgotten it.

On April 12, 1954, Ernie had been brought in by the struggling Dumont television network to host a late night show opposite Steve Allen. Kovacs' biographer, Diane Rico, recalls just how determined Ernie was to show off his demonic comic skills:

"Ernie, who was producing and writing the show, decided that his cast and guests should make an appropriate entrance. Spoofing those extravagant movie premieres in which stars dripping with furs and diamonds are mobbed by screaming fans and flashing cameras as they emerge from chauffeured limousines, he had a remote unit stationed outside the Dumont studios to photograph the talent as they arrived in his sponsors' delivery trucks."

Long before David Letterman, Kovacs literally turned viewers on their ears by screening commercials upside down. He reminded viewers that there wasn't much choice on the other local channels: he played an old 30's movie clip of cops shooting it out with robbers. Then he re-ran it 26 times in a row.

Kovacs, on local late night, was breaking rules before they could be made.

Variety reviewed the show, declaring, "Once the opening-night confusions, bedlam and uncertainties are out of the way it should settle down to perhaps the most frantic hour on the video circuits. There's no pretense at making sense."

Kovacs enjoyed playing practical jokes on the viewers. He once instructed the control room to slowly lower the sound throughout the program. Listeners had to get up every ten minutes or so to turn up the volume on their TV sets. Then, suddenly, the control room turned the volume back up again, exploding speakers in hundreds of bedrooms.

Ernie wanted to buck NBC's powerful national *Tonight Show* and got on Steve's back in a number of ways. First and foremost, Ernie scrambled onto the airwaves a sneaky five minutes before *The Tonight Show* began. Now and then Ernie would get in a few digs at Steve via print interviews, insisting that he was the original and Steve Allen prone toward copying.

Steve's and Ernie's sense of humor may have overlapped on occasion, but there were vast differences between the two. Both, for example, had developed a character called "The Question Man."

Ernie's "Question Man" simply asked strangely silly questions: "If camel's hair comes from a camel, does mohair come from a mo?"

This character was a parody of radio's "Answer Man," who could find the answer to a most any question from listeners.

Steve's parody of the "Answer Man" was to create a semi-brilliant fellow who could come up with the *question* to most any answer!

Answer: Clams Marinara, Beef Stroganoff and Frog Legs Sauté.

Question: Name three famous gangsters.

Answer: A loaf of bread, a jug of wine and thou.

Question: What's on a cannibal's menu?

Answer: 33 1/3, 45 and 78.

Question: What are the measurements of your unmarried sister?

It was a strange coincidence that for the role of "Question Man," Steve wore a bushy mustache that made him look a bit like Ernie Kovacs.

Some similarities were hardly intentional. Both men, for example, featured their wives in sketches. Jayne Meadows was excellent at parodying glamorous starlets and Edie Adams did the most devastatingly hilarious impression of Marilyn Monroe of all time.

Kovacs had no shortage of comic ideas. One of Ernie's most enduring comic creations arrived during the heat of his creative battle with Steve Allen. This was the collection of musicians in gorilla masks dubbed "The Nairobi Trio."

On April 21, 1954, they first appeared miming a silly little tin-whistle tune called "Solfeggio." During the number, one of the trio systematically began to bop another on the head. This subtle twist on monkey-mask comedy and slapstick violence became a cult favorite, a symbol of Kovacs' bizarre anti-humor.

Kovacs was undisciplined and unpredictable. One night he'd reach into his vault of scripts and re-work a bit of Spike Jones-styled comedy ("The 1812 Overture" performed with odd noises courtesy of chomped celery and eggs sizzling in a frying pan). Another night he'd present the cutting edge of black comedy, the panel show "Whom Dunnit." A typical guest was one "Dr. Harvey Serene," a not too serene fellow who had just been shot in the stomach. The panel's job: guess who shot him.

Ernie: "I'm sorry, panel, but your time is up. The contestant is dead."

Now, in the midst of Steve Allen's war with Ed

Sullivan, Kovacs had leaped from local late night to NBC, taking over two nights a week of *The Tonight Show*. The question was whether Ernie was going to leap over Steve.

At NBC, the worry was whether Ernie one night would try to dive through a camera and leap into somebody's bedroom. He was wild all right, too wild. He wasn't much for conferences, meetings with censors or carefully scripted shows. Some evenings a sketch would run on forever, other nights he'd be winging it, trying to fill up time. NBC thought Ernie had learned his lesson over the many years he had been producing zany shows for one local station or another. But irreverent Ernie could not be tamed. Whether local or national, he was too full tilt crazy to go straight.

Steve's battle with Ed Sullivan was where NBC's real problem was. As the months dragged on, the decision was made to pull the plug on *The Tonight Show* completely. The idea was to push Steve Allen's energies into a head-to-head war with Sullivan one night a week and dump the erratic Kovacs.

The demise of *The Tonight Show* didn't bother Steve or Ernie. NBC's consolation prize for Ernie was a second chance with a daytime show opposite the aging Arthur Godfrey. Ernie was happy as long as he could bring Bill Wendell with him, and get plenty of air time for Edie Adams.

Steve was glad to concentrate on his prime-time battle with Ed Sullivan. Especially when there were so many things that could go wrong. On one of Steve's first shows, John Cameron Swayze did a commercial for Timex. Trying to show how waterproof the watch was, Swayze slipped it around the propeller of an outboard motor and submerged it in a tank of water. The motor was turned on, the water foamed, and when the camera zoomed in on the propeller, the watch was gone.

Swayze said, "Well, it worked beautifully all afternoon at rehearsals... we'll repeat this experiment and show it to you next week!"

Steve Allen looked into the camera and ad-libbed, "So you think there's going to be a next week, John?"

The important thing for the show was getting the best guests. After a few more weeks of frustration, learning that Ed had tried to steal away a guest, Allen broke his usual polite silence and called Sullivan "nothing but a pirate."

With Steve a prime-time player, it was up to NBC executive Pat Weaver to look after *The Tonight Show's* interests. He had his hands full in handling a vicious power struggle with Robert Sarnoff, whose father was the hotshot head of RCA, which in turn owned NBC.

Daddy Sarnoff was grooming Robert to take over at NBC. It didn't matter that Pat Weaver had been instrumental in creating hits throughout the NBC lineup, not only *The Today Show* and *The Tonight Show*, but a successful mid-day show called *The Home Show* hosted by Arlene Francis. Now, amid executive backstabbings and power plays, the new thinking was that Weaver's best years were behind him.

Weaver thought he was building a dynasty. *The Today Show*, *The Home Show* and *The Tonight Show* would be the backbone of the network, establishing viewing habits that would not change year after year.

The new thinking was, well, to try something new.

Robert Sarnoff was in, and *The Tonight Show* was out. Ernie Kovacs ended on January 22, 1957, and the last show with Steve Allen aired on January 25.

Instead of replacing Steve and Ernie and continuing with *The Tonight Show*, the new young network execs went with something new and different... *Tonight: America After Dark*. It was a good title for a show that could only premiere in America under cover of darkness.

The idea was to duplicate *The Today Show* at night: to cover hard news, information, and then add some entertainment features. A typical night might have coverage of a new jazz club followed by a live report from the site of an airplane crash.

It was as if someone was flicking the dial back and forth between David Letterman and Ted Koppel, pulling the viewers back and forth between comedy and tragedy.

At that hour of the night, bewildered viewers simply turned the set off and went to sleep.

The nominal host of this mess was announcer Jack Lescoulie. He was soon joined by a singer named Judy Johnson, and a fleet of reporters and columnists, including Earl Wilson, Hy Gardner and Irv Kupcinet, all firing stories in from various cities around the country.

Every five or ten minutes, there was a report from one of the newsmen covering a crime or trend. If there was nothing too exciting going on (and there rarely was), the cameras would stake out a Hollywood party or premiere and try to get a few non-commital words from any celebrity in attendance.

Earl Wilson occasionally sought out Jerry Lester's old pal Dagmar for a laugh, but these were few. If all else failed, Judy Johnson or Gretchen Wyler or someone would start singing, backed by the house band, the Lou Stein Trio.

The flabby show stretched back to ninety minutes and that made critics even more numb. When it was obvious that NBC had laid a late night egg, the executives were quick to remedy the situation.

The Lou Stein Trio was fired.

Somehow, the ratings for *Tonight: America After Dark* did not improve.

This called for another strategy session of NBC executives.

They fired the replacement band, the Mort Lindsay Quartet.

When it became clear that something far more drastic needed to be done, The Mort Lindsay Quartet was fired in favor of the Johnny Guarnieri Quartet.

The show staggered through the winter and spring months and began to gasp for breath during the smoggy New York summer of 1957. Host Jack Lescoulie was replaced by Al "Jazzbo" Collins, a man whose main claim to fame was recording some of Steve Allen's "Hip Fables" on 45 rpm.

The jockeying and bickering among the other cast members intensified. Instead of one program, it was every man for himself. Hy Gardner, for example, called his segment *Hy Gardner Time*, ready to spin it into its own late night program at any moment. News-man Bob Considine countered with the hard news *Considine's Corner*, hoping that NBC would take the hint and give him the entire late night time spot.

NBC's nightmare show had to be put to a restful, permanent sleep. The head of programming, Mort Werner, wanted *The Tonight Show* back in something approaching the original Steve Allen format. Producer Dick Linkroum remembered the odd-man-out when the debate over replacing Steve first began. The choice had been between Ernie Kovacs and Jack Paar.

Why not try Jack Paar now?

Paar's name was written down, but almost as soon as it was, agents and executives came out of the woodwork to nominate their own choices.

Former *Tonight: America After Dark* columnist Earl Wilson heard of the situation and quickly advised Paar to be on his best behavior and not do anything controversial or crazy that would spoil the deal. This was easy for Paar to do, since he was out of work at the time.

Paar, who had replaced Walter Cronkite on *The Morning Show*, had ultimately failed against *The Today Show*. CBS gave him another chance in the afternoon, then pulled the plug. Paar had developed a reputation for feuding and fighting even then. He had fired his band leader Pupi Campo in 1955 and announced, "He hasn't any talent... He couldn't read music or lead a band on TV... he doesn't know what to do." Campo had to wait six years, but he finally won a lawsuit charging Paar with slander. He collected $15,000.

Paar drifted to local radio and was not a success. But then again, he had failed in radio three times, first as Jack Benny's summer replacement, and later in summer replacement shows for Eddie Cantor and Don McNeil.

It had gotten so ridiculous that columnist John Crosby wrote: "What, I keep asking myself, does Jack Paar do in the winter time? Live on the nuts he stores in the summer time? I have learned to tell the season by Jack Paar. When Paar appears it's time to lay away the winter clothes in mothballs and get out the tennis racquet."

Fred Allen never forgot the ingratitude Paar had shown Jack Benny that first summer. Now, when asked about Jack, Fred got his revenge: "Oh," he answered, "you mean the young man who had the meteoric disappearance?"

Paar was desperate for this new chance. He came down from Bronxville and pitched himself to NBC. Mort Werner had enjoyed Jack's work on the old CBS *Morning Show*. He liked Paar's low-key but sharply satiric personality. Of course, nobody was more in agreement than Jack Paar.

CHAPTER FIVE

HERE'S JACK PAAR... THEN, WHERE'S JACK PAAR!

On July 26, 1957, NBC and mortician Mort Werner quietly buried their big mistake, *Tonight: America After Dark*.

Several of NBC's late night alumni were there to see it go. Dagmar was a guest that night, and so was Ernie Kovacs.

The show was re-titled *The Tonight Show*, for its premiere on July 29, 1957. With a considerable lack of enthusiasm, NBC gave new host Jack Paar a 24-week contract. The standard would have been a 26-week contract, but 24 weeks would bring them both to January 1, 1958 — when the show could neatly be canceled if it was doing poorly.

By that time, it was doing, to use a Paar-ism, "just peachy." NBC was slowly winning back the affiliates that had defected over the past year.

Jack Paar became the show's most controversial host. Each night viewers would tune in, wondering whether he'd insult a guest or fawn over one, and whether he would sizzle with wiseguy sarcasm or simper and weep with sentimental emotion.

"He really did cry on TV when he felt like it," Earl Wilson recalled. "He almost cried the time I called him a few years before and alerted him that NBC wanted him as a successor to Steve Allen... "

Earl Wilson remembered Paar saying "I need that job. I've been so down and so discouraged. I've been about to get out of the business."

Now he had one of the most high-profile jobs in all of television, exposed to the nation for over an hour and a half a night, five nights a week. Although it had been a while since Steve Allen helmed the program, Paar was immediately compared to the old *Tonight Show* host, and not favorably at first.

Many critics were expecting entertainment in Steve's style: the crazy stunts, the zany sketches, the friendly personality of the host. Unlike Steve, Jack Paar had little comic versatility.

His pleasant, mildly handsome face could not register funny expressions. His ordinary demeanor was not suited to sketch comedy. As Hollywood had learned long ago, Paar was no actor. One night a trick chair collapsed underneath him during a stunt and he flopped to the floor injuring his arm. He limped off the show and guest Cliff Arquette had to take over.

Paar had such a strong ego and such a set personality that there was no way he could effectively submerge himself into a "Question Man" like Steve or an "Art Fern" as Johnny Carson would later do. Paar was best as himself.

Paar preferred verbal humor. He opened with a monologue. He later recalled, "Most of the really hard creative work went into the monologue or opening comments on the news of the day. I think that Johnny Carson and I were the only ones really good at that form."

Then he introduced the guests, who came out for light-hearted chat. The show might stop for a song or two from a guest, but the emphasis was on talk. There were fewer sketches or comic turns for the host to impersonate various characters.

Basically, Paar's format, low on demanding versatility from the host, was the one that most, from Merv Griffin to Pat Sajak, would follow. Paar modestly notes, "If you are referring to the late night program that became the most imitated show in television and that consisted mainly of conversation and personalities, then I am guilty."

Paar always knew where his strengths were. He was sincere and intimate with the guests and the home viewers. He was a good talker and a good listener. This style had helped him to meet his second wife, Miriam, at an Army dance. He didn't try to impress her with zany comedy or a fast tap-dance step. Paar told the woman that they shouldn't dance at all, just sit instead.

"I'm interesting to talk to," he said.

That was basically his concept for *The Tonight Show*, the way to save it and himself.

He wanted a show that would spotlight the brilliant raconteur, the egotistic crackpot, the earth-shaking prima donna and the most controversial and opinionated person alive: the many sides of Jack Paar.

Along the way, the show would also spotlight other people besides himself. Paar went after everyone from Eleanor Roosevelt to Albert Schweitzer, earning the respect of the press and linking himself with the day's fine minds and great thinkers. He wasn't the intellectual that Steve Allen was, but, like Larry King a generation later, he was humble in the face of power.

Paar's earnestness impressed the politicians, who saw his show as an easy way to reach out and touch the average viewer without confronting major issues. Paar wasn't about to throw a nasty curve to a guest like John F. Kennedy or Fidel Castro. One night he had Vice President Nixon on the show, and Nixon asked for Paar's autograph.

On the average night, Paar filled the panel with movie and TV personalities clearly beneath him. With these demi-celebs, he could get in prickly digs, becoming the confident King of the night. Opposite an inarticulate sports figure or a bland singer, Paar was urbane, witty and the life of the party.

Paar mixed up the action and it fascinated his viewers. What was Jack Paar really like, this fellow who could be so confident and insulting one minute, so stuttery and vulnerable the next? Never had there been such a display of emotion on television. In what ever mode Paar was in, he wore his heart on his sleeve.

Viewers had known very little about Steve Allen's personal life (besides his constant mentions of wife Jayne Meadows). In general, most TV personalities kept viewers at a distance, believing that familiarity would breed contempt. But Paar would often stop the program to show his latest home movies and vacation snapshots. It seemed there was little happening in his Bronxville home that didn't turn up in his opening monologue.

One night he told America about his daughter's first training bra. In confessing little details about himself and his suburban lifestyle, he created the earnest catch phrase "I kid you not." He spoke intimately to his audience as if everyone was a friend, or analyst.

The most obvious sign of his vulnerability was his self-conscious stammer. He was sometimes incapable of getting through even one monologue joke without nervous stops and starts. Paar hated impressionists who dared to mimic him, especially since they turned his mild manner and fluttery stutter into the stereotype of an effeminate fool.

One doesn't need an impressionist to get an idea of how shaky Paar could be as he stumbled along trying to choose the right words to convey all his emotions. Here he is in all his neurotic glory, trying to get through a few simple lines of observational monologue comedy. He's describing his stay in England:

"You know, I was up this morning at seven-thirty.

"Really.

"I was.

"Truly, that's so. And I was out in the park outside the hotel.

"And I was there. And I was walking around.

"And there was a guy like Trevor Howard, you know, with tweeds on, walking the dog, and I said, 'Hello.' And he said, 'How are you.'

"And I said, 'I'm — I'm an American.' And he said, 'None of us is perfect.'

"So for the rest of the day I called myself a Southern Canadian."

Jack's contradictions were many. His style was soft-spoken and conversational, but he could also be strident and sarcastic without a trace of stammer. He could be charming and witty one night, then with a different set of guests appear petty, rude and foolish. This may not have been the way to host a polite panel show, but this was a *talk* show. Paar was in essence hosting a nightly gathering at his "house," complete with home movies, guests who should not have been invited and the atmosphere that "anything might happen." Some guests were quietly invited to leave, the subject of catty insults. Others were embraced and urged to come back over and over, long overstaying their welcome.

His "regulars" were more like kook neighbors: airheaded bimbos comically self-absorbed in themselves, strangers to the neighborhood with odd accents and malaprops, crabby intellectuals and non-celebrity "raconteurs" who only had "the gift of gab." Most of these sychophants were unknown to America before Paar turned them into stars.

One of the few "old-time" performers" with any previous stardom was old Cliff Arquette. One night on the show Paar happened to muse "whatever became of" that wonderful character actor. As it turned out, Arquette was alive and fairly well, and ready to do the show.

Arquette resurrected his "Charley Weaver" character, an old lovable codger from the tiny town of Mount Idy. By this time, Arquette could not remember lines well, but devised the idea of simply reading "Letters from Mama" on the show. Something like this:

"Dear Castor Oil (Mama always said I was hard to take), Things are fine in Mount Idy (she goes on). Leonard Box was arrested yesterday. Somebody told him his wife was as pretty as a picture, so he hung her on the wall. Elsie Krack dropped by yesterday. My, she looked lovely. She just had her hair done. She waited at our house until they sent it over.

Well, son, I must close now and go help your father. He just kissed a bride and got himself a black eye. I know everyone does it, but not seven years after the wedding. Love, Mama."

Paar loved surrounding himself with "sitting ducklings," foolish, preening women who were fun to flirt with and sting with ad-libs. A pair of regulars quacked in funnee foorin oksents: the Hungarian starlet Zsa Zsa Gabor and a French singer with a tousled little-boy hairstyle, Genevieve.

Paar liked his double-entendre now and then. To a busty blonde comedienne/starlet Joyce Jameson, eyeing her low-cut gown: "My dear, I'm afraid your net doesn't quite cover your gross."

His most popular silly female guest was ditsy Dody Goodman. Her closest brush with fame prior to Paar was a role in 1955's *Shoestring Revue*. Dody sang a novelty song about an ardent suitor who sent her flowers. And then "the rock garden came. One rock at a time... here followed a garland of fungus, and then as a tropical treat, he sent me a plant that proceeded to pant and later began to eat meat!"

Dody was perfect for Paar. She arrived for an

audition dressed like a crackpot. Paar recalled that she "spoke in a distracted manner that defied description... To answer a simple yes or no, she would twist her mouth into a knot, scratch the end of her nose, and open her large blue eyes to the size of fried eggs."

"Are you putting me on?" Paar asked.

"A little," Dody replied. It was the put-on tradition that, in variations, would yield comedy between Carol Wayne and Johnny Carson, Eva Gabor and Merv Griffin, and Terri Garr and David Letterman.

A week after New Year's, Dody came on Paar's show and ended by saying, "Good night, and a Merry Christmas to all. I know it's too late to say that, but I just thought of it!"

Another time, she kept saying to Paar, "You have a speck on your eyelash." He dabbed at his eye and she insisted, "You still didn't get it." She too dabbed at his face. Then she cried out, "Oh! It's on MY eyelash!"

Jack got plenty of laughs just reacting to Dody's silliness. But when he sensed that Dody was getting too many laughs herself, he became characteristically moody. The more he contemplated Dody's rising stardom, the more he thought about shooting that star down.

The irrepressible Dody was a bit too irrepressible. One night, after interrupting Jack once too often, Paar had enough. He met with her manager and cried, "Look what your girl did to me on the show last night — cutting off my lines. We've got to get rid of her!"

Paar had made her, and he could un-make her. He dropped her from the show, announcing, "I felt like the owner of a department store who looks around and sees a little ribbon clerk has set up her own counter in his store, with her own cash register and everything."

Paar always expected to have the most laughs by the time the evening was over. One night Jack E. Leonard was on a roll, with Paar calling out, "Keep going, you're doing great!" Then he refused to book Leonard again. Paar told his listeners point-blank: "You'll be seeing a lot of him in the future, but not on my show!" Fat Jack grumbled, "He's as miserable as any human being. You can quote me."

Curmudgeonly comedian Henry Morgan was not a Paar fan. On his radio show he started a "Hate Jack Paar Club." Paar scoffed, "Mr. Morgan has a personality. Unfortunately it shows through."

Paar developed a reputation for feuding with stars, and his most notorious encounter came in December of 1960 when Mickey Rooney turned up on the show and Paar turned up the heat.

Rooney was in an ebulliently good mood, alcohol induced. He was celebrating the success of his fifth marriage.

Paar promptly brought up his first marriage, demanding to know, "What was Ava Gardner really like?"

Cocking a bleary eye at the mild-mannered host, Rooney shot back, "Well, Mr. Paar, may I say this? She is more woman than you will ever know."

"I think you're loaded," Paar said.

Rooney answered in triumph, "I'm making a puzzling situation out of myself to you!"

Unable to get much satisfaction from pickled Mickey, Jack played to the audience, drolly confiding, "Don't stir him up or we're dead!"

The audience squirmed while Rooney launched into a rambling critique of last night's show.

"I stayed up until I couldn't sleep any more," Rooney told Paar. "I didn't enjoy your show, Jack... Pretty rotten, pretty rotten."

With the polite testiness of a librarian, Paar replied, "Are you enjoying it tonight?"

The tipsy little actor declared, "Not necessarily. I'm not a fan. I don't care to watch your show."

To which Paar replied, "Would you care to leave?" Mickey walked off the show.

Paar got the last word: "It's a shame. He *was* a great talent."

In the momentary confusion, someone in the audience asked if Rooney was really drunk.

Paar answered, "I wouldn't light a match in here for weeks."

Rooney's career took an immediate skid with this latest proof of instability. Reporters dogged him and taunted him. Finally he admitted, "I had a few drinks before I went on the show. How else can you stand Paar?"

Paar sassed, "Mickey called me and threatened to punch me in the nose. But I didn't want to be hit in the knee."

It all might seem mild today, but at the time the concept of a real *talk* show was new. Merv Griffin remembers:

"What appealed to me about Jack and *The Tonight Show* was the spontaneity; you never knew what was going to happen next, and I didn't dare miss the show because if I did, that would be the one everyone was talking about next morning."

People were still buzzing over the night in September of 1959 when Debbie Reynolds was the guest. Reynolds had the reputation for telling friends and reporters how good in bed various stars were and what their attributes were like. She was evidently trying to unzip some evidence on Jack. The aggressive actress suddenly attacked Paar and pulled off his jacket. He flopped down under his desk and Debbie whipped off his tie and showed it to the audience. Then she went down, below camera range, to strip off his shirt. Paar managed to come up for air, crying, "Were you this rough on Eddie Fisher?"

Back then, television viewers rarely saw unrehearsed interviews. It was a shock to see famous people acting just as foolishly as everyone else. Many a star was caught saying the wrong thing with Paar.

When Red Skelton guested on *The Tonight Show*, Paar wanted to know how Red was able to keep his weekly show so funny.

Red smiled and answered, "All my jokes are put in my head by the voice of God."

Out in TV land, his hard-working writers were watching. A few days later, when Red expected to see the week's new script, he found a book of blank pages and a note: "Dear Red: Please have God fill in the empty pages. Thanks. Your writers."

Paar's own writers often feuded with him – as did his stage hands, his executive staff, and a most everyone who came in contact with his erratic paranoias and petulance. The man who had helped Paar get *The Tonight Show* job in the first place, producer Dick Linkroum, didn't last six months.

In the course of the midnight madness, early regulars like Tedi Thurman and Bill and Cora Baird's puppets vanished while "finds" like singer Trish Dwelley and Betty Johnson were banished. At any time, any of the "regulars" from Dody Goodman to Elsa Maxwell might be suspended for some minor slight or other, or permanently banned.

Paar bounced a director before finally settling on Hal Gurnee (now with David Letterman) and there was some question as to how long band leader Jose Melis would stick around. Only a few weeks after he started his show, Paar dumped his announcer. This was Franklin Pangborn (best known for his comic snitty fussbudget roles in 1940's movies). Paar felt the "little gay guy" was a good announcer, but he wasn't showing enough spontaneous enthusiasm during the actual program. Hugh Downs was Pangborn's replacement.

Even the mild-mannered Downs was amazed at what he saw every night. What surprised Hugh was not Jack's sometimes testy attitude toward rivals or guests, but the way he reacted to the audience. He said of Jack, "He has more reserve and hostility toward an audience than anyone I've ever known. Sometimes I expect him to come out with a whip and a chair."

The regulars Jack admired were neurotic, openly hostile and misanthropic. Oscar Levant was a favorite. The hypochondriacal pianist/raconteur was practically a psychotic recluse when Paar re-discovered him. Levant's career had been going downhill for years and he had recently made a shambles of a local show in California. One night he excoriated a sponsor for withdrawing from his show and told his viewers, "Let's fight the power game! I don't need Philco! Who needs Philco!"

Another night he found hosting his own show so boring he took an on-screen nap. For an aching minute, Levant remained inert, with his eyes closed. A staff member finally tried to wake Levant and told him that his next guest was waiting. Levant didn't even bother opening his eyes. He just muttered, "Wake me up when he leaves."

Levant once said, "Happiness is not something you experience, it's something you remember."

When he wasn't indulging in self-flagellation, Oscar feuded with anyone whom Paar had missed. Levant said he would not watch Dinah Shore: "I can't stand seeing her on account of my diabetes."

Levant feuded with Paar's other guests, saying that Zsa Zsa Gabor's "face is inscrutable but I can't vouch for the rest of her."

Paar: "There is a fine line between genius and insanity!"

Levant: "I've managed to overcome that fine line."

Levant summed it up this way: "My friends either

dislike me or hate me."

Another curmudgeon, Alexander King, was unknown before he began appearing on Jack's show. King was an admitted morphine addict and former thief, twice jailed and married four times. As such, he had fine credentials for entering show business. Now an author of bilious memoirs and essays, after one appearance with Paar his latest obscure book hit the bestseller list.

Paar could simply sit back and let King ramble. As Brother Theodore would later do for Merv Griffin and David Letterman, Alexander King provided caustic commentary that left the host shaking his head with horrified amusement. Something as mundane as a visit to a kidney specialist could bring out the poison poet in Alexander King:

"I wanted to reach a purely human level of sympathy and understanding with him. I wanted him to like me. I'm like an ancient iguana full of splenetic wrinkles. I wanted this character to respond to my personal charm. I covered him with the slime of my amiability until he looked web-footed. I got no response. This squat, ovoid, red-faced man permanently submerged in his urinous misgivings had finally turned into a kidney."

The day after appearing on *The Today Show*, publicizing his latest book, 'Rich Man, Poor Man, Freud and Fruit,' Alexander King dropped dead. If he had been a true friend of Paar's, he would've stuck it out a little longer and keeled over for *The Tonight Show*.

Happily for Jack, others staggered from the show like the walking dead. Paar encouraged stars to get into blood-feuds with each other on his show. British comedienne Hermione Gingold disliked fat, dumpy Elsa Maxwell and was given every opportunity to hurl insults. She once declared of Elsa, "I admire anyone who can go so far on so little." And, when Elsa huffed over Elvis Presley autographing a female fan's breast, she announced, "You could write a three-act play on her bosom!"

Mostly, the feuding was supplied by Jack himself. One night after Elsa departed, Paar said, "The balloon left here in a cab for the Waldorf." At one point he had Maxwell on his show once a week, and he seemed to come up with insults about her even more frequently: "Once I told her, I said, Elsa, your stockings are crooked. And she said 'I'm not wearing any.'"

Jo Coppola in a March 1958 *New York Post* story wrote, "Petty rivalries, jealousies, foibles and ambitions penetrate the sweet talk." Whether it was Paar, Dody Goodman or any number of regulars, "without the feuds that have broken into print or the excuses given by either side as to the cause of the bickering, the Paar circle often acts as if it came from a long line of woodsmen. I see no other way to account for the axes they grind in public."

Paar fought with practically every columnist who wrote a line about him. Harriet Van Horne, of the *World Telegram*, once reviewed Paar's show and gave it a lot of praise — except for a moment when Paar dragged out his 11-year-old daughter Randy and the two mimed to a recording of "I Remember It Well" by Maurice Chevalier and Hermione Gingold. Van Horne said the bit was "fairly amusing" but "I've never thought it a wise idea for stars to shove their offspring into the spotlight. Miss Paar appears to have talent... She also has a lovely face with an upturned nose and wide eyes. But it's sad to see such a pretty little girl so alarmingly overweight. A high-protein, no-bonbon diet would seem to be indicated — at once!"

Paar said on *The Tonight Show*, "All right, let's take Harriet Van Horne. Harriet Van Horne has her picture in her column. She is very attractive from her picture, very feminine. Actually she is about as feminine as Gorgeous George. She recently reviewed a show that I did. I couldn't care less about her review, but in the review... she remarked about my daughter's weight. She said that my daughter was pretty fat, that we had better keep her away from bonbons. Now what the hell right has this broad got to talk about my daughter's weight?"

Paar went on to bicker with another columnist. He flattened Dorothy Killgallen with one line: "You have no chin!"

Paar and Walter Winchell battled for years. Paar insisted he was slighted in an early Winchell column. Winchell pointed out many columns that praised Paar. Winchell felt Paar was thin-skinned.

"I think Winchell's life is pretty sad," Paar answered, "He morally is in no position to comment on anyone else... he's a vicious old man." Another time he challenged Winchell to appear on his show: "I would like him to ad-lib with me — not to read. He can ask me any question of a personal nature and I would like to have the same privilege."

The feud boiled over when Paar's guest Elsa Maxwell also attacked Winchell and intimated that he never even voted in an election. Winchell demanded an apology. He got one, but he also got a promise of more abuse: "If Walter Winchell keeps attacking me and is unfair, then I will see that Winchell is paid off — but only with laughter. Laughter he cannot stand."

Winchell fired back: "The Reverend Paar... enjoying an American privilege ('the right of reply') previously charged us with being an immoral person; that we are 'a senile, old man' and in the next breath 'that we are lecherous'... He added that we had questioned his virility... That one elusdes us... When was that? We think the distraught fellow was depressed over a recent line credited to comedian Henry Morgan: that Paar 's teevee's oldest little girl...'

"The anguished Paar, in defending his manhood, told his network that his virility was known only to his wife. Does St. Paarnard mean that Walter Winchell couldn't make that statement? When The Associated Press called for comment we said: 'My morals, I am sure, are not as pure and virginal as Paar's — but is anybody's? But what is Jack Paar really sore about? He has never forgiven us for catching him in a lie that he was forced to retract the next night. He permitted a guest to carelessly state that she could prove that Winchell has never registered or voted in his life..'

"Paar is a mean, sick and malicious Little man."

Jack laughed at Winchell, saying that Winchell could never appear on TV because he had a ridiculously high voice caused by wearing "too tight underwear." The feud with Winchell got so bad that political patriarch Joseph Kennedy got involved. Kennedy called up Paar one night and shouted, "Stop replying to Winchell on the air. He's dead as an important columnist. You are making people read him again. If you mention him one more time, I will come and kick you in the ass."

Other columnists were ready with more feuds and fusses. One day Earl Wilson headlined: "Multimillionaire J. Paul Getty wants the Jack Paar TV show killed and Elsa Maxwell barred from the air because of cracks about him."

Jack was blameless. "I'm unhappy with strangers," Paar once said. "When I walk into a room where I think people may dislike me, I find myself doing the very things that would make them dislike me — overstating, being smart-alecky, letting myself get emotional. All because I'm a terribly shy guy."

Once a fan came up to him and said, "Mr. Paar, you keep me awake every night!"

He answered, "Haven't you tried Nembutal?"

Jack's main writer, Jack Douglas, recalled that

Paar could sometimes be surprisingly easy to deal with. "Here's the arrangement I had with Paar. I'd just give him the sheets [of jokes] and let him pick what he liked... He would never say 'boo' about what you did. He would never criticize."

Not about the jokes he got. Maybe about the laughs others were getting. Paar was ready to fire Douglas for getting too many laughs during on-screen appearances promoting his various comedy books.

In May of 1959, after Douglas had a bestseller with his book *My Brother Was an Only Child*, Paar became jealous. After Douglas appeared on TV with Mike Wallace, Paar fumed that Douglas was not concentrating enough on jokes for *The Tonight Show*. Paar was concerned about rumors that Douglas was going to get his own talk show. Douglas told reporters, "I'm not a threat to him. Nothing was ever said to me about doing a show opposite him."

Douglas had been friendly with Paar for a dozen years, and was one of his most loyal writers. Ultimately Paar sent Douglas a memo demanding his resignation. The memo added, "You have misused me and your expense account... It would be best if you would remove your files from our office."

Douglas told the press: "I have a contract with NBC and if they want to fire me, they will have to do so. Paar has sent me equally nasty memos over the 12 years. At the time he wrote it he probably meant it, but with Paar you never know." He added, "He'll chew up anybody in a letter and then forget it... Maybe he wasn't angry at me at all, but at somebody else. Who knows?"

It took a while for the two men to patch up their feud. Especially since Paar always felt he could easily find other gag writers.

Star-struck Dick Cavett broke into late night TV as a gag man for Jack. As Jack Douglas recalls,

"Cavett used to hang around NBC... (he) just button-holed him one day and gave him some material and said, 'Please read it.' Doing a thing like that to Paar! Holy Christ! He'd fall apart completely. But somehow he read it, and he liked it, and that's how Cavett got the job with Paar, and that's how he got started."

But once Cavett began working for Paar as a talent coordinator, he saw things differently. He recalled, "it was a little like living at home with an alcoholic parent." In Cavett's opinion the moody star acted like someone with "a low-grade paranoia."

Writer Terry Galanoy chronicled the goings-on and wrote that during rehearsals Paar "stalked the stage like a hunted man, refused to sign autograph books or talk to strangers or join the crew at meals or after the show."

One of Paar's nastiest battles was with Ed Sullivan. Sullivan had warred with Steve Allen and now it was Paar's turn. Ed was angry when big stars would extract huge amount of money for appearing on *The Ed Sullivan Show* and then perform for scale on *The Tonight Show.*

Sullivan had dueled Steve to a draw. He figured to do better with Paar. Sullivan threatened stars and told them not to stray over to *The Tonight Show* before, or within a few weeks after, a booking on his show. Paar bristled and fought back, filling one show with top stars who were indignant over Ed's black-listing attempt.

Paar launched attacks on Sullivan and Ed responded by calling him "an emotional man who feels the whole world is against him."

Triumphantly, Paar announced, "Sullivan is more incoherent, more emotional and more nutty than I am!"

Paar publicly dared Sullivan to come on *The Tonight Show* and talk about the booking war. On March 13, 1961, Sullivan was supposed to battle

Paar live on the air. He didn't show up. "Ed Sullivan is a liar," Paar told his audience, the biggest audience he'd ever gotten for a night's broadcast. "If that is libel he must now sue and go to court. Under oath, I repeat, Ed Sullivan: you lied today!"

Sullivan hastily told *TV Guide,* "I couldn't go up against Paar in this "discussion" business he insisted upon. I've never pretended to be a comedian, quick with the gag lines. Paar's a very good comic. In any 15-minute discussion, he could kill me."

Sullivan insisted that he wasn't objecting to guests appearing on Jack's show to talk. He just didn't want them to *perform* for that low $320 scale fee. Paar fumed that Sullivan had told dozens of performers and agents that anybody who appeared on *The Tonight Show* for $320 would only get $320 for doing *The Ed Sullivan Show.*

Paar, mindful that Sullivan had paid *him* $5,000 for several appearances in the early 50's, tried not to escalate the feud. But he couldn't help himself. He wrote a letter to Sullivan — and then read it aloud on *The Tonight Show,* insisting, "I am appalled that you raise the question of money and that you challenge me to pay performers what you pay them. Ed, I don't have money to pay performers. This show is a low-budget freak that caught on because performers want to come on and want time to entertain people without the monkey acts and Japanese jugglers waiting in the wings."

Sullivan declared that he was sick of paying comic Sam Levenson $7,500 and then hearing the same jokes recited on Paar's show for $320. He was angry that singer Pat Suzuki grabbed $5,000 from Sullivan, then sang songs for Paar's $320.

Sullivan complained to the *New York Herald Tribune,* "Paar himself said on camera he didn't understand how he could get stars like Pat Suzuki for $320 when she got $5,000 from me. I was in the odd position of being indicted, right in front of Miss Suzuki and the NBC network, as a dope!"

Most stars were distressed getting caught in a loyalty fight and a tug-of-war between Ed and Jack. It was a no-win, embarrassing position.

Jack Benny knew them both and didn't want to be told what to do by either of them. The mild-mannered Benny shocked Paar by suddenly opening the wound on national TV. He lectured Paar, "If you're going to be mad at someone, be mad at Eichmann or somebody. I know you called Ed all those names, but you did not mean one of them. Ed didn't call you names because he at least has some sense!"

The lovable, sensible Jack Benny was a living legend even then, and so respected by everyone, including Paar, that there was no comeback to his comments.

"This is the sweetest guy in the world," Benny told the audience. As Paar sat there in embarrassment, Benny continued, "He goes crazy in one minute! Calls everybody everything and then goes home and cries and is sorry that he did."

Benny declared, "We want you both to make up and call of this silly feud!" He told Jack, "Tell everybody you're sorry!"

"I'm sorry, I'm sorry!" Paar finally said.

Paar and Sullivan actually made up.

That was rare for Jack. His feuds could last years, if not decades. He was always ready to go after the original *Tonight Show* host, Steve Allen.

Paar's grudge began when he was doing his rapidly failing daytime program for CBS. He insisted Steve and/or his writers were lifting ideas and jokes. He wrote Steve a letter, ending with a sassy wisecrack: "Please look into this or I'll go over your head to Jayne."

A few days later, he got an answer, what Paar called "a long, ponderous... tedious lecture on comedy" from Steve. Then, on *The Tonight Show*, Steve gave Paar a little satiric tweak of the nose. During a routine that involved reading book titles and then the authors, Steve noted that new volume: *Death In the Afternoon* by Jack Paar.

In 1958, Paar was often asked how he'd replace Steve Allen. He told columnist Jack O'Brien, "I don't know how to imitate Steve Allen. All *I* know how to do is *entertain.*"

In 1960, with *The Tonight Show* the unquestioned hit of late night, Paar penned *I Kid You Not*, a memoir that focused mainly on the antics of his daughter Randy and the joys of his safari trips to Africa. But he did take the time to address Steve Allen:

"He is the most self-promoted thing since the Tucker automobile. He has done so much public soul-searching he's beginning to sound like a saint. But I still don't think he can walk on the water. He'll have to take the Staten Island ferry like the rest of us. Steve is the greatest living non-authority on comedy. Whenever there is a scholarly discussion of humor, Steve raises his hand. I wish he'd just leave the room."

Steve dismissed Jack's fretting. After all, Jack was not only neurotic, but probably jealous. Steve was enjoying some success against the formidable Ed Sullivan and received a 1960 Peabody Award for *The Steve Allen Show*.

Jack kept at it. Twenty years later, Jack wrote another book, and once again picked at his old wounds until he could bleed them out on paper: "I fear for his safety. I must write his peachy wife, Jayne, of my concern. You see, if Steve insists on being 'Mr. Show Business' and trying to do everything, there is a danger. When next the circus comes to Los Angeles, I am afraid that Steve is going to try and get up on that high wire and do a few back flips. The chances are he may fall and break his glasses!"

Steve Allen still wasn't taking Jack too seriously. "Jack Paar," he mused, "has gotten himself into awkward situations over the years by taking undue umbrage. Oh well, I suppose it's better than taking Valium."

Lenny Bruce, who had been given key national exposure from Steve Allen, was not welcomed by Paar. Lenny muttered, "Paar has a God complex. He thinks he can create performers in six days."

Merv Griffin admitted that, with Jack's tactics, he deserved the title of "TV's most famous terrorist." What alarmed Griffin and others was the way Jack not only terrorized worthy foes, but even his own guests, who were subjected to sudden wisecracks.

Cartoonist Al Capp recalled, "Paar wanted you to succeed so much that he would help you to the point of tripping you up."

Part of Paar's peculiar nature was to give left-handed compliments to guests. Woody Allen didn't know what to think when Paar introduced him with this:

"An Indiana humorist wrote a wonderful line about somebody else one time that applies, I think, to our friend Woody Allen. He would have said, "Woody Allen looks like the kind of guy who would come up on the stage if a magician asked him to."

Woody's friend Dick Cavett recalled in his autobiography the time that Paar gave a similarly odd introduction to Jonathan Winters, saying "Jonny Winters is pound for pound the funniest man on earth" and that Winters had made the stagehands roar with more laughter than anybody'd ever heard.

In Cavett's analysis, "What Jack is doing here is saying, 'This guy is capable of being great, he has been great all over the place in the past, and if he isn't tonight he must have something against me, because eyewitnesses can testify that he can be if he wants to be.'"

A newspaper columnist of the day, Leo Guild, recalled that the opinionated Paar couldn't wait to launch into character assassination: "Before I could ask a question, Paar told me how much he disliked Walter Winchell, how much he disliked Jim Backus, Harriet Van Horne, NBC and Dorothy Killgallen."

Guild could see the complexity behind Paar: "There was a sincerity about him. When he hated, he fidgeted and scowled. When he talked of things he liked, he slumped in his seat and grinned."

Paar squabbled with his backstage associates — on the air. While today it's common for David Letterman to drag his cameras backstage and comically shout to his stage manager or co-producers, back then it was a novelty. It was also an embarrassment, since Paar did it with undisguised irritation.

One talent coordinator on the show was blasted by Paar on the air for not being out somewhere looking for new talent. Paar later fired the man, a longtime friend, for being too much of a drinker. He launched into an on-air tirade later, calling him a "Judas" when he mistakenly believed the man had leaked unfavorable anecdotes about him to *Newsweek*. Years later, in typical Paar fashion, he nostalgically re-hired the man.

All of this was bizarrely new to American TV audiences. There had been an occasional flare-up in the past, for example, the time lovable Arthur Godfrey fired his singer Julius LaRosa on the air. But Paar was doing this kind of thing all the time, giving vent to all his emotions, which could range from endearing and hilarious to ridiculous and petty.

Throwing a party every evening could destroy even the most outgoing host or hostess. And here was Paar, doing it in front of millions of people, with big names and high risk, walking a tightrope of his own nerves. A nation not yet jaded by Phil Donahue, Geraldo Rivera and a half-dozen late night hosts watched each night in absolute fascination. Movie stars, comedians and celebrities, not accustomed to routinely being interviewed as they are today, worried and fretted over being unexpectedly stung by a cool Jack Paar wisecrack.

As the show's popularity soared, Paar was so well known that his announcer, Hugh Downs, only had to introduce him with two words: "Heeeere's Jack."

Paar knew he was helming a hot show and he knew that NBC was making a lot of money from it. Paar began to resent the situation, and feud with NBC. He was called a prima donna for his contract demands. Disgruntled executives couldn't believe it when Paar boldly slapped their faces with his irreverent jokes. Nobody had ever done such a thing before.

Typical of Paar's sass was the time he stood before a big industry banquet and told the brass, "You fellows have made astonishing progress. I can remember the days when commercials were no louder than the rest of the show!"

Paar's feuding reached new levels of hysteria. When he felt slighted by an article in *TV Guide*, Jack slammed the magazine's owner Moe Annenberg on the show, intimating the man had criminal connections and had gone to prison for tax evasion. When NBC president Robert Sarnoff tried to hush him, Jack snapped, "I should think that you would be concerned about a story that is harmful to your most successful program!"

While his audiences cracked up over his jokes, insiders wondered when the jokes would make Jack crack. They got their answer at the evening taping of the February 11,1960, program.

A toilet joke flushed Jack Paar down the drain.

Jack was delighted with a silly risqué story that turned on an oddity of British slang. In England, the term for the bathroom is the "water closet," abbreviated to the even more circumspect "W.C."

That night he told his audience, "I debated for a moment whether I should do this for you because — I tell you it's funny — terribly funny — but there is a question of slight taste involved here. I debated the whole thing for about thirty seconds, and I decided to do it... It is apparently true... It was sent to me and it's probably one of the funniest things I ever had in my little hand. May I read it to? I do this only with full knowledge that we're an adult group gathered at this hour, and we're not here to do anyone any harm ever. Well, occasionally, but that was last week. Now here we are."

Then he told the story:

"An English lady, while visiting Switzerland, was looking for a room, and she asked the schoolmaster if he could recommend any to her. Hhe took her to see several rooms, and when everything was settled, the lady returned to her home to make the final preparations to move.

"When she arrived home, the thought suddenly occurred to her that she had not seen a 'W.C.' That's a water closet to the British. We would call it a bathroom or ladies' room, men's room. I guess a bathroom.

"So she immediately wrote a note to the schoolmaster asking him if there were a 'W.C.' around. The schoolmaster was a very poor student of English, so he asked the parish priest if he could help in the matter. Together they tried to discover the meaning of the letters 'W.C.' and the only solution they could find for the letters was a "Wayside Chapel." The schoolmaster then wrote to the English lady the following note:

"I take great pleasure in informing you that the "W.C." is situated nine miles from the house you occupy, in the center of a beautiful grove of pine trees surrounded by lovely grounds. It is capable of holding 229 people and is open on Sunday and

Thursday only. As there are a great number of people... I would suggest that you come early, although there is plenty of standing room as a rule. You will no doubt be glad to hear that a good number of people bring their lunch and make a day of it, while others, who can afford to, go by car and arrive just in time. I would especially recommend that your Ladyship go on Thursday when there is a musical accompaniment.

"It may interest you to know that my daughter was married in the W.C., and it was there that she met her husband. I can remember the rush there was for seats. There were ten people to a seat usually occupied by one. It was wonderful to see the expressions on their faces.

"The newest attraction is a bell donated by a wealthy resident of the district. It rings every time a person enters. A bazaar is to be held to provide plush seats for all the people, since they feel it is a long-felt need. My wife is rather delicate, so she can't attend regularly.

"I shall be delighted to reserve the best seat for you if you wish, where you will be seen by all... "

Paar's audience chuckled over the letter, and Paar smiled and said, "You're my kind of people."

NBC's censors weren't his kind of people. They clipped the routine out of the tape, which made it seem as if Paar had said something outrageously filthy.

Paar had not even used a "bathroom word."

Compare it to the toilet humor Johnny Carson routinely used years later. In describing the possibility of government officials testing urine for drug use, he quipped, "How do we know that the President and members of the cabinet will really take a urine test? Are you gonna believe the CIA? You're never gonna know until *The Washington Post* leaks it..."

In another monologue, Johnny spoke of a curious

ailment: "The Vanna White Flu. It gives you a vowel movement."

But at the time, Paar's "W.C." joke was considered the height of bad taste.

Outraged that his innocuous routine was cut, convinced that his honor was impugned, Jack went on the attack during the next broadcast.

He said that the situation was "a question of free speech," and that it was shameful that "less than an hour before the birthday of Abraham Lincoln, the man who freed the slaves," he was being persecuted for telling a joke.

"I've been up thirty hours without an ounce of sleep," he cried. "I've been wrestling with my conscience all day. I've made a decision about what I'm going to do... My wife doesn't know, but I'll be home in time and I'll tell her. I'm leaving *The Tonight Show*. There must be a better way to make a living than this, a way of entertaining people without being constantly involved in some form of controversy... It's rough on my wife and child, and I don't need it... I took over a show with 60 stations, there's now 158. The show is sold out... I love NBC, and they've been wonderful to me, but they let me down.."

His moist gaze fell on the audience and he said, "You've been peachy to me, always."

And then he walked out.

"Is he gone?" Hugh Downs asked, looking toward the wings.

The mild-mannered announcer remarked, "Jack frequently does things he regrets."

Realizing that the show had to go on, Downs brought out the evening's guests, seasoned pros Orson Bean and Shelley Berman. They entertained the crowd while agreeing with Paar's point of view.

This was national news. This was breathtaking scandal. Emotionally exhausted, Jack flew down to Florida, hiding from the press.

For weeks, guest hosts filled in, some of them indicating a readiness to take over full-time if needed. A flurry of activity went on at NBC as executives shouted and screamed at each other over whether Paar should stay or go.

Columnists wondered what would happen to Jack, and how his loyal audience could take life without him. Columnist William F. Buckley, Jr., had a different perspective: "The mistake is often made of assuming that the audience of Jack Paar is as loose-minded as he is."

Finally, on March 7, Jack returned. He stood basking in the glow of a minute-long ovation and demurely murmured, "As I was saying before I was interrupted... " The audience laughed and applauded. "There must be a better way of making a living than this. Well, I've looked. And there isn't!"

Not long after, Paar visited England and appeared on a talk show. The host asked, "Why did you flounce off your show?" Paar shot back, "I didn't *flounce.* That's only done at the BBC." Pointing out the difference between an effeminate British gait and the stalwart, John Wayne-like walk of a real man, Paar stood up and demonstrated, saying, "An American walks off like this."

And he walked off the show, leaving behind a thoroughly perplexed host and audience.

But back home the pressure continued to mount, and he couldn't even hide behind the private door of a bathroom. Paar was such an enormous star he was even besieged in restrooms. He once wrote of the the agony in trying to use the urinal with fans watching: "Finally you reach the porcelain and find that — with all eyes on your performance — you cannot! What to do? They are all watching! You panic because now they might think you are some kind of weirdo or voyeur looking around. You press the handle of the urinal, you whistle, and you wish you could get the battery-jump starter from the trunk of your auto. You think encouraging thoughts, hoping that it's a mental block, but find that your sphincter muscle has never heard of you... I tell you it's very hard being a star in a men's room."

Paar began to seek relief. He wanted Fridays off. Then he wanted Mondays off. On the air, Paar promised controversy no matter what the cost, declaring, "I am totally unable to hide what I feel... There will be a rock in every snowball!"

He saw himself as one of the most powerful men in show business. "I have made Walter Winchell, Dorothy Killgallen... and the rest of that ilk a laughingstock in this country. They have been de-fanged." But Jack's obsession with columnists was getting ridiculous. Even his sidekick Hugh Downs became disgusted, and after a Paar tirade aimed at newspaperman Irv Kupcinet, Hugh turned on Jack and said, "what you did tonight was wrong."

Paar's vacations began to seem like "tryout" times for would-be hosts. Ultimately Paar knew the strain was too much for him. He announced that he would retire from the nightly grind. He professed no interest in who his replacement might be and snickered that the network executives "looked, held meetings, but as of now, they have not found anyone. So if you know of anyone, please get in touch with NBC. There may be a finder's fee."

Actually, there was a pretty short list of replacements for Paar. At the top of it were two quizmasters: Johnny Carson of *Who Do You Trust?* and Merv Griffin, host of *Play Your Hunch.*

CHAPTER SIX

HERE'S JOHNNY! WHO'S JOHNNY?

The more Jack Paar thought of it, the more he considered Merv Griffin the best replacement. While Johnny was one of the guest hosts picked by NBC, Paar discovered Merv himself. It wasn't difficult. Griffin was hosting *Play Your Hunch* in the same studio that Paar used for the evening's *Tonight Show* broadcasts. One day Paar happened to arrive early and was surprised to see how well the smooth young Griffin was presiding over the screaming quiz contestants.

Paar delighted the audience by stopping the show and coming out on stage. "What are you doing!" he cried.

"We're taping a show," Merv said.

"This is *my* studio," Paar deadpanned.

"Only after four o'clock. It's my studio in the morning... "

"What are those people doing?"

"*Play Your Hunch*... it's our show."

"So this is what you do during the day. Well, sorry to bother you, Merv, I'll be on my way."

Later Paar gave Merv some advice: "Just always remember one thing about talk shows and you'll be fine: YOU always be prepared but let the show unfold. Let it be chaos — planned chaos. Chaos pays off on a talk show. You want an electric undercurrent that keeps the audience from knowing what is going to happen next. You be ready with your next question, but know when to let the show run itself."

Paar liked booking Griffin as a guest host, and
Griffin's ratings were good. The press reacted well to
him. Merv figured he was going to take over for Paar.
He recalls now, that "the network executives, however, had already signed a replacement, long before I
showed up on the scene... "

NBC wanted Johnny.

Jack Paar is prone to re-writing history. In his
last book, he went so far as to write: "Johnny was
my choice." Then, a typical left-handed compliment:
"I wanted to get away so badly that I would have
accepted, if I was asked, to be replaced by Vincent
Lopez or Yogi Berra."

At the time, Johnny wasn't sure he wanted to follow Paar. Johnny had been burned a few times in his
professional career already and was still concerned
about his own naiveté in the business. After all, he
hadn't even been in New York City that long as host
of the quiz show for ABC. There was still a lot of the
shy Nebraskan in Johnny.

Carson was born in Corning, Iowa, but in early
childhood moved with his family to Nebraska. The
shy kid practiced magic tricks that became his way
of getting attention. After graduating high school,
Johnny went into the Navy's V-12 program. Fresh
out of officers' training school, he was assigned to
the South Pacific. He arrived to discover sailors
ripped to pieces by a torpedo. The young ensign had
his first job: directing the retrieval of the bodies.

On Guam, Johnny amused sailors with card
tricks as "The Great Carsoni" and went on to try ventriloquism, buying a sidekick dummy that he
prophetically named Eddie. Johnny loved show business more than the Navy, and mentioned it — to the
Secretary of the Navy himself, James Forrestal.

Ensign Carson was entrusted to deliver a message to Forrestal, and when the powerful naval officer asked young Johnny if he planned to make the

Navy his career, Johnny said no and whipped out a deck of cards instead. Within minutes, Ensign Carson was making his boss smile with some sleight of-hand tricks and that mischievous Nebraska grin.

When Johnny came marching home, he attended the University of Nebraska, majoring in journalism. He got a job at radio station KFAB, appearing on a serial, *Eddie Sosby and the Radio Rangers*, at 7:30 in the morning. To earn extra money, Johnny resurrected his magic act. He got big bucks: sometimes $25 a show. His assistant was Joan Wolcott. Friends called her Jody.

They had been dating for a while. At first, she was not impressed. The first night out with the college senior, she found Johnny "cold, aloof and distant." A year after graduation, 1949, they married.

Johnny's graduate thesis was "How to Write Comedy Jokes." It was something unusual: a taped lecture by the young student spliced with clips from the radio stars he especially admired: Jack Benny, Fred Allen and Bob Hope.

Back then, Johnny said: "A good comedian can keep you home from bridge parties to listen to his program, [and] can get you to buy his sponsor's products. But there are many reasons for a top comedian's success and one of the most important is in the writing... "

The trio of Benny, Allen and Hope would provide Johnny with most of his influences and inspiration. Jack Benny was likable; one of the family. "If an audience likes a performer," Carson said, "he can get away with anything. If they don't like you, it doesn't make any difference how clever or witty you are. It just won't work... Jack's audience always cared."

Benny's comic style was to let the jokes bounce off him. Carson would later admit, "Basically, I, like him, am a reaction comedian. I play off of the things that are happening around me... When things happen around me, I can play off them by reaction, timing, pauses and looks... "

Bob Hope appealed to Carson's aggressive instincts. Hope was the wisecracking wiseguy. Hope could get away with a line about politics or politicians and still be the patriotic All-American boy.

And there was Fred Allen, radio's greatest wit, the man who sparked joy and envy in other comics by the ease of his ad-libs. When Jack Benny couldn't handle Fred's quickness during a radio sketch, Benny cracked "You wouldn't have said that if my writers were here."

Carson practiced his comedy style working for local radio stations. Once Johnny became comfortable, the wiseguy streak started coming out. Johnny just couldn't help it. When he had to pause between platters to read a commercial for the Friendly Savings Bank, he made them very friendly: "Drop in any time. At two or three in the morning... help yourself!"

Carson balanced old-fashioned manners with scampish stunts. Disc jockey Johnny resented the fake "celebrity interviews" he had to do. To promote a star, record companies send out a trick record and a script. The disc jockey reads questions from the script while the disc plays the star's answers. It seems like the star was actually in town chatting with the local disc jockey. Over the years everyone from Henry Mancini and the Smothers Brothers to Julian Lennon and Genesis have released these "open ended" interview records for disc jockeys.

Back then, Johnny dutifully did these celebrity interviews. Only he re-arranged the questions. One of the "guests" coming to Omaha was Patti Page:

Johnny: I understand you're hitting the bottle pretty good, Patti. When did you start?

Patti: When I was six. I used to get up at church socials and do it.

Johnny joined WOW-TV and won his own TV show: *The Squirrel's Nest*. He had experimented with television briefly in college and was part of the cast for an experimental closed-circuit broadcast, "The Story of Undulant Fever." He played a milkman concerned over unpasteurized milk.

The Squirrel's Nest not only became an experimental showcase for Johnny's talents, he learned how far a star could go off-camera. Bill Wiseman, Jr., the assistant general manager of WOW, saw this side of Carson firsthand: "There was the time when Johnny received a memo from WOW's accounting department. Johnny had used the company phone to make a twenty-cent long-distance call to Council Bluffs."

The company auditor wanted Carson to either explain what that call was for, or pay the twenty cents. As Wiseman recalls, Johnny did neither. "And so it went on, for months, I guess. The auditor was stubborn and Johnny – well, I don't know whether he was stubborn or just having fun. Finally the auditor got tough. You know, pay or else!"

Johnny still wouldn't pay. "The next afternoon an armored car pulled up in front of the station. Two uniformed guards with drawn revolvers got out and stalked into the station with an envelope that could be surrendered only to the auditor, who came a-running! He signed, opened the envelope, and found a check in the amount of 20 cents, signed by John Carson."

To make his point, Johnny had spent $25 renting the armored car and the two guards.

To pay his $72 monthly rent, "The Great Carsoni" could still be prevailed upon to perform. Johnny was one of the best magicians in Nebraska. When a teenage magician appeared at the Lions Club in Lincoln, Nebraska, the announcer actually apologized to the crowd: "We have a disappointment for you. We couldn't get Johnny Carson today. But we have a young man who someday is going to be just as good."

And out stepped young Dick Cavett. Cavett recalled in his autobiography that the two future talk show stars crossed paths way back when. Anxious to watch the master, Cavett attended a performance of "The Great Carsoni" at a church affair and met Carson backstage:

"He looked slightly annoyed. People are always nosing around when a magician is setting up, and the magician rightly would like to catapult them through the nearest window." When Cavett, explained that he was a budding magician himself, Carson "became quite friendly." Johnny showed the teenager some card tricks, and Dick felt "aglow" from his "contact with a star."

Johnny was a slick pro even then. During his act, he introduced the celebrity in the audience, the young magician Dick Cavett and had Dick take a bow. Cavett and his friends lingered to catch a glimpse of the superstar after the show. "How we envied him as he glamorously pulled out into the night in what looked like a 49 Chevy!"

Carson was soon ready to drive out to California: "I made an audition movie, using WOW's film and WOW's cameraman late one night after the station was closed."

In 1951 Carson left his wife and his young son, Chris, back in Omaha, finding his way to California only after an Oklahoma blizzard left him stranded in the bitter cold. A detour down through Texas battered him with the fiercest winter that state had seen in decades. The miles burned holes in his tires till each one had to be patched.

Carson's self-esteem took a beating as he peddled his tape from door to door. It reminded him of years earlier: "I sold vacuum cleaners door to door for about a day and a half. Couldn't take the rejection."

This time he took it. From San Francisco he went down to Los Angeles. With some help from an ex-Iowan neighbor named Bill Brennan (later a CBS vice president), Johnny got a job as staff announcer at WNXT. Carson quickly discovered that "staff announcer" was short for "staff announcer, handyman, messenger and anything else we can think of." Some at WNXT showed open hostility toward the rube from Omaha. Carson bristled, but accepted a role he knew by one word: "flunky." He and his family settled in California.

In 1952 Johnny tasted his first moment of glory. The folks back home heard him speak to a nationwide audience. He announced the immortal words, "This is the CBS television network."

Johnny made the painful transition from local big shot to competent city pro. Now with two young kids to support, he was barely getting by. He finally was able to convince the local CBS TV station that he could handle a half-hour show for them and produce it cheap. They asked, "How... cheap... is it?" Budget: twenty-five dollars. The show premiered on October 4, 1952.

Carson's Cellar was the essence of low budget, but it had the youthful enthusiasm and schooled comedy smarts of Johnny Carson. He wasn't going to let the tight budget prevent him from securing big stars and big attention. On one show, he had a member of the stage crew rush past the camera. "That was Red Skelton," Johnny announced to his viewers. "Too bad he didn't have time to stay and say a few words!"

Carson's wiseguy antics surprised and amused the older comics. Fred Allen became the first star to really appear on the show. The "real" Red Skelton came down soon after. *Carson's Cellar* is surprisingly similar to the style Johnny later used on *The Tonight*

Show. He opened with a smart monologue and followed with loose and laughable sketch material.

A typical show opened with an announcement: "KNXT cautiously presents... *Carson's Cellar*... and here's the guy who has to account for this half hour, Johnny Carson!"

Johnny came out: "Thank you very much for coming into the cellar tonight. It's a little bit cold tonight." He presses his fingers together, Jack Benny-style. "In fact I think that's why we got one young lady out there. Before the show I said, 'Why did you come to the show?' and she said, 'Because it was cold outside.' But I like to have an honest audience... "

Carson deadpanned the line just like Jack Benny. Johnny once admitted to Jack's wife, Mary Livingstone, "I realize now that, in the early days of my career, I was too much like Jack. I tried to emulate him, which was wrong. But I idolized Jack... I can show you things I did in the early days... in which I was so close to his style, it embarrasses me now."

After a Benny-like wave of his arms, he tries to get the studio audience involved with him: "Did you see the game yesterday?"

He puts his hands into his pockets. "USC-UCLA. Of course yesterday was a big football weekend all over the country.... 96,000 people at the Coliseum. And I had a couple of tickets to the game. Of course the game was sold out two days ahead of time. You couldn't buy a ticket at all. You could buy a ticket, but the only way you could get it was from a ticket scalper. Those are the fellas, you know, who buy up the tickets at regular prices and just before game time they sell 'em for a lot more money. And tickets were going for 20, 30, 50 dollars a seat! Fifty dollars for a ticket." Johnny pauses with a deadpan look of exasperation. "That makes me kinda mad." He pauses a beat. "I'm kinda disgusted." A Jack Benny look of wistful chagrin: "I got a lousy ten dollars a seat for mine!"

Carson's sketches had the same hip-vaudeville feel as later routines on *The Tonight Show*. One typical effort, featuring guest star Jack Bailey (best remembered as host of *Queen for a Day*), offers Johnny as a manic quizmaster hosting *Take It Or Nothing*.

"If any one of our contestants say the secret word tonight, they win $100!" Johnny shouts happily. "The secret word is prognostication."

Johnny brings out Jack Bailey, who immediately notes, "I had a prognostication I might be on the show." An announcer's voiceover: "Ladies and gentlemen, the secret word has been changed to contingency." Johnny resumes his fast-paced banter. "All right now, let's get on with the game. Sir, I hope you're ready to earn some of those big prizes tonight."

Bailey shrugs. "Well, I always hold myself in readiness for any contingency... "

The announcer: "Ladies and gentlemen, the secret word has been changed to tranquility."

Johnny turns to the female contestant. "How about you Miss, are you having a lot of fun tonight?"

"I'm not exactly a sea of tranquility!"

The announcer: "Ladies and Gentlemen, there will be no secret word tonight."

There are consolation prizes, at least: "Here's something you'll treasure for years to come. You'll get a whole year's supply and you can use them indefinitely."

Then to the bewildered audience: "Are you havin' fun, audience? You betcha! You bet you're havin' fun!"

More prizes: "First, a beautiful pair of hammered, aluminum shower clogs. You also receive a lifesize picture of Buster Crabbe that glows in the dark. And a whole year's supply of marinated Ping Pong balls for every member of your family. And a beautiful deep-fat fryer that fries deep fat to a golden brown. If you like fried fat you'll love the Wilson Deep Fat Fryer!"

In May of 1954, Johnny moved on to network television, hosting a quiz show called *Earn Your Vacation*. It was earning him enough money to support his wife (and now three children), but he found more satisfaction in writing jokes for Red Skelton.

During rehearsals on August 18, 1954, Skelton hurled himself into a prop door. Which didn't open. With just 90 minutes before air time the producers were frantic. In a scene right out of a bad 1930's movie, they wrung their hands, wondering, "Who can take Red's place?"

They called Johnny, who was relaxing at home, waiting to see Red deliver some of the jokes he'd written.

Carson raced to his car and began the half-hour drive to the studio. Along the way he occupied himself by thinking up some light gags to explain to the audience what happened to Red. And who the hell Johnny Carson was.

And just like that bad 1930's movie, the young star was a rousing success. The nervous CBS brass were relieved and delighted with the performance of the bright young comic. And almost immediately plans began to formulate to give Johnny a variety show just like Red's. The result was like a very bad 1930's horror picture. Carson was always a little pessimistic about television. He said, "There's no place in TV to be bad. In vaudeville there was room to be bad and to learn. Even in radio you had the chance. In his early radio days Fred Allen was canceled but came back."

CBS wanted to give their new star a little bit of added exposure before he went prime time. They brought him to New York to be a substitute host for two weeks on a morning talk show. The host of that show was an ex-stand-up comic by the name of Jack Paar.

Co-workers from that era remember Johnny as extremely quiet. His visit to the big city awed him. He stayed in a New York hotel directly across the street from the show's office. He did his job and came back. All business. No problems. Asked if he was taking in any of the sights in the Big Apple, he answered, "I pretty much stay in my room."

A prime-time show was what Johnny wanted, but at the same time, the enormous risk and the tension to succeed turned some of the moment's pleasure into agonized pain. Rather than appearing happy and excited, as onlookers might have logically expected, Carson was serious, worried, tense and withdrawn.

People began to describe him as "cold." He just didn't have the time to present a warm facade to everyone. He was trying to chart a path with as much cold calculation as possible. Johnny guessed and second-guessed himself through all the rehearsals, going through the schizoid simultaneous egotism and insecurity that dogs so many who choose to confront an audience of strangers.

Television in 1955 was a fast and furious mix of quiz shows, sitcoms and dramas, mostly half-hours. Johnny's show was scheduled for Thursday evenings at 10 p.m. On that night viewers could tune in at 7:30 for *The Lone Ranger*, then watch *Love That Bob*, or Groucho Marx's *You Bet Your Life*. At 8:30 there was *People's Choice* (a sitcom about a talking dog) or *Stop the Music*. More half-hour quickies followed between 9 and 10, including *Dragnet*, *Star Tonight*, *Down You Go*, *Four Star Playhouse* and *Ford Theater*. Restless audiences could spin the dial endlessly while network executives played Russian roulette with the results.

By 10 p.m., Johnny's time, many viewers were already played out. His competition was a travelogue, *Outside U.S.A.*, on ABC, and the formidable *Lux Video Theater* on NBC. When *The Johnny Carson Show* premiered on CBS Thursday night, 10 p.m., June 30, 1955 the critics were "amused." Young Johnny is a "nice guy", wrote Jack Gould.

Johnny's show was formatted like most comedy-variety shows of the era. There were sketches and parodies of popular TV shows. The gags were broken up by the weary but traditional spots for the regular boy and girl vocalists (Jack Prince and Jill Corey). Johnny expanded on the kind of thing he'd done for *Carson's Cellar*. He did sketches on everything from a dentist pulling a whale's tooth to a gun-shy daredevil worrying over being shot out of a cannon. Johnny even resorted to celebrity impressions, including a parody of Steve Allen and his "heh-heh" laugh.

Carson's Cellar had been experimental. In prime time, Johnny tried bucking the network big shots. He put in some material that was considered not ready for prime time. In more recent decades, Steve Martin, Andy Kaufman and Albert Brooks challenged the standard stand-up techniques. Brooks, in one *Tonight Show* appearance, actually read the phone book for laughs.

Johnny was showing that kind of comic bravado back in 1955. Writer Philip Minoff remembers: "Carson one night bragged to his audience that he could hold its attention simply by executing an elementary tap-dance. He launched into a lumbering "Tea-for-Two" step, and the people out front didn't take their eyes from their sets for the next three minutes. For there, on a large movie screen behind Carson, flashed a crazy montage of everything from dive bombers to storm-tossed battleships!"

Critics chuckled mildly. Jack O'Brien in the *New York Journal-American* noted that Carson "has a sudden smile which explodes either in sincerity or in masterful imitation thereof. His manner is restrained... Probably Carson will labor along under the label of "another [George] Gobel," for his pleasant, almost aimless appeal has much in common with Gobel... humor more on the giggle side than guffaws."

In *The New York Times*, Jack Gould noted: "C.B.S. apparently intends to use Mr. Carson as its answer to George Gobel... The construction of last night's show was disconcertingly similar to the pattern of Mr. Gobel's program... such copy-catting is a serious mistake... The young man is no Gobel; he has neither the uncanny timing nor the performing experience... What Mr. Carson does have is a singular youthful charm and an impish twinkle in the eye. He seems like the proverbial nice guy down the block."

Johnny's ratings weren't bad, but CBS was panicking. They felt the Gobel trend was ending. They wanted Johnny to be more like a bombastic Red Skelton or a Jackie Gleason. Johnny reluctantly agreed, telling a reporter that his show would now have "a novelty act, lots of chorus girls, production numbers, etc. This way the burden isn't on the comedian, as it was on Sid Caesar a few years back... He went crazy trying to get new stuff to do each week." Producer Ben Brady agreed with CBS that this was best. For, after all, Johnny "is generically not a strong stand-up comedian."

Carson says, "When I was signed everybody told me I was great. Then when I started the show, everybody had just a few ideas for improving it. They killed it. I had eight different writers in 39 weeks. And seven directors. Imagine that. Seven directors. They couldn't all have been wrong... there was interference from the sponsors. Before long I found myself and my material subjected to the opinion of businessmen. It was frustrating, believe me."

He remembered a typical moment of inane insanity dealing with CBS executives:

Exec: Johnny, what your show needs is a feeling of importance.

Johnny: What's a feeling of importance?

Exec: A feeling of importance is... a feeling of importance.

After 39 weeks he was dumped. Even his manager walked out on him. Johnny's worst suspicions about friendship and loyalty were confirmed. So was the never-to-be-forgotten chagrin of having his own comedic instincts ignored. After the show ended, Johnny remarked, "I have no great hates, although today I wouldn't want Ben Brady to produce my coffee break."

When Johnny would get *The Tonight Show*, he made a point of never being swamped with production numbers or upstaged by dancers. He rarely performed in a sketch with a large cast. He would prove to be, for thirty years, a strong stand-up comedian: the only one to endure night after night for three decades.

Carson had a short-lived daytime show and then in desperation auditioned for a quiz show called *Do You Trust Your Wife?* The title was changed to *Who Do You Trust?* and it became an unexpected daytime hit.

The show was loosely patterned after Groucho's *You Bet Your Life*. The focus was not on winning things, but on the patter between the quick ad-libbing host and the wacky contestants.

Carson got some mileage from Max and Will Berkowitz, twin undertakers from Cleveland, and even more from Valerie and Leila Croft, blond identical twins. He got double the laughs from a woman who insisted it was possible to breathe through the toes. He learned something many comics never do: share the laughs.

One time, a movie heavy named Harold Huber turned up as a guest. "How do you feel about having been slain in over 100 films?" Johnny asked.

Huber answered, "It's a living."

The quiz show was making Johnny a household word, but it wasn't quite the same as having his own comedy show. "Some day," he sighed, "people will want to laugh again. They'll pull back from their television sets and ask themselves: How long is it since I've had a laugh out of this thing?"

As with Groucho's show, Johnny's program relied on pre-interviews to bring out the juiciest topics to discuss on the air. For example, in the course of the staff pre-interview, it was discovered that a contestant worked in a department store, and had recently divorced her husband. Johnny was clued to ask where she worked, and whether she was married.

Then came the scripted ad-lib: "What did you do, take him to the exchange department?"

Interviewing a musician who worked in the musical *Subways Are for Sleeping,* Johnny was handed a quickie ad-lib: "What do you play, a train whistle?" And when interviewing a woman whose husband worked as a meat smoker in a deli, Johnny was given: "Couldn't he get cigarettes?"

Johnny often came up with his own fresh ad-libs. He also learned how to make his scripted answers *seem* ad-libbed. To be a good comedian meant being a good actor.

The show was a training ground, giving Carson valuable insight into dealing with average people. His comedy was moving away from impersonal gag sketches and monology. He was learning to get laughs interviewing people. Without these five years of contestant interaction, he might have failed as a talk show host, as many pure stand-up comics have.

He learned that "almost without exception... the best contestants are those you actually have to coax. The more eager they are to be on, the duller they turn out to be."

He got along especially well with housewives. He told Harriet Van Horne: "They're good-natured and quick-witted. And they're not afraid of looking ridiculous. It also might surprise the program directors to know how smart most housewives are. I hate to hear this condescending talk about the twelve-year-old mind of the daytime viewer. A lot of housewives are college graduates. They read books, they travel, they're hep."

But Carson was restless. "Sure, I don't want to do this kind of thing all my life," he said at the time. "I may do a straight dramatic film for Columbia... I'm signed up for guest spots with Garry Moore, Dinah Shore and a few others. You have to keep your hand in the nighttime scene. There are some things you can't do in a daytime show. There's also talk of a night spot for me at ABC."

Indeed, in 1961 ABC made a tentative offer to Johnny for a talk show opposite Jack Paar. He turned it down, but asked if they'd be interested in *Who Do You Trust?* at that hour. After all, Groucho's quiz show was on in prime time. A late night quiz show could be something unique.

Carson pitched his idea not only to network executives, but to the public. He mentioned it in interviews, and in an interview with the *Newark Evening News* contrasted his proposed quiz show with the antics of *The Tonight Show* and Jack Paar:

"I don't have celebrities on my show. I work with *people*. I've got the greatest staff of gag writers in the world — the people who come on my show... The emphasis is on the contestants. Do you know what the people watching us are most interested in? Other people. The little chats we have with the contestants have more audience appeal than all the gimmicks of the game."

Carson was getting used to the game of television. Working a daily grind, Carson learned how to be amiable and pleasant even when he wasn't in the mood. In his office he had a dart board that he used all the time. "It's a good way to work off the aggressions," he told staffers. He also had a small drum set, which he admitted was "a form of therapy."

The show was Johnny, not quiz money. Asked years later to describe the actual mechanics of the show, he shrugged and said, "I don't even know what the hell the point of the game was."

CHAPTER SEVEN

EXIT JACK. WILL JOHNNY BE "UP TO PAAR"?

When Johnny Carson was approached as a possible new host for *The Tonight Show*, he shook his head. "I just wasn't sure I could cut it," he said later.

Carson had been a guest host on *The Tonight Show*. He had proved to a lot of people that he could do the job. But he still wasn't sure himself. Johnny had guested on major prime-time shows. Hell, he'd even starred on one, hellish though it turned out to be. He had made his Broadway debut while handling his quiz show duties, starring in *Tunnel of Love* in 1958.

His manager told Johnny how much the NBC brass and even other comics were impressed by his smooth ad-libbing style.

At Friar's Roasts, Johnny had proved he could duel with the best. He fended off bald insult comic Jack E. Leonard by calling him "The Mean Mr. Clean." Fellow comics doubled over with delight. When Jan Murray made a long speech eulogizing the late Al Jolson, lamenting that his children would not grow up sharing the joy of Jolie's voice, Carson interrupted: "They grew up while you were talking!"

The Friars, guys like Buddy Hackett and Joe E. Lewis, enjoyed the young comic who could match them gag for gag. Phil Silvers once stood up and said, "Johnny is the only Gentile on the dais and immediately after his speech we are going to circumcise him!"

Johnny bludgeoned back. Talking about Friar Alan King, he said, "All I've been reading about in the papers is Alan King and I'm tired of it! Alan King has guest shots. Alan King's producing four shows. Alan King has a Rolls-Royce. Just once I'd like to pick up the paper and see "Alan King Has Gonorrhea.""

Carson was scalding at a roast for Don Rickles. He declared, "I am one of Don's very close friends. And I think that's important to Don. Because queers need friends! Let's get it out into the open. About eight years ago when I first met Don, the entire top of his head was covered with thick, curly black hair. He was going down on Kay Arman, and that's enough to make Smokey the Bear turn queer!"

At a dinner for Robert F. Kennedy, Johnny cracked, "I would have preferred a written invitation to this affair, instead of being rudely awakened at 4 a.m. by the FBI."

Carson was a little more restrained when he first began major guest-hosting duty on *The Tonight Show*. He subbed for Paar for a full week beginning on May 26, 1958.

Carson wasn't about to make waves, saying "Nobody's going to get an ulcer on this show. I don't expect to 'slay' anybody, but then I never did. My specialty is light satire of the easy, relaxed school, and I've a feeling it's the one form of comedy that'll probably survive on TV... On the Paar show, thank heaven, you can't rely on material, not when you have to entertain for an hour and forty-five minutes each night."

Johnny was successful on *The Tonight Show* right from the start. Earl Wilson wrote, "Johnny is now NBC's secret weapon to succeed Jack Paar in case Jack really quits." Still, Johnny needed to be coaxed.

Comics loved him. Network executives were high on him. And insiders reported that since he was far from being a temperamental man like Paar, most of

Johnny's staff seemed to be able to work with him. Johnny was friendly with *Who Do You Trust?* producer Art Stark as well as associate producer Mary Dodd. But as Dodd remembers, "He was uncomfortable socially. What they call his distance and coolness in the days when I knew him I would've categorized as shyness and insecurity."

As all offices do, the *Who Do You Trust?* gang threw parties for various minor occasions. At one holiday party, everyone was gathered around celebrating. Johnny excused himself and went into a small office nearby and began making phone calls.

"We pretty much forgot about Johnny," one of the partiers remembers. "I needed to use the phone, and I picked it up. Johnny was on the line — but he wasn't talking to anyone. There was no one on the line. He was sitting by himself with the phone, just making up conversation. He did that because he just couldn't be comfortable at the party."

With small groups of people, and those he knew well, things were a bit different. Says Mary Dodd: "As long as there were no other people around he would be like anyone else. You don't expect any of your friends to keep you in stitches. He was witty, very pleasant and a pretty ordinary down-to-earth man."

Dodd continues, "He didn't come on like a brash young comic. After all, he wasn't a New Yorker, he hadn't done the Borscht Belt. He was from Nebraska. He was a nice young Middle West kid. Johnny didn't have any friends here. Any male friends. He had his wife and children."

Over the years of the quiz show, producer Art Stark became a friend off-camera, as did the show's announcer, a Philadelphia TV personality Stark had hired: Ed McMahon. Ed was always what he seemed to be on camera: gregarious and affable. He and Johnny would often have lunch together and soon were close friends. Ed knew New York and was able to show Johnny around. Carson found a companion to help him through the deteriorating stages of his marriage to Jody.

Ed recalled, "On Fridays we used to do two shows, a live one at three-thirty in the afternoon and at seven we taped a show for the following Monday. This gave everybody a three-day weekend. Between those two shows Johnny and I got into the habit of strolling next door to Sardi's little bar for a couple of relaxers, which we felt we needed before doing the second show. We only had about two hours. How much can you drink in two hours, especially if you're talking business? The trouble was that Johnny, as he's said many times on the air, isn't the world's greatest drinking man. Give him three shots and he gets very frisky. And sometimes when we'd come back to tape the Monday show, tongues got tangled and things got said that had to be bleeped."

As Paar became flakier and flakier, and the word came down that it would be either Merv or Johnny, Johnny had to make a decision.

Skitch Henderson recalled a time Johnny guest-hosted. Skitch walked over and said, "I hear you're being favorably considered as the new host." Carson just stared at him for a moment and walked away.

Columnist Ben Gross of the *Daily News* talked to the "boyish 5-foot-10 1/2-inch 153-pounder" about doing a talk show.

"I'd like to do one," Carson admitted cautiously, "but only if the circumstances are right."

"What's the big difference between day and night on TV?"

"...At night you can do satire and talk about topical things because the audience is in the mood for that type of humor. But not during the day, when you're playing to so many housewives."

"You mean that they aren't intelligent?"

"Of course they're intelligent. But satire requires

concentrated looking and listening and most women during the day are too busy with children and household chores."

Johnny experimented with satire whenever he could get a prime-time or late-night assignment. On Steve Allen's prime-time show, Johnny mentioned a topical news item: Gangster Mickey Cohen's car was stolen. His dog was in it at the time. Johnny joked, "The car had not been found, but the police recovered the dog – holding up a liquor store."

The following day he received threatening phone calls from a gangster who said, "Watch your step! Don't make jokes about Mickey Cohen."

Meanwhile, TV producers were censoring the monologues he did on variety shows. He had a line he just couldn't use back then: "Where are tomorrow's comedians coming from? Based on recent observations, from the Democratic and Republican parties."

Maybe the only place where a gag like that could be told was late night, on a show where controversy was welcomed: *The Tonight Show.*

The controversy of Jack Paar's reign ended with a memorable final show.

His farewell was a major event. For fifteen minutes Jack remained in his dressing room while others performed and Hugh Downs read tributes to the "towering personality" and celebrities filled the stage. On tape, everyone from Billy Graham, Richard Nixon and Robert F. Kennedy to Bob Hope, Joey Bishop and Jack Benny bid him a final goodbye. Paar was in tears more than once.

Just to show that bygones were not bygones, he took one last opportunity to attack Dorothy Kilgallen, who was going to India "to fight a mongoose." Then he called Walter Winchell a phony who wears his patriotism "like a bathrobe."

At the end, a tearful Paar was serenaded by

Robert Merrill singing *Pagliacci*. A *Tonight Show* title card was flashed on the screen:

"No More to Come."

Paar was tearful, but he had reasons to be cheerful. Jack's salary on *The Tonight Show* netted him $4,000 a week. Now, following Steve Allen's lead by trying a weekly prime-time series, he would have a less strenuous job and job and a slight pay increase: $30,000 a week.

For doing *Who Do You Trust?* Johnny Carson had toiled for $500 a week. Now, Carson was able to ink a contract for $100,000 a year, the magical salary figure of the era's greats, like baseball star Mickey Mantle.

March 29, 1962 had been Jack's farewell.

On March 30, Johnny Carson didn't take over.

Not on the 31st. Not on April Fool's Day.

His big break was being held up by ABC. When Paar left, Johnny's contract had a half year still to go. When ABC refused to let Johnny leave, he publicly called them "The network with a heart." Frustrated and tense, Johnny was sentenced to six months of waiting.

On March 28, the day before Paar's departure, Bob Williams of the *New York Post* asked Johnny about taking over *The Tonight Show*. Carson said: "What can I say? That I'm worried? How would that look in print?"

While he waited, NBC went with guest hosts, including some of the most famous names in show business. Johnny knew that any one of them could catch fire and become a candidate to replace him the moment his ratings dipped. Maybe some weasel contract lawyer would even help break NBC's contract!

The nervous young quiz show host had to sit and keep waiting. Waiting while reporters asked: "Johnny, what are you going to do? How can you replace Paar? What will your show be like?"

A reporter for the *New York Herald Tribune*, Richard K. Doan, remembered Carson during this difficult time. Carson lit a cigarette and began to answer one of Doan's questions. Then he looked down and saw a cigarette already burning in his ashtray. "Who's nervous?" Johnny said.

Columnist Kay Gardella witnessed Carson edgily recite all the pitfalls of the job to her: "The job primarily, on a nightly show, is to be a catalyst... The trick is to keep things going... I know it's a tremendous strain doing a nightly show. You could dig a ditch for twelve hours a day and not be as tired. It's the hottest spot on television."

But Carson wanted it: "It's also the only place left where you can experiment... It's a comedy laboratory. Sure, I could remain secure by staying in daytime TV and not running the risk of failure... but there's something more to show business than security. I suppose it's ego... "

He knew he was no Jack Paar. Carson told Gardella, "It would be difficult to continue that kind of rapport with the people. I'm going to try to make it an entertaining show."

As the months passed, Carson's feelings wold saw between elation, frustration and fear. Sometimes they came to rest in the numb middle-ground of ambivalence. To Margaret McManus he shrugged, "I guess I'm glad to be leaving [*Who Do You Trust?*] after so long a haul, although you develop an affinity for something you've done this long. I can't tell how I'll feel on the last day. After a few weeks of *Tonight*, it might look darn good to me."

Of the impending show, he allowed, "You have to know that you cannot be brilliant on every show. There will be nights when you won't be funny and times when you can think of nothing to say. There will be times when the show just hangs there and you must sense this quickly, and do something, anything, to change the pace."

He was so unsure of himself that even doing an opening monologue, Carson's strong point, was in doubt. "It can be a trap," he told one reporter. "We'll probably vary the opening."

Ed McMahon was coming along as Johnny's side-kick. He asked Johnny, "How do you see my role in this show? What's my stance? How do I fit in?"

Johnny answered, "Ed, if you mean, what are you going to do, let me put it to you this way. I don't even know what I'm going to do. So let's just play it by ear and see what happens."

Carson ended his contracted duties for *Who Do You Trust* on September 7, and had barely three weeks to pull together the premiere of *The Tonight Show*. He had three weeks before taking over the most prestigious, pressure-filled five-times-a-week job in show business. All he had to do was be funny and effortlessly charming, score big ratings and make everybody forget about Jack Paar.

One day at the strange new office of *The Tonight Show* Johnny opened a copy of the *New York World-Telegram* and was greeted with a headline in inch-high type: "Will Carson Be Up to Paar?"

The first sentence read: "Several hours before air time on the night of Oct. 1, Johnny Carson will step out before a studio audience in Rockefeller Center and run a risk few performers care to undertake: laying a big, fat egg."

CHAPTER EIGHT

JOHNNY'S A HIT: JACK'S IN A SNIT

While Johnny waited to take over *The Tonight Show*, the ratings began to dip. Without Jack Paar viewers didn't seem to be interested. The guest hosts included everyone from Groucho Marx to Jerry Lewis, from Mort Sahl to Soupy Sales. Even Paar's sidekick Hugh Downs got a chance while Carson played *Who Do You Trust?*

Many of the hosts eager to host *The Tonight Show* had second thoughts after they got their first chance. It wasn't as easy as it looked.

In April of 1962, Merv Griffin suffered through his "first time." His knees knocked together as he waited to go on. He was nervous throughout the monologue, worried that his mild jokes would get zero laughs.

"I'm thrilled to be filling in for Jack Paar tonight," he said. "But I realize people in the audience here and at home have no idea who I am. It's eleven-thirty at night and I happen to be a daytime person. If your wives are sleeping, men, wake 'em up and they'll explain who I am, because I spend mornings with them while you're at work, on a game show called *Play Your Hunch...* "

In his autobiography he admitted that after the show broke for a commercial, he broke for cover. He rushed to his dressing room, telling the producer, "I have to leave... I don't know how to do this show, you'll have to get someone else... This isn't going to work... Get me out of here... "

Griffin had to be shoved back on stage that night in April of 1962.

On another night in April, while waiting for his late night chance to come, Johnny guested on *The Timex All-Star Comedy Show*. Buddy Hackett was the star of the evening, but he didn't want to be billed as host.

"Me, a host?" Hackett bellowed. "Ya gotta get the right type! A fella who won't offend anybody, a colorless personality... He should be neat and not too bright. A real loser!"

Hackett turned to Johnny. Carson stepped forward and said in deadpan chagrin, "Hi there. This is your host: Johnny 'colorless, neutral, neat and not too bright, a real loser' Carson."

Johnny made sure to get a lot of color for his first show. On the night of his *Tonight Show* debut, he brought in Joan Crawford, Tony Bennett, Rudy Vallee and Mel Brooks.

Opposite him, CBS's New York affiliate ran a 1935 George Raft movie called *Rumba* and ABC offered *Father Was a Fullback*, a 1949 Fred MacMurray comedy. CBS and ABC were still not ready to challenge NBC with a network show, but that didn't mean Johnny could relax. The important thing was to equal Jack Paar's ratings.

October 1, 1962.

This was the date that Johnny had moved to his first real home in Avoca, Iowa. This was the date that Johnny had married his first real sweetheart, Joan "Jody" Wolcott. Now it was the date for the most important night in his professional life.

Before the show Johnny received two gifts. He received a pair of cuff links in gold that depicted St. Genesius, the patron saint for actors. And from his new girlfriend, Joanne Copeland, he received another pair of cuff links. These were custom-made with NBC cameras on them. Johnny wore one of each, hoping this would double his luck.

One of the greatest comedians of all time came out on that October night to face the expectant audience. It was Groucho Marx. He introduced Johnny, and Johnny nervously pointed out that he had been waiting for this moment for over six months. "Now I'm aware of what you ladies must go through in a pregnancy. The difference is, I didn't get sick. But I'm the only performer ever held up and spanked by General Sarnoff."

Like an important Broadway show, the debut of the new *Tonight Show* was hot entertainment news. *The New York Times* critic Jack Gould delivered the big verdict:

"The permanent replacement for Jack Paar is off to an attractive start," he pronounced. "The format of *Tonight* remains unchanged, but Mr. Carson's style is his own. He has the proverbial engaging smile and the quick mind essential to sustaining and seasoning a marathon of banter."

The critic was impressed with Carson's feisty honesty: "At the outset he said he was not going to describe every guest as an old and dear friend, an indication of a refreshing attitude against prevalent show-business hokum. A healthy independence without overtones of neuroses could wear very well."

In Chicago, Johnny racked up phenomenal numbers, grabbing 58 percent of the viewing audience. Reports were high all over the country. *Variety* reported that "The Johnny Carson version of *The Tonight Show* is heady stuff... "

Johnny kept wearing his mis-matched cuff links and the good luck continued.

Checking back on the show a few months later, Jack Gould reported that "Mr. Carson... has worked out a style much his own. Chiefly the program is a showcase for one of the quickest minds on the air. When a colloquy gets going he can come up with an inverted quip that is often hilarious. He leans to an impish quality and admittedly savors the double entendre, occasionally to his own disadvantage. But for light laughter his batting average night after night is extraordinarily good."

Jack Paar read the reviews. A fickle public loved John as they'd loved Jack. Paar had been the "King" of late night TV and Johnny had modestly told reporters "just call me The Prince." But the ratings anointed Carson as the new royalty.

Reporters asked Paar about Carson constantly, and to make matters worse, for several awkward weeks Jack taped his show directly across from *The Tonight Show.*

Johnny had won the biggest battle of his career: succeeding on *The Tonight Show.* Now he faced a new show biz stress test: the personality feud.

It was Jack Paar vs Johnny Carson, man to man.

Paar's star was dimming. It wasn't that his new prime-time show wasn't exciting or entertaining — it was just a compact version of what he'd always done. By comparison, Johnny was completely new, a fresh face. He was on five nights a week and that made him the viewer's friend instantly. The easy, likable young man was so much more "comfortable" to watch at night than the nightmarish Paar. Johnny was quickly becoming a habit.

Johnny tried to avoid a confrontation. Interviewed by Herbert Kamm, Carson admitted that he and Paar were not close. "When I was signed as his permanent replacement early this year, he didn't write or call, and I didn't feel it was my place to do it. I've never seen Jack Paar socially any place and I was never a guest on the show when he was presiding. He might be an interesting guy to know. I just don't know. I really don't have the slightest idea what he's like."

He generously told the press that Paar was irreplaceable: "It would be foolhardy to try and top Jack

Paar. The only way it could be done is to walk on stage and drop an atom bomb."

Somehow that, and other Carson compliments, sounded a little left-handed. "He took a show that was absolutely nothing... and he made it the most talked-about show in television history," Carson said. Then he added, "Whether you like him personally or not had nothing to do with it. He did one hell of a job."

"I've always had respect for Jack," Carson told John P. Shanley in *The New York Times*. "Disregarding the emotional aspects of the show, it was seldom dull."

And finally, there was this unusual remark: "I don't think Jack is an easy man to get to know. I think I am very easy to get to know."

Daily News columnist Ben Gross asked Johnny, "Isn't it true that it was Paar who suggested you as his successor?"

"I've heard reports to that effect but really don't know," Johnny replied. Actually, it was well known that NBC's Mort Werner was the man who ultimately made the decision. Carson was asked how he got along with Paar.

"Well, on my opening night he sent me a nice wire, and since then I've run into him at the NBC studios. He's been most cordial. We get along well, but we've never really had a social relationship."

Jack Paar had a different story.

In *The Saturday Evening Post*, Jack insisted that Carson was so unsure of himself he went to Paar for help. Paar complained, "Johnny would be hanging around the studio where we were taping, and he'd say, 'Well, what do you think Jack? How's it going?' And all I could say was 'Johnny, I hear it's great... '"

Paar inferred that Johnny's show was past helping, "Frankly, it isn't my cup of tea," he said. He added that he couldn't even sit through a show. "I don't mean to sound condescending, it's just that I can't stay awake that late."

Cool Johnny blazed white-hot. After *The Saturday Evening Post* hit, Carson hit back:

"Controversy is something that must come naturally and honestly," he said. "I don't deliberately start arguments and never shall."

Then, in front of his *Tonight Show* audience, Johnny showed his disgust for Paar's comments: "I didn't hang around his studio like a cocker spaniel, any more than Goldwater goes swimming at Hyannis Port."

He denied even talking to Jack about *The Tonight Show*, insisting that the longest conversation they had was when he wished Jack well with his first season in prime time.

Carson couldn't understand what could've made Paar so steamed. Then he said that if anything embarrassed Jack, it might've been the time they happened to meet in the men's room. "Maybe that's what embarrassed him," Johnny said. After hitting low, he cried foul. "Paar says he's honest," Johnny deadpanned. "But how could someone as childish as Paar know right from wrong? I don't want to get into an argument," he added, "it's like getting into an argument with my children. They get petulant and the truth gets all mixed up."

Paar fired back: "Other than recommending to NBC that he replace me, I have never done or said an unkind thing publicly or privately about Johnny Carson. Further, I have ignored or chosen to disregard snide references to me by Carson. If Johnny needs a feud to help his ratings, he will find this like tickling. He can't do it himself. I don't need it, as my last national rating was 48 per cent of the audience, our highest of the year."

On Paar's prime time show in February of 1963, guest Oscar Levant described Johnny: "He's quite amiable about being dull." Carson took pity on the renowned hypochondriac and refused to "pick on a man who has emotional problems."

The feud sputtered on. By April of 1963 Carson had no praise for Paar at all: "When it comes right down to it, Paar didn't do anything different from Steve Allen."

Ironically, if anybody was going to show up Carson, it was Steve Allen. Following his prime-time show, Steve was offered a new syndicated talk show, and it was becoming even wilder and zanier than the old *Tonight Show* had been.

Allen started, it up in June of 1962, getting a jump on Johnny's premiere. Almost immediately Steve literally topped himself when it came to crazy stunts. An ice cream manufacturer was the guest on one show. Steve shouted, "Make me a banana split." Instantly, stage hands hauled him off, stripped him to his shorts and threw him into a giant dish, where he was deluged with ice cream, bananas, chocolate syrup and whipped cream. With nuts.

It was on this syndicated show for Westinghouse that Steve was persuaded to perform the "Human Explosive" trick. He was shuttered into a wooden box full of strategically placed dynamite. Then it was exploded, nearly sending Steve skyward. He recovered to perform even more stunts. He set himself on fire while wearing an asbestos suit, covered himself in red ants, and went wing, walking on a vintage airplane.

Johnny was younger and even more athletic than Steve, and he tried his own stunts, opting for a George Plimpton slant: What would it be like to play major league ball with Mickey Mantle, wrestle Antonino Rocca or free-fall 10,000 feet from a plane? Of the last stunt, Johnny recalled, "NBC thought it was a little hairy, my doing it, that is, but what could they do about it? I hadn't told them in advance what I was planning."

Johnny took big chances, like the time he let a blindfolded machete wielder slice a watermelon while it lay on his stomach. He also indulged in a different kind of eye-catching stunt. He practiced a snake dance with the exotic Margo, took hula lessons from the new Miss U.S.A. from Hawaii, and exercised with fitness buff Debbie Drake. When they were stretched out on a mat together, he cracked, "Do you want to leave a call?"

Steve's show enjoyed a comfortable rating and continued on for several years. There was no problem between Steve and Johnny. After a while, there was no probem between Paar and Johnny. In June of 1965, Jack's prime-time show faded away. Paar, the nemesis of both Johnny and Steve, bought WMTW-TV in Poland Springs, Maine, for three and a half million dollars. He disappeared into a reclusive existence.

Johnny was glad to be rid of Jack, happy that the old talk show host was probably "off somewhere communing with a moose."

Paar made a very determined effort to be forgotten, rarely granting interviews. But when he did, somehow Carson's name came up. When Merv Griffin began his late night talk show in the mid-60's, Paar immediately went on the attack, perhaps figuring that the gentlemanly Merv wouldn't engage in a public war himself.

Paar told *TV Guide* that Carson was no Merv Griffin: "He started with 180 stations and followed the most successful commercial show in television... Merv Griffin had to begin from zero. Griffin has, in my view, the best-booked show and he obviously has read a book."

Paar told Tom Shales that his *Tonight Show* "was a more literate show than it is now." And in *The New York Times* he asked, "Can you prove to me that Carson has ever read a book?"

Jack later mellowed slightly. In 1983 the ex-star wrote a memoir. Caustic and nasty as ever, he skewered everyone from Steve Allen to Groucho Marx. Then Paar wrote, "I have enormous respect for Johnny Carson... not just because of his talent... Only he and I know what it's like to do what is the most difficult show in television ever!" He added, "Johnny replaced me many times going way back to my *Morning Show* on CBS. I doubt if anyone will ever come anywhere near Johnny's success... "

Then Paar's opinion of Carson flickered the other way, within a month. He wanted to promote his book on Carson's show, and when producer Fred De Cordova was slow in getting back to him, Paar got spooked. "He has a thing about me," Paar moaned to reporters. "Who the hell are they! I invented that kind of television. Fuck them, I'm not going on at all."

In May of 1986, Jack was coaxed out of retirement to appear on an NBC special honoring the network's thirty stellar years of broadcasting. The idea was to bring together the hosts of *The Tonight Show*, including Jerry Lester of *Broadway Open House*.

Surprisingly, Johnny, Jack, Steve and Jerry appeared for publicity photos together. In a charming bit of mutual revisionist history, the story went out in press releases that Paar and Carson had "never even met" until the anniversary gala! Johnny was quoted as walking up to Paar with a handshake, a smile, and a "Hi. We've never been properly introduced. I'm Johnny Carson."

"He couldn't have been nicer," Paar told everyone.

In November of 1986 Jack came back for an NBC special, showing kinescopes of his shows with the Kennedys, Judy Garland, Richard Nixon and "discovery" Bill Cosby, who actually made his *Tonight Show* debut during Carson's era. In a tense publicity move, Paar agreed to go on *The Tonight Show* to promote the program.

Johnny and Jack had never met in a talk show setting before. The only time Paar had been on *The Tonight Show* since he left it was in 1968, when Joe Garagiola was subbing as guest host.

No one knew what to expect. Johnny gave Jack a nice introduction, and Paar came halfway through the curtains. He stayed there as if there was Velcro on his hands. Already overcome with emotion, Paar stayed in the spotlight and acknowledged the applause until Johnny came out from behind his desk, embraced him, and brought him over to the couch.

Jack said, "Dr. Livingstone, I presume?"

Then he looked over to Doc Severinsen and asked, "Who are you?"

Doc answered, "I'm a friend of Jose Melis!"

"We should lay a couple of things to rest," Carson said. "Jack and I are not what you'd call close friends... the longest conversation we had was maybe five or ten minutes, some years ago when we first met, and that was about it."

And that was about all Johnny could say. Nervous and hyper, Jack cut off Johnny's questions and launched into a rambling monologue, a patient trying to get through all his latest recollections and anecdotes within the therapist's allotted hour.

"I'm sorry to go so long," Paar said during one story, but it was obvious that he was too excited to sit still for any serious questions.

"Why do I feel I'm guesting on your show?" Johnny asked with a smile. Paar smiled and begged him for some indulgence. He had more stories to tell. Johnny politely listened, his hands in front of him on his desk like a schoolboy. "Why'd you give up *The Tonight Show*?" Johnny asked during a break. "You could've been here today... "

"Well," Paar parried, "you needed the work."

The audience laughed and Jack carefully pointed out, "Nobody will ever ever equal what you have done on this show."

A master at telling stories and anecdotes, his voice intimate and his manner confiding, Paar had amused the audience with his harmless recollections about his grandchildren and his career. But the great "meeting" between Johnny had produced neither a warm fifteen minutes of *The Tonight Show* memories or a crackling war of ad-libs.

When Jack bid farewell, choking back a self-deprecating "I talk too much," Johnny seemed relieved. His face pinkened, an improbable smile twisted over his lips and he started breaking up as he said, "That's the longest conversation I've had with Jack Paar in thirty-two years!" And he was relieved it was over.

The next night he couldn't resist getting in a few lines about the anti-climactic meeting. "I was almost late tonight," he said. "Jack Paar is still backstage. He was talking about his trip to Guam with Randy..." He did a light impression of Paar's small, sincere voice: "Jack *does* like to talk, you know... "

A week later Jack told *The New York Times* that Johnny was "a great, great clown." He added, "I go to bed early. I've seen Johnny Carson maybe five times in my life."

He had little to say about the new talk show stars of the 80's, except for Joan Rivers: "I don't care for her, or for that kind of.aggressive tastelessness." Of the others he said, "I'm better than any of them alone, if I have something to talk about."

But it was too late now, and it was too late then. Soon after taking over *The Tonight Show*, Carson had been making many viewers forget about past hosts. And he would stay on the air long enough for nearly two generations to question when there ever was a different host of *The Tonight Show*.

In 1962, as they'd done with Jack Paar, fans began to ask: "What's Johnny really like?"

In an issue of *Esquire*, a month after his premiere

on *The Tonight Show,* Johnny offered a rare insight into himself. He drew his own self-portrait and answered a kind of questionnaire about himself.

Carson's cartoon-doodle of himself looked like a drawing of a twelve year-old, not an adult. The hair was mashed forward "pudding bowl" style, the ears were large and the nose crooked. The eyes were enigmatic. The mouth was sketched into a goofy half-smile. The head sat on a bare, squared outline of a neck and shoulders.

Rather than answer *Esquire's* questions with the kind of glib and evasive wisecracks he used during "questions from the audience," Carson was remarkably serious and truthful:

What would you really rather do?

"I once thought of being a doctor... "

What's your most paradoxical quality?

"The outward relaxed appearance often does not match the inner feelings. Sometimes after a program someone will comment on how relaxed I seemed to be... when in truth, I felt like I was coming unglued."

What are the chinks in your armor?

"A certain restlessness... the inability at times to finish one project before taking on another one."

What's your boiling point?

"I can get pretty angry at myself at times... perhaps because I let petty things annoy me. Other than that: strangers who want to tell me a dirty joke."

What's your personal panacea?

"To be by myself for a while... and try to bring my problems down to their perspective."

He mentioned that he had the fear that his good fortune, health and luck would run out. And when asked for his "secret satisfaction," he responded with a golden rule drilled into him from childhood:

"I believe the only real satisfaction anyone can have is by doing something for someone else. If you can do it anonymously, so much the better."

CHAPTER NINE

"Six long months passed and Johnny was the biggest thing alive. And we loved Johnny and we owned Johnny and no one knew how Johnny felt inside."

Joe Jackson – *Blaze of Glory*

Johnny seemed to be pleased with the way the show was going but, he told columnist Jack O'Brien, "I'm too close to it. We've come up with some new people and we've done some interesting things. Apparently NBC is perfectly happy, because a peaceful silence seems to reign and they all smile when they pass me in the hall.

"Of course," he added, "I'm never completely satisfied even when things go great. I still have an urge to polish and change things so the show will be even better next time... You have to satisfy *yourself* first of all."

The toughest part was getting started. Then getting over the feuding with Paar. Now came the grind of maintaining quality night after night, handling all the different guests, standing in front of America with an untried bunch of jokes and making them work.

There were nights when Johnny wished he hadn't shown up. One night, Robert Merrill came on the show and sang an operatic piece. Johnny was impressed. "Is this guy still writing operas?" he asked. Merrill replied, "He's been dead seventy-five years." Carson wasn't so good with the latest music, either. He had to ask producer Art Stark and Skitch

Henderson who Simon and Garfunkel were when they were booked on the show.

Carson learned how to avoid asking the foolish question or embarrassing himself with the gaps in his own knowledge of politics, opera or literature. He polished his interviewing style to a fine buff and bluff – the giveaway to his fierce self-control and inner tension being the trademark tapping of his pencil or the habit (picked up by impressionist Rich Little) of speaking through clenched teeth. He was getting smoother and smoother, even more of a pro than when NBC deemed him ready to take over the show on October 1, 1962.

Another show had premiered on October 1, 1962. It was a daytime talk show hosted by Merv Griffin. The staff included ex-*Tonight Show* veteran Dick Cavett and future *Tonight Show* writer Pat McCormick.

Merv recalls, "Since Johnny Carson's version of *The Tonight Show* had debuted on the same day as *The Merv Griffin Show*, a natural rivalry existed between the two shows..." After Carson handled the Paar flare-up, there were some minor skirmishes with Griffin. On Johnny's show one night, comedian/actor Mickey Shaughnessy happened to mention *The Merv Griffin Show*. The plug was bleeped out of the tape.

Merv couldn't believe it. He and Johnny were both on the same network, NBC. One talk show was on in the day, the other at night. He was so irritated, he reported the incident on his show. There wasn't enough time to start a feud, though. The daytime version of *The Merv Griffin Show* folded after six months, on April Fool's Day, 1963.

The New York Herald Tribune's critic, John Horn, reviewed Johnny's progress in July of 1963: "Mr. Carson still doesn't know which of his predecessors to be, Steve Allen or Jack Paar." The critic missed Paar's "genuine affection" and the zaniness of Steve

Allen, complaining: "When he is not up to Paar, Mr. Carson tries to be Mr. Allen. He reads mock book titles and other lists of jokes, gets into plastic splints and other gimmicks, dons wig or mustache to play skits or be a character interviewed by Mr. McMahon..."

Johnny was developing his sketch style, which, quite different from Steve's, involved risqué humor. With Mamie Van Doren as the guest, Johnny played "Kit" Carson, Western hero. In one scene he described an encounter with a bear, saying he tried to shoot the bear in the leg. Mamie felt his leg. Johnny then explained, "I figure I missed his leg so I aimed for his chest." Mamie began to grab him around the chest.

Ed McMahon: Did you finally shoot him?

Johnny: Yep.

Ed McMahon: Where?

Johnny: You gotta be kidding!

When critics objected, Carson huffed, "If you can't say a few sophisticated things at twelve o'clock at night without being called dirty, we're in trouble."

The Tonight Show was a hot ticket, an R-rated ticket, a show that had a strict policy of not allowing anyone under eighteen in. They might hear an expletive that would be deleted on the tape delay. They might even see Johnny running around with his pants off. Ed recalled, "Sometimes when he had to make a quick change for a 'Mighty Carson Art Players' sketch or something else, he just wore his shirt and jacket because it takes too long to drag off a pair of trousers." The secret would be concealed by Carson's desk. Once the studio audience saw even more of Johnny. He was doing a bit as Shirley Temple and playfully flounced his ruffled skirt. The first few rows could see that he'd forgotten to wear anything underneath.

The more confident Johnny got, the wilder and

more spontaneous, the jokes. One night Johnny set fire to McMahon's script. Another night, while the camera was on Ed McMahon during an Alpo commercial, Buddy Hackett stripped naked just out of camera range. Johnny tested the censors regularly. Paar couldn't do scat jokes? Johnny could. He once described how his path to work was a minefield thanks to dog owners not cleaning up after their pets: "And that's how The Twist started."

For every double entendre scored, viewers seemed to cheer for the next one.

Johnny was enjoying the glitter and sophistication of his New York City lifestyle and giving all America a peek. Carson surrounded himself with the hip jazz musicians he admired, like drummer Buddy Rich. He invited the slickest nightclub comics to drop by, like Hackett and Don Rickles. He traded come-on lines with hot starlets and sex symbols.

Like a typical New York sophisticate, he became a night person and dreaded the dawn: "I get up between nine and ten in the morning. I don't believe in jumping out of bed and shouting 'Hey, hey, another day.' I just grumble and sulk for a while. I don't really start to function until noon or afterwards."

Carson had been stepping out with starlets even in his California days. By now, his marriage to Jody had fallen apart completely. She had accepted the infidelities as the price the wife of a glamorous star had to pay. Once when she asked to go out with him for a star-studded night on the town, he shot back an old radio gag instead: "Why take a ham sandwich to a banquet?"

One night, Johnny and *Tonight Show* producer Art Stark had dinner with Mary Tyler Moore. Johnny told Art, "That's the kind of wife I should have." He made a cameo appearance in a mild Connie Francis movie called *Looking for Love*, but his looking stopped when he began seeing Joanne Copeland.

One of four sisters (there was Barbara Glee, Carole Lee and Shirle Mee), Joanne had been a cheerleader at San Mateo College and had the Vanna White-like job of guiding contestants around the set of a quiz show called *Video Village*.

The sprightly brunette became Johnny's cheerleader and quickly settled into his bachelor apartment at 1161 York Avenue, re-decorating it to match the level of sophistication expected of a *Tonight Show* host. Supportive, unthreatening, she barely reached five feet two inches and weighed 95 pounds. She was so petite Johnny once remarked, "She looks like she would wear Donald Ducks on her underpants."

One insider recalled that John and Joanne were an item quite early. Joanne "made herself one-hundred-percent totally available to him. He was married; most women wouldn't do that. She knew what she wanted and I think she wore him down." Joanne was, without question, Johnny's greatest fan. They were married in August of 1963 and moved to 450 East 63rd Street, and then in 1967 up to the thirty-fifth floor of UN Plaza with a spectacular view of the East River.

Johnny had some stability now, and his show was settling into a comfortable groove, but the tension of the five-night grind was still tough, the constrictions of city living tight. Everywhere he went he was bothered by autograph seekers. He couldn't go out shopping with his three sons: "In twenty minutes they have us backed against the wall... 'Hey, come here and take a picture with my idiot cousin.'"

Many were surprised to find Johnny so shy, but, as he often pointed out, "On the show, I'm in control. Socially, I'm not in control."

Johnny's tensions showed, but people weren't noticing. He couldn't eat a big meal. Sometimes dinner was just a snack: popcorn and milk. He kept up his energy by endlessly nibbling on Sara Lee chocolate cake. He had a habit of humming to himself. He smoked too much. He drummed the pencils on his desk and had a bunch made up with erasers on both ends. Another nervous eccentricity was his inability to stay on the phone. Joanne mentioned, "I've yet to hear him talk to anyone for more than five minutes."

Fans wondered if Carson was some kind of fraud. On the street he seemed distant and tense. They were accustomed to seeing the always-smiling, warm and ingratiating Johnny. They didn't think twice when they walked past the other 90 percent of the population that sulked through the streets in a self-absorbed frown. But it seemed so out of place on the face of a star. Reality was unreal.

Johnny filled the apartment with distractions: a drum set, telescope, barbells, archery equipment, fencing foils, guitar, eight color TVs and a sauna. Johnny and Joanne had two terriers, Fluffy and Muffin, each a gift from the other. Joanne spent her time being the perfect hostess and keeping the apartment immaculate.

She had some interesting theories on design. The wife of a *Tonight Show* staffer recalls, "Books were coming into *The Tonight Show*. It seemed like every book ever published would come in, and Johnny brought back shopping bags full. The first time I was in the apartment, decorated by Joanne, I was shocked to see all the books arranged according to color."

Joanne made sure the apartment was a refuge for Johnny. It was just him and her up there. She was the "total woman" before the term was invented, asking, "Is there anything I can do to improve?" She told reporters, "He's under so much pressure. Everybody is after him for something." So she was there for him. "I orbit around him," she said.

The pressures on the show continued, despite Joanne's orbiting. Feeling "edgy and restless," when he had a week off, instead of staying home he went on to a new challenge. He began to headline in Vegas. He told jokes that would never make it to *The Tonight Show*. On TV commercials, he quipped: "I'd like to see somebody run up to the Jolly Green Giant and say, "Ho-ho-ho yourself, you big queer!" On topless Vegas shows: "Women don't like topless shows. They say to their husbands, 'You'd get sick if you had to look at that all day.' But Carlo Ponti hasn't had a sick day in his life."

Questions and answers with the audience:

"Johnny, why don't you put your damn show on earlier so my wife will come to bed with me?"

"Have you ever thought of putting on a better show than I do?"

Others thought of putting on a better show, but it didn't seem to happen. Steve Allen's syndicated series ended in 1964 and a new show hosted by Regis Philbin premiered. He unveiled a new strategy: the "guest star of the week" to co-host. The first week it was Ann Sothern. By the second week his days were numbered.

1965 saw Carson in firm control of *The Tonight Show*, now dictating new terms to NBC, like: Monday nights off. Carson came up with a pair of top-selling novelty books, *Happiness Is a Dry Martini* and *Misery Is a Blind Date*.

They were filled with the new hip humor that viewers had come to enjoy; the gags promulgated the "booze and babes" lifestyle of Vegas and New York City:

"Happiness is discovering the prune juice your doctor ordered you to drink has fermented."

"Happiness is going to the opera and finding out your balcony seat is directly over Sophia Loren."

The Tonight Show was becoming to "fill" super-slick with Carson. Seemingly spontaneous lines were scripted well in advance. One night Barry Goldwater was the guest, the man who had been crushed by Lyndon Johnson in the presidential elections a few years back. Johnny began to ask a question when he stumbled over a word.

Flustered, he said to Goldwater, "Did that ever happen to you? When you just can't get out what you mean?"

Goldwater answered, "Yes, for three and a half months two years ago."

It got a big laugh. Goldwater was quoted in the newspapers for his witty remark. But not only was Goldwater's gag line rehearsed, so was Johnny's "stumble" to set it up.

Johnny was so smooth he rarely stumbled unless it was pre-arranged. He had developed a trademark of gracefully turning bomb jokes into big laughs by his reactions and takes. He had become the best monologist in America and, as such, was given the plum assignments that had gone to men like his idols, Jack Benny and Bob Hope.

Carson performed at a White House function for Lyndon Johnson. He joked about usually being seen late at night: "I've done more for birth control than Enovid."

Jack Paar's old nemesis, Dorothy Kilgallen, instantly began a feud. She blasted Carson for uttering a tasteless joke and made it the subject of a front-page column.

Cool Carson erupted. At a dinner for the White House Photographers Association, he said, "For Dorothy Kilgallen to criticize me for bad taste is like having your clothes criticized by Emmett Kelly. I don't know why Dorothy should take offense at a joke I made. I didn't when her parents made one... I don't see why she would object to a joke about birth control. She's such a living example *for* it. She's the only woman you wouldn't mind being with if your wife walked in."

Kilgallen kept her silence.

Carson continued to make *The Tonight Show* the setting for racy gags. By now, he had educated the audience into playing along with him. One night Zsa Zsa Gabor talked about wearing a skirt so skimpy "you could see all the way to Honolulu." The audience was already roaring as Johnny shook his head, saying, "I'm not going to touch that line." When Tony Randall voiced his annoyance with canned laughter, Johnny mock-innocently asked, "What's wrong with a few titters?" The audience giggled knowingly.

Johnny admitted, "Once they get to know you better, once they like you, it's amazing what you can get away with."

The audience was with him, allowed to be part of his "show biz" world, sharing the fun of being at a swanky party with celebrity guests. Johnny winked and let them in on the secrets of putting over a monologue, muttering "Watch this segue," or smirking "I'm the prince of blends." He let them take over as straight man:

"It was really wet today."

"HOW... WET... WAS IT!"

"All I know is twice on my way to work I was photographed by Jacques Cousteau!"

Since the network wouldn't permit a lot of strong political humor or adult subjects, Johnny had to fill his monologue with weather jokes, bits about the NBC commissary and running gags about his side-kicks. One on bulky Ed McMahon:

"I found out something about him I did not know. Did you know he was decorated for heroism during World War II? It happened in Germany. In order to give his buddies time to escape, Ed threw his body in front of a huge German tank. And the Germans lost two hours driving around him."

One on Doc Severinsen's fey and fashionable clothing: "You look like a recruiting poster for the

Beige Panthers."

Now and then, he tried for something just plain weird:

"We had a little excitement in midtown New York last night. It seems the Jolly Green Giant got ahold of some fermented broccoli. And the next thing anybody knew, he was squatting in the middle of Fifth Avenue, turning Volkswagens upside down to try and find out their sex."

The Tonight Show was so popular that ten million viewers were tuning in. In 1965, *The Best of Carson* aired on Saturday nights. Johnny was uneasy about the overkill. Prophetically he said, "They should turn that time over to some young comedians, or an experiment."

Seeing the ratings get even bigger for *The Tonight Show*, the networks and syndicates began a frantic search for someone to syphon off some of the action.

ABC brought out the first network competition, head to head: *The Les Crane Show.* An ancient ancestor to Phil Donahue and Tom Snyder, Crane attempted controversy instead of comedy, but to *Newsweek* and other critics, he came off as "a combination of egotism and logorrhea... an oppressively strong personality."

By contrast, Westinghouse was now syndicating a talk show helmed by Merv Griffin. Around the country, Merv was rarely given a late night slot opposite Johnny, and that seemed just as well. *Newsweek* found him "at best, mildly funny." He'd "not yet proved himself able to carry the show alone." Only Carson had the magic: "He is a sharp, original wit."

Sharp? One night Ed Ames was the guest on Johnny's show. He was playing an Indian on the TV series *Daniel Boone*, and demonstrated hatchet throwing. Ames took aim at a cowboy drawn on a huge wooden board. Accidentally he sank the hatchet right into the cowboy's crotch.

As the crowd howled, Ames tried to retrieve his weapon. Johnny held him back, waited for the crowd to quiet down, and said, "I didn't even know you were Jewish!" The laughter exploded louder than ever. "Welcome to Frontier Bris!" Johnny shouted.

At the time, this was the essence of Carson, what *The Tonight Show* was all about: a moment of spontaneous outrage topped by quick ad-libbing.

One night Ray Milland told an anecdote about movie-making. The man who was always "wide-eyed in Babylon" told the audience that movie "romance" was often not too romantic. He described the time he was making *Jungle Princess*, doing a romantic love scene in a swimming pool with Dorothy Lamour.

The actor recalled, "I had to go to the bathroom. I thought, 'Oh God, not now! Not now.' But the call of nature had to be obeyed. "As she put her arms around my neck and started kissing me, the cold water of the pool did its work and I let go."

The audience chuckled good-naturedly.

But, as far as the FCC was concerned, both Ray Milland and Johnny Carson had gone too far. Had Jack Paar opened the water closet for a flood of john humor?

The FCC's commissioner, Robert Lee, complained, "There have been four or five incidents on his show over the past year which would raise some eyebrows... I don't want the industry to degenerate into indecency! I'm not a prude. I haven't been offended and maybe nobody has. After all, Carson has a sophisticated show at an hour when the kids are in bed... but I do feel that late night shows are getting pretty close to the line of indecency."

"I don't know what to say," Carson remarked coolly. "I'm baffled by his terminology. I don't know what he means. He could not define what indecency was. I can't define it either. So what are we talking about? Mr. Lee says he wasn't offended, so who was?"

He added, "He sounded like a hell of a nice guy to me."

NBC confirmed there were no phone calls or letters after the Milland appearance. Johnny went on the air and said, "Welcome to NBC's rendezvous in the bedroom. I'm Johnny Carson. I say that because the FCC has been mixing me up lately with Lenny Bruce."

He told a gag about Flipper being named in a paternity suit by a Christmas seal. After the laughs, he said, "Sorry about that, Commissioner Lee!"

The FCC couldn't stop Carson. Neither could NBC, for that matter.

Back then, the local news was just fifteen minutes. Under Paar, *The Tonight Show* had stretched from 11:15 p.m. to 1:00 a.m. NBC kept it that way, but in 1965 many local affiliates had expanded their news to 11:30. That meant they picked up the show *after* Carson's monologue.

One night Johnny simply didn't come out for the first fifteen minutes. He let Ed McMahon and band leader Skitch Henderson fill in. Then he explained that in most towns the only people watching at 11:15 were "four Navajos in Gallup, New Mexico, and the Armed Forces Radio on Guam."

NBC capitulated. The show moved to ninety minutes. Skitch Henderson told a reporter, "Johnny is very easy to work with if you don't get in his way."

Ed McMahon had to learn that the hard way. One night, Johnny was talking about a new science report. He deadpanned to the audience that, according to scientists, mosquitoes don't just bite anyone. They go for those warm-blooded "passionate people" first.

Instinctively, Ed McMahon slapped himself on the arm. "It killed his punch line," Ed recalled with remorse. "I had to apologize to him during the next break... I stepped out of line."

Carson wanted Ed fired. He told his producer, Art Stark. Art said, "How is it going to make you look if you fire Ed?" He remembered how badly Arthur Godfrey's popularity suffered after the kindly host booted his singer, Julius LaRosa.

Carson kept Ed McMahon. But not long after, Art Stark was gone. Stark had been with Johnny since the *Who Do You Trust?* days, but Johnny wasn't about to be questioned too often by anyone. And Al Bruno, Carson's longtime manager, was also bounced. Staffers questioned Carson's sense of loyalty. After all, this was not the first such incident. Carson had bounced Bill Brennan as his director on the prime-time *Johnny Carson Show*. And Brennan had gotten Johnny his first job in television!

They had no idea of the Machiavellian plots that were brewing all the time at *The Tonight Show*, schemes that had left Johnny fretting over who to believe and when. Johnny's secretary, Jeanne, was a wonderful and trustworthy girl who always looked out for his best interests. When she kept denigrating Art Stark, implying that Johnny shouldn't be bossed around by anyone, even his old pro producer, she had to be trusted. It was a coincidence that the new producer was her boyfriend, Rudy Tellez.

One change had nothing to do with politics. In 1966, after Skitch Henderson left the show, the new bandleader became Milton DeLugg. He simply lacked the charisma to share the spotlight with Johnny and Ed. In 1967, Carl "Doc" Severinsen took over the bando. His colorful nickname came via his father, who was a dentist. His father was "Big Doc" and he was "Little Doc." When Doc began sporting very colorful and charismatic clothes, Johnny had a running gag for over two decades. Soon Doc was injecting his own unique blend of both hip and corny comedy into the proceedings.

Carson was taking the heat and the pressure and

he had to make the decisions. The heat and the pressure were intensifying through 1966 and 1967 as more and more Johnny-come-latelys arrived on the scene. All over the dial, guys like David Frost, Merv Griffin and Dick Cavett were aiming to take over as the King of late night.

CHAPTER TEN

TALK SHOW MANIA: JOHNNY, MERV, DAVID, DICK AND SOMETIMES STEVE

In March of 1967, New York's Governor Nelson Rockefeller appeared on *The Tonight Show* and shocked the nation by announcing his displeasure with current New York Ssenator Robert F. Kennedy. His choice for a replacement: John W. Carson.

"You've got very good ratings," Rockefeller told Johnny. And then, alluding to Kennedy's long hair and his many years living in Massachusetts, added "You'd have to let your hair grow. But you wouldn't have to worry about residency."

The studio audience buzzed with excitement, but Carson resented being put on the spot. "I'm flattered... but I'm not sure I'd be very good in politics," he said.

Backstage, Carson told a throng of reporters that Rockefeller couldn't have been serious. "I thought he was just being cutie pie."

But after the show Rockefeller said he was serious: "I think it's a tremendous idea... There's a great potential there, believe me. I'd like to get his reaction and then we'd discuss it later."

Robert F. Kennedy fighting Johnny Carson for the U.S. Senate? It could have been one of the most amazing races of all time. It would be a night-and-day battle, too, since both men lived in the same building. But Johnny declared, "Who am I to be a pundit? I have opinions like anybody else, and I might even be better informed than the average person because this is my business, to keep up on what's happening. But who am I to foist my opinions on the public? Why should they care?

"Besides," Johnny finally said, "you can't win. I say something like, 'I'm for easing the divorce laws', and a good part of the people listening will always think, 'Ah, he's for loose morals.'"

The politics of television was enough trouble for Johnny. In April of 1967 he went on strike supporting his union, AFTRA. When NBC showed an old rerun of his show, he charged that NBC had breached his contract by re-running the unauthorized show. He vowed not to return to the show, even if the strike was settled.

After five years, the Carson habit was an addiction for late night viewers. *Newsweek*, in its April 24 issue, declared *The Tonight Show* "a 90-minute verbal tranquilizer" that let millions of Americans "slowly find their way into uncluttered sleep... " It was also, the magazine noted, netting Carson $700,000 a year and was one of the prime sources of revenue for NBC.

Ben Gross, in the *Daily News*, wrote that Johnny was not that concerned about re-runs and that he really wanted "more money." Headlining his piece "Success Changes Carson and All Other TV Stars," Gross insisted that it was impossible for Johnny to have "risen from comparative obscurity to the status of a millionaire national celebrity" without changing. "Such a lack of change would be against all human nature... it would be a miracle if Carson weren't affected by such success... Any way you look at it, he is not the same fellow he was when he first appeared on *Tonight* in 1962."

Reporters uncovered another twist to the story. NBC president Julian Goodman, during a routine meeting, was asked to okay a publicity stunt to take the steam out of the premiere of *The Joey Bishop Show* on ABC. How about having Johnny pull a Jack Paar act by storming off the show for some reason or other, only to come back the night of Bishop's debut?

Some reporters believed that Johnny, the master of timing, was timing his return for maximum publicity. Bishop's show was now only weeks away. Bishop would be using his "rat pack" connections to land big stars. Not only that, Bill Dana and his "Fourth Network" talk show was hitting syndicated stations on May 1. Dana would be based in Las Vegas and trying to grab all the flashy celebrities in town.

Bishop, born Joey Gottlieb in the Bronx, was a tough veteran of the stand-up comedy scene in nightclubs since the late 40's. Tony Martin worked with Bishop, and later Frank Sinatra became a vocal supporter, which helped Joey land more and more nightclub work. But what really helped Joey Bishop was the exposure he got as a regular with Jack Paar.

Bishop recalls, "When Frank Sinatra takes you on the show, they say, 'He must be good, otherwise Frank wouldn't have him on.' So there is a point of acceptance, a stamp of approval, immediately. What Jack Paar did was make it *national* for me. Remember, in those days, if Jack Paar had you back three or four times, you were a hit."

Bishop had supported Paar during his feud with Ed Sullivan and had been one of the stars to tape a personal farewell for Jack's last show. Bishop was one of the few comics who seemed able to ad-lib on Jack's show without making the host jealous or competitive.

One night, a sportswriter was discussing the upcoming rematch between Ingemar Johansson and Floyd Patterson. He said of Johansson, "He's an original."

Bishop said that Patterson was "going to find out

he's an original and put him on canvas."

No doubt Paar would be happy to see Joey come in and knock off Johnny Carson. No doubt ABC felt they had another Jack Paar on their hands.

ABC theorized that Bishop had a perfect late night personality to rival Johnny. He was fast with ad-libs and a smooth entertainer, but just low-key enough to be ingratiating night after night. He also had Paar's sentimental streak, ready to air a sob story about an entertainer in the midst of bad luck or a tragedy.

And like Paar, Bishop oozed caring sincerity. "Complete honesty," he once said, "that's my strategy. Don't bullshit an audience. You can never be a star until you can take an audience by the hand. That's very important to remember. An audience must trust you implicitly."

Like Carson, Joey Bishop could tell a mildly risqué joke in an amusing and acceptable way. One of his classics was his line about winter in his old neighborhood:

"We were very poor when I was a kid. I remember one winter it snowed and I didn't have a sled. I used to slide down the hill on my cousin. And she wasn't bad!"

Now Bishop was getting his chance, and NBC wasn't even sure Johnny was going to show up!

Carson insisted that the real issue was his union. "What is the price that should be paid for a re-run when it is used while your union is on strike? That's the main point... I know of no business except the broadcasting industry in which a performer becomes a scab to himself and his union because of videotape... NBC's trying to make me look like an ungrateful wretch."

Johnny left New York for Fort Lauderdale, Florida. When Jack Paar walked off the show, he had headed South too.

The strike was settled, but Johnny remained in Florida. He wanted further negotiations with NBC, and added that he wasn't going to budge just because Joey Bishop was about to premiere: "The whole thing would look like a gigantic hoax if I marched back as he opened." Carson reiterated that "money [was] not the main consideration although naturally this always comes up." He wanted more control over his show and who was on his staff; less network interference.

True to his convictions, Johnny remained out while ABC launched its attack on *The Tonight Show.*

Joey opened with Danny Thomas, Debbie Reynolds and Governor Ronald Reagan. Bishop was so humbled by Reagan's appearance, the Governor quipped, "Another ten seconds of this and I'll go back to *Death Valley Days."*

From exile, Johnny read the newspaper reviews. Columnist Harriet Van Horne spoke for most reviewers when she wrote: "Though he's a quick wit and an able performer, he lacks the poise, the what-the-hell assurance that has distinguished all the successful night-owl hosts — Steve Allen, Jack Paar and the incumbent Carson... Johnny Carson has nothing to worry about."

NBC was still worried. Overnight in New York, Bishop's ratings were better than *The Tonight Show* (as guest-hosted by Jimmy Dean) and the syndicated *Merv Griffin Show* combined.

NBC announced that Bob Newhart was their choice to take over as guest (and perhaps permanent) host. They intimated that they were going to keep Johnny on ice for the two remaining two years of his contract. Let him face a two-year blacklist and be another forgotten man, like Jack Paar!

Paar, insisting he'd never return to the show, did take the opportunity to question Carson's morality. After all, Jack didn't want cash when he walked away from NBC, he wanted respect for his water-closet joke.

"I can't believe that it's money," Jack told writer Al Salerno. "But if it is, it's wrong... it eventually will get him in a jam with the public."

Carson insisted he was ready to dump TV entirely. He claimed to be booked for stand-up work, including a booking for April 29 in Baltimore and July in Las Vegas.

The war between Carson and NBC was being played out while noise was coming from Joey Bishop and Merv Griffin on another battlefield. Carson was unyielding. NBC's strategists were confused. Could Johnny be bluffing? Could he really be intent on quitting the show? How easily could Bob Newhart come in and keep *The Tonight Show* on top?

Jack Gould in *The New York Times* pointed out that Johnny Carson was vital to NBC and his demands weren't so outrageous. Gould wrote that Carson was "almost indispensable. Economically, the program fills up 7 1/2 hours a week, less repeats, and in being presented between 11:30 and 1 a.m. conveniently falls outside the bounds of any stringent codes on the number of commercials that can be inserted... and in cold cash at the moment the show represents a gross of upward of $25 million yearly for N.B.C."

NBC surrendered, re-negotiating Carson's contract and adjusting the salary to $20,00 a week plus a million-dollar life insurance policy.

Carson gave out a prepared statement: "I return with new enthusiasm to *The Tonight Show*. I am grateful for the many many people who have been kind enough to say they missed me. Television makes friendships possible with a host of unknown persons. I hope to repay their generosity with the very best that is in me."

On April 25, having given Bishop a week's head

start, Johnny returned. Bishop anticipated him — and on the first night of the head-to-head competition, Bishop's guest was none other than Jack Paar.

The gunfight around midnight was the talk of the town.

Johnny chose to ignore the competition. In his opening monologue he mentioned his negotiations with NBC, instead. He talked about the Passover holiday and said, even though it was a time for eating unleavened bread, he'd wanted "more dough."

On ABC, Paar was ready to prove that viewers would want to choose him over Johnny. He eagerly took over for Joey Bishop and controlled the program, telling anecdote after anecdote, convinced he was the most charming of raconteurs.

The New York Times noticed that Paar "inadvertently drew further attention to Mr. Bishop's mounting plight as a host who is ill at ease in the presence of guests." Johnny, along with Buddy Hackett and Peter, Paul and Mary, easily outpointed Bishop and Paar.

The overnight ratings gave Carson 41 percent of the audience, Bishop 12 percent. CBS, running movies, got 22 percent. The rest went to independent stations like Group W, where Merv Griffin even topped Bishop with 16 percent.

A few weeks later, Bill Dana and his syndicated late night show from Vegas crumbled like old halvah.

To some in the industry, the demise of Dana and the limp ratings of Bishop still didn't mean that Johnny could not be topped.

In 1969 Johnny Carson's hold on late night TV led CBS to one conclusion: fight fire with fire. Instead of movies, CBS vowed to hunt up a Carson killer. They went to Jack Paar. He told them to go someplace else. They begged Philadelphia-based daytime talk show host Mike Douglas to try it, and he begged off.

Douglas knew the power of Johnny. Both had been managed by the same man, Al Bruno. In a head to head war, Douglas knew he was unarmed. Ever since Bruno had the temerity to add Douglas to his stable of clients, Carson had a grudge against the singer. At an Emmy Awards show, Johnny pointed to him and said, "There's a man as indigenous to Philadelphia as cream cheese, and just as funny! Mike Douglas!"

So who had a pleasant personality? Who had been around just as long as Johnny? Who had the experience? Merv Griffin.

Merv's syndicated evening show was doing well. In his heart, Griffin knew he could sneak into the dark of late night and bump off Joey Bishop. He wasn't sure about trying his hand against the fastest wit in America, Johnny Carson.

Merv was flattered but frightened by the CBS offer. Like an amateur poker player caught in a high-stakes game, he feigned nonchalance as the chips stacked higher and higher. "You can't afford me," Merv told them, laying his cards on the table. "I know Johnny's salary. You'd have to double it!"

CBS called Merv's bluff and pushed the cash across the table.

"Suddenly I felt sick," Griffin recalls.

Through the blistering heat of a New York summer, Griffin practiced his sharpest questioning and quickest grin. He took over the empty Cort Theater and it became a fort where he, his new staff and CBS huddled and strategized.

Johnny meanwhile huddled with his lawyers. New challenge? That meant new contract! On July 2, 1969, George Gent of *The New York Times* reported that Carson's new contract, lasting through April of 1972, was worth probably "between $75,000 and $85,000 a week" making him "the highest-paid television performer in history."

The next day Carson blasted Gent for mentioning money. On the air he fumed, "I think it is damn unfair to me and damn unfair to performers. I want to disclaim it once and for all."

He told Jack Gould, the ranking TV reporter at the *Times* that his salary was closer to $20,000, and insisted, "I am not the highest-paid performer in television. As I said on the air, I think how much somebody makes is your own business. I don't like being evasive but I just don't want to discuss the matter."

On July 4, the *Times* ran a headline: "Report on Income of Carson Erred." And underneath: "$75,000 Figure Found to Be Unlikely — Data Are Secret."

"Investigation yesterday left no doubt that even with all the emoluments, Mr. Carson's revenue from *The Tonight Show* would not reach the $75,000 weekly sum."

But the *Times* wondered that, if Carson was denying that he, of all people, was not the highest paid TV performer, "that naturally invites the question of who is." Meanwhile, Merv Griffin would later claim that his weekly salary to take on Johnny was $80,000 a week. By contrast, Joey Bishop was getting $25,000.

With three men fighting it out in the midnight hours – Griffin, Carson and Bishop – that left an opening in the evening hours, the talk show slot Griffin had held down in most parts of the country.

Two years earlier, David Frost impressed critics when he guest-hosted for Griffin. Over the July 4 holiday in 1968, Frost scored again guesting for Carson. Brought back again, on September 30, he made headlines with a controversial show that included a discussion on birth control and the Pope.

Actor Robert Shaw commented, "As far as I'm concerned all of that business about infallibility is nonsense." Frost recalled a nineteenth-century Pope who said one afternoon, "I'm not infallible." And then at 7 o'clock he said, "I'm sorry. I made a mistake. I am infallible."

NBC received over a hundred phone calls. Vacationing in Florida, Jonny offered no comment. He figured if Frost wanted to be controversial, maybe he should do it on his own show.

When Merv left for CBS, the Westinghouse syndicate handed Frost half million dollars a year and a five-year contract. Then he literally prayed for strength. After the negotiations were completed, he had his chauffeur drive him to the nearest church.

At one time *The Tonight Show* was practically the only game in town, any time of the day or night. But with television growing through the 60's and hundreds of stations now in place, there was big money to be had and the talk show format was very cheap to produce. There were daytime shows like the one Mike Douglas hosted.

And in the evening, "The Talk Show Wars" had begun. The fighting got dirty. Staffers were lured from show to show. *Tonight Show* comedy writer Walter Kempley had been getting $1,000 a week from Carson. Frost bought him for $1,300. Dick Carson, who had desrted Johnny to direct the ill-fated *Don Rickles Show*, turned up as the director on Merv Griffin's show.

Staff defections irked Johnny, who was in a no-win situation. With the intense responsibilities of being both the star and the real boss of *The Tonight Show*, he had so much on his mind he often walked by people without the perfunctory smile and chit-chat. Johnny was not the one to shout to the secretaries on a rainy day, "Nice weather for ducks!" While most understood the pressures on him, others pronounced him a cold fish and deserted, only giving him more cynical reasons to feel that he was surrounded by people he couldn't trust.

On the night of September 10, 1969, while TV

audiences watched *The Tonight Show*, Sal Pepe, a worker in the Rockefeller Center building smelled smoke. He sounded the fire alarm and followed the trail through the deserted corridors of the seventh floor. He came to Johnny's office. "When I got to Carson's door", he said, "I could feel the heat from inside. Then when I opened the door the flames shot out at me and I had to jump back."

Firefighters arrived moments later, and worked hard to put out the blaze. The room was now smoking wreckage, the walls charred, the furniture wrecked, everything burned black.

The flash fire had originated somewhere in Johnny's office and had not spread elsewhere. When he arrived, Johnny immediately went through the sopping, smoldering wreckage to check on the portrait of Joanne that had hung in his inner office. It was destroyed.

He went through his desk, the smell of burnt wood still acrid in the air. Johnny managed to pull out two small survivors — his pair of good-luck gold cuff links.

By the time the reporters found him, Johnny had a half smile planted on his face. And they laughed appreciatively when he looked over the wreckage, paused and said, "I wonder where Joey and Merv are tonight?"

The deadliest fighting was between the staffs of the Griffin and Carson shows. There wasn't enough room in town for both of them. The powerful *Tonight Show* staff was especially tough. The attitude was: "If you talk to Merv, then you'll never talk to Johnny again."

Variety investigated the situation and found a few performers willing to talk. Jack E. Leonard, Myron Cohen, Hugh Downs, Lorne Greene and singer Noel Harrison were among the stars who admitted to being intimidated by *Tonight Show* personnel.

The trade paper intimated that aside from keeping away big stars from Merv Griffin, *The Tonight Show* was snatching away up-and-coming performers once they broke in with Merv. Once a "minor leaguer" showed talent on Merv's show, that performer was promoted up to the big-time *Tonight Show* — on condition they never went back to Griffin.

The battle to attract and keep important guests continued to be a major problem, especially with so many talk shows. It bothered Johnny when he had to sit opposite some uninteresting star and promote that person's latest movie. He resented having to work hard to keep the ad-libs flowing, realizing that the responsibility for making the show worth watching was his.

"So you have, say, Eydie Gorme on," Carson remarked. "You ask her about her kids. What the hell else are you going to ask her about besides singing?"

One night, with Eva Gabor on the panel, Marlon Brando mumbled, "How long are we going to have to listen to this crap?"

"I could not give a shit what Bianca Jagger is doing, or what Jackie O. is doing," Carson admitted off stage, "but those are the people you constantly read about... Some of them don't have anything except their manufactured celebrity status."

Johnny found himself locked into booking certain types of guests for *The Tonight Show*, feeling a responsibility to present a balanced, funny but basically soothing and reassuring late night program.

It was precisely this dilemma that inspired David Frost.

Frost had come to fame in England as the host of *That Was The Week That Was*, the anti-establishment comedy show that was the *Saturday Night Live* of its day – only with meaner intent. He was respected as an intelligent, politically aware show host and when he brought his talk show to America, he was confident he could attract the controversial authors, writers and performers who had avoided "chat" shows before.

On July 1, 1969, Frost was a guest on Merv Griffin's show. Griffin's viewers saw him again on July 4 when the gentlemanly Merv announced him as the new host of the syndicated show. Then on July 7, 1969, *The David Frost Show* premiered, featuring Prince Charles, Ed Sullivan and the Rolling Stones. Immediately, Frost sent out a warning that he could attract big names. He also proved to be fast with his wits. When Sullivan suddenly asked, "Why have you never married?" Frost replied, "You present variety and I enjoy it."

When it came to fielding questions from the audience, Frost was ready.

"How do you feel about unwed mothers?" someone asked.

"Not responsible."

But as a responsible talk show host, Frost was interested in getting a variety of guests. He booked Dr. Spock, Golda Meir, Prime Minister Wilson's wife and Adam Clayton Powell. He became the critics' darling, the most controversial of the four talking head-liners.

Powell claimed there was a conspiracy in the slaying of Dr. Martin Luther King. Frost demanded facts. He wanted to know who paid for the "hit."

He told Powell, "Give more facts of where the money came from."

"I know where it came from," Powell said, "and I will not tell you." Then he added mysteriously, "But when we leave here, I'll tell you."

"No, no, no, don't let's have private chats. Let's talk to the people," Frost shot back. "Tell them!" Powell backed off. "I'll shut my mouth," he said.

Frost cried, "That's the most irresponsible thing you have ever done."

That kind of point-blank accusation was absent from the talk show scene.

Johnny didn't want to hear about Frost's relevance. "Bullshit. That's my answer... controversy just isn't what this show is for. I'm an entertainer, not a commentator. If you're a comedian your job is to make people laugh... I get irked when the press says my show doesn't do enough relevant things. Neither does Dean Martin or Flip Wilson. That's up to Bill Buckley. That's my idea of what a talk show is."

Buckley's show, *Firing Line,* was not on in prime time or late night. Frost continued to score with important guests and quotable comments. Sometimes a quotable comment came from an unlikely guest. While it has sometimes been attributed to him, it was actually his guest Raquel Welch who one night declared, "The mind is an erogenous zone."

Sometimes a guest strayed into the wrong zone entirely. Mentioning other talk shows was a prickly sore point on Frost's show as it was for everyone else's. Frost invited Jacqueline Susann on his show. She was known for trashy best-selling novels, which led Frost to wonder exactly how she saw herself; as a serious writer of literature or as an entertainer? How did she feel she fit in with other authors?

Susann said, "To answer that would be as bad as if I had to say where do I place you. Are you like Johnny Carson? Like Merv Griffin? I think you are unique. I am so glad you're here. We need you here. And you're different, and human."

John Simon, also a guest that night, took up the question. He didn't wish to label her "Dumb Jackie Susann or (expletive deleted) Jackie Susann or Swinish Jackie Susann," but he did want to know something. "*Miss* Susann," he asked, "do you think you're writing art, or do you think you're writing trash?"

"I'm writing stories," she muttered.

She still had to prefer being on Frost's show to being anywhere near Carson. One night in a restaurant she ran into Carson, who was in one of his states of intoxicated obnoxiousness. Their brief encounter ended when she splashed her drink in his face.

On Frost's show, a most any faux pas would be more akin to spilled champagne. A pair of his most memorable evenings involved homosexual "outings" and "in-ings." Gore Vidal was not about to get deeply involved in a discussion of his homosexuality. Asked if his "first time" was with a male or female, he answered, "I was too polite to ask." But when Frost questioned him about other varieties of sexuality, Vidal's eyes lit up. "I'm all for bringing back the birch," he told Frost, "but only between consenting adults!"

Frost had more success pinning down Tennessee Williams. The writer had not yet discussed such matters openly, but he did give a winking nod to Frost. He demurely admitted, "I don't want to be involved in some sort of a scandal but I've 'covered the waterfront.'"

Not foolish enough to present nothing but egghead authors and politicians, Frost sought out big-name movie stars, winning them over with a preposterously gushy interview style. With these guests he was always crying "Mahvelous" and "Supah" at everything they said, asking them safely probing questions like: "What is your definition of love?"

When Dick Cavett arrived on the scene, he said, "I don't know how David Frost could bring himself to ask those godawful, formula-interview, what's-your-most-embarrassing-experience-questions night after night?"

But at the time, Frost was doing quite well with it, and as Merv and Johnny looked on with envy, it was David Frost, O.B.E., who snared some of the guests who never, ever did talk shows. In 1968 the Beatles appeared live with Frost. They were never on with anyone else. In 1970 Elizabeth Taylor was on the show with Frost. She wouldn't sit down on Johnny's couch until over twenty years later; to salute him on his retirement. Frost would later nab ex-President Richard Nixon for an historic series of specials, once again frustrating the competition.

Of all the talk show hosts, Frost was most attuned to the new music scene. Carson loved big bands and Merv was still prone to a chorus of "I've Got a Loverly Bunch of Coconuts," but it was David Frost who championed the cause of John Lennon and gave him a forum to sing his newest and most controversial songs and discuss his immigration problems.

Frost didn't have to rely completely on his staff to find out what was hip or controversial. He had an inquiring mind and sought out the truth for himself. One day he opened up a newspaper to read about a concert given by radical folk singer Phil Ochs. As Ochs's biographer Marc Elliot, points out, "It was the first time [Phil] had been invited on a major TV show. Frost, although syndicated, was on more than a hundred stations across the country. It would mean more exposure at one time than he'd ever had before... After the taping he thanked Frost profusely, shaking his hand, telling him how grateful he was for the chance to be seen... "

Johnny was occasionally persuaded to try a controversial guest, but the results seemed to backfire on him. Atheist Madalyn Murray O'Hair was on the show and the audience booed her, which disgusted the always gentlemanly Johnny. He had politicians on but was rewarded with devious tricks: "They'll tell you what they want to tell you and no more... I had Agnew on, and he bored the shit out of everybody and moralized." Governor Ronald Reagan appeared, and could have given *The Tonight Show* the biggest scoop in all of television. But it was two days later that he told the press he would run for president.

Mort Sahl once asked Carson to give Jim Garrison some air time to discuss new theories on the Kennedy assassination. Johnny agreed, but then network lawyers got involved and pressured him to avoid libelous terrain. Of that night's fiasco, the *Village Voice* huffed: "Carson interrupted his guest about every minute and a half to have him qualify what he was saying or repeat that it was only his opinion. As a result, it was impossible for Garrison to complete a sentence, let alone present a coherent argument."

Carson realized that *The Tonight Show* had to remain what it was, and considering the ratings, that wasn't so bad. If he felt strongly about a political issue, he could always tell it to a print interviewer. He did just that for his *Playboy* interview with Alex Haley. Harley, Carson said, called Vietnam "an unpopular war. And it keeps going on and on. I'm a father with a boy coming out of high school next year, and I don't look forward to his marching off over there. I don't think anybody dissenting against this war has any business being called un-American."

Frost could have the accolades and discuss politics. Besides, that was just a syndicated show. As for the new challenge on CBS from Merv Griffin? Well... just what *was* Merv Griffin going to do?

Merv tried a little of everything for his premiere. He went with Hedy Lamarr for glamour, Ted Sorensen for relevance, Moms Mabley for laughs, and young Woody Allen – supplying film clips from his very first movie *(Take the Money and Run)*.

Joey Bishop tried to sabotage Merv's evening by bringing on the Smothers Brothers, who had recently been thrown off the air by CBS in a censorship dispute.

Johnny simply called on his pal Bob Hope and beat out the both of them.

The ratings showed Johnny commanding a 34 percent share of the viewing audience, Griffin an 18 share and Bishop a 13 share. Some of Griffin and Bishop's defenders argued that Carson had an unfair advantage. NBC was the strongest network with 206 affiliates, as opposed to CBS with 151 and ABC with 135.

Advertisers went with Johnny, paying $17,500 for a minute of show time. Merv was able to command $10,000 and Bishop $7,500.

Griffin, quickly passing Joey Bishop in the ratings, began to make the race between first and second closer.

The stakes got higher. Joey Bishop had to mutter one of his catch phrases: "Son of a gun!" He was removed; Dick Cavett became the new hope for ABC.

Bishop figured at least he'd lasted longer than anyone expected. And he came away in better shape than Johnny: "I'm married to the same woman and don't drink."

The pressure to get exclusives with guests increased. There were three late-night shows competing at night, all emanating from New York. Added to that, David Frost was a major factor with his syndicated series.

When Senator Hubert Humphrey came to New York, there was a not-so-friendly truce between David Frost's people and the staff at *The Merv Griffin Show*. The idea was to share this big catch. Both shows were taping simultaneously. Humphrey would do twenty minutes with Frost, then catch the last half of Merv's show and do twenty minutes there.

To the horror of Griffin's talent coordinator, Frost and Humphrey continued to talk past the twenty-minute mark. So during a commercial break, she rushed onto the stage and grabbed Humphrey, announcing that he had a commitment with Griffin. Like a pair of bank robbers, they hustled into a waiting limousine and burned rubber.

For Johnny, it seemed that every star and non-star came directly to him with a plea to get on his show. He didn't mind it when big-time sex symbols and starlets tried to influence him with a one-night stand. That was fun, and as far as Joanne and love and marriage was concerned, just a physical thing, nothing serious.

What was more serious was the continuing encroachment of the press, photographers and fans. Again, Johnny wanted to be polite to them and understood their needs, but he desperately needed to cool down in private darkness after the hot spotlight was on him.

Some stars avoided everyone with limousines and bodyguards. Johnny didn't want to become as isolated as a king, hidden behind an entourage, but as the King of late night television, he had no choice, pretentious as it might be. For example, he loathed the star routine of being escorted into theaters or films through a special entrance and placed in a special box. "I don't like that idea, the special treatment bit," Carson complained to interviewer Phyllis Battelle.

But what could he do about it? "You can't stand in line at the box office, not when everybody else in line sees you in their bedrooms every night... All of a sudden you're engaged in conversation. People grab you by the arm and haul you over to meet their idiot cousins who'd be 'great on *The Tonight Show*' and you can't say 'Oh God, I hate it,' because if they didn't come up to you you'd be in real trouble."

Like so many comics, his humor was fueled by

his anger. His silly, stupid sketches were driven by one simple principle: "Stupid things are what irritate me the most."

While he was mindful of snaring the best guests and just leaving the crumbs to Cavett and Griffin, Johnny took a firm position about the stars he'd have on the show: "I can't go out there and fake that I'm in love with somebody when I'm not... People I disagree with completely just don't get on the show because if I've got hostility I'm gonna kill 'em — and I don't see the point in getting somebody up in public and start zinging them."

There were many people Johnny didn't want to deal with for one reason or another. They ranged from Elliott Gould to Milton Berle and included personalities who espoused loathesome philosophies, from LSD advocate Timothy Leary to slick con man Clifford Irving. While he might have gotten big ratings for booking scandal celebrities like Linda Lovelace, Elizabeth Ray or Charles Manson, Johnny always said no.

One man whom Johnny said yes to was Jerry Lewis. Jerry seemed especially excited to be a guest on *The Tonight Show* one night. But the next morning, Johnny realized that it had been an elaborate practical joke. Jerry had also stopped by *The Merv Griffin Show* and *The Dick Cavett Show*, becoming the first and only celebrity in late night history to score an unassisted triple play.

CHAPTER ELEVEN

TALK SHOW INTRUDERS ARE IN THE DUST, BUT CRIMINALS ARE ON JOHNNY'S TRAIL

As vicious as the booking wars were during the fight for *The Tonight Show* in the late 60's, the battlefield didn't extend beyond the studios. The four hosts were not bitter enemies in real life. This was quite different from the days when Jack Paar was sneering at Steve Allen and, snarling at Johnny Carson.

Dick Cavett and Johnny had a relationship of mutual respect. It had begun back in Nebraska when Carson was "The Great Carsoni" and Dick an apprentice magician eager to learn. Cavett had left Jack Paar, but returned as a gag writer when Johnny took over *The Tonight Show.*

When Dick brought in jokes that were good, Johnny sometimes complimented him, a rare thing for the harried, hurried host to do. When Johnny didn't like the material, he simply told Dick. "I think you're capable of better work than this."

Johnny and Dick were often on the same wavelength. Cavett impressed his boss not only with his comedy knowledge, but his taste and tact in handling matters both personal and professional.

In his autobiography, Cavett mentioned Johnny's problems on the show: "I have heard that he has been manipulated and screwed more than once by trusted associates, to the point where he is defensively wary to what some find an excessive degree. I see this as a perfectly reasonable response... "

When interviewers came to him for the dirt about Johnny, Cavett had a reasonable response. Asked about Johnny's coldness, Cavett replied tartly, "He is so cold, one day he was napping in the nude in his dressing room, and I shoved a thermometer up his ass and the mercury froze." That ended the interview.

For this, and other reasons, the relationship between *The Tonight Show* and *The Dick Cavett Show* was calm, and Johnny even turned up one evening to be interviewed by Cavett.

Carson's relationship with David Frost was always pretty cordial, too. Carson also did a rare ninety-minute interview for *The David Frost Show.* Carson didn't consider the syndicated talk show to be such tremendous competition. Frost wasn't on directly opposite him, like Dick and Merv.

Merv Griffin and Johnny Carson also had mutual respect for each other. Their careers were similar. Both had a love of big band music, both had hosted quiz shows and both moved on to host NBC talk shows beginning the same day in 1962 Johnny on the night shift, Merv during the day. Johnny's brother, Dick, was the director on Griffin's show.

All four men had something in common at the turn of the 70's. The talk show wars were killing their private lives.

With Cavett, working on the show was a see saw of mood swings. Some days he considered himself the luckiest man in the world. Other days depression took him over and he felt as if he was on, to quote his idol Fred Allen, "a treadmill to oblivion."

Griffin was nervously overeating and had ballooned thirty pounds. He was stoking his tobacco habit, going through three packs of cigarettes a day. His marriage was beginning to unravel.

David Frost's long-standing relationship with Jenny Logan was scuttled soon after he began the grind. In the midst of the dizzying turbulence, Frost made headlines romancing Diahann Carroll. This didn't last either.

Willi Frischauer, Frost's biographer, saw Frost's temperament changing during the show's run. He "seemed nervous, giving his colleagues the impression that he was wrestling with problems. He obviously realized the magnitude of his undertaking... gregarious at most times, David now preferred to keep his own company. He did not seem overeager to go down to the studio... "

Johnny's marriage to Joanne was skidding to an end and all he wanted was peace and quiet, which he couldn't find in New York City. New Yorkers always pridefully say, "You can get anything here, any time of the day or night." The exceptions are peace and quiet.

Johnny had no defense against a window washer who dragged his clanking scaffold past the bedroom window every morning at 8 a.m. His "luxury" building was an acoustic nightmare of noises thanks to cheap walls, floors and pipes. The incompetents and imbeciles running the building couldn't fix a thing, and shrugged that everyone had to put up with city noise. Carson had to sue the landlord and tangle with lawyers to get satisfaction, reporting that the noise was "destructive of the health, comfort and property of those exposed to it." For good measure, he demanded $25,000 compensation.

Johnny often attacked Con Edison, the power company, in his monologues. There was good reason. They too had often disturbed Johnny's rest, drilling early in the morning and then stopping at noon. "And nobody knows what for. But I do. They're using it for a training ground... A guy comes to work and Con Ed says, "You don't know how to dig? Well, go over to our practice area."

If there wasn't aggravation at home, then it was

at work. Before ABC did it successfully, NBC tried football on Monday nights. The games ran late, cutting into Carson's time slot. Johnny threatened to walk off the show if NBC didn't shape up. He knew the importance of viewers, automatically dialing up the show the same time every night. He said, "It is not fair to treat my show like a late-night filler. This show is about the biggest moneymaker that NBC has, grossing about $27 million or $28 million a year."

Then there was continued annoyance from the NBC censors. After they made dozens of changes in a minor "Tea Time Movie" sketch with busty blonde Carol Wayne, he took his case directly to his viewers, angrily insisting, "You can find obscenity in anything!"

Using the sound of a censor's "bleep," he recited nursery rhymes that were filled with innuendo:

"Jack and Jill went up the hill to BLEEP." "Little Miss Muffet sat on her BLEEP." "Mary Mary, quite contrary, how does your BLEEP grow?"

The audience broke up. "I think that gives you an idea," Carson added.

Carson was delighted when he was able to put something over on the censors. For months he dropped in references to the "Fakawi Indians." It got the band hysterical and always broke up the comics on the show.

The censors didn't understand the tribal name because they hadn't heard the old joke: a Cavalry troop were out hunting the fearsome Fakawi Indians. They hunted over forests and deserts but could never find them. They used an Indian guide who led them deeper and deeper into nowhere. Finally, the exasperated Sergeant asked the guide, "Where the Fakawi?"

One Monday night in March, Carson had to ask that question about Muhammad Ali. Where —— *was* he? Just before showtime a member of the boxer's entourage phoned to explain that the champ couldn't make it. Not normally prone to give Jack Paar-like tirades, Carson couldn't help himself. His monologue turned into a lecture:

"This is the second time it has happened and I think [twice] is enough. I think if you can't make this show, you ought to have a little better explanation than 'I'm not going to be there' forty-five minutes before the show!"

Four days later, Carson checked into the New York Cornell Medical Center. The hospital reported him in "fair" condition, suffering from hepatitis.

Gossip columnists weren't buying the story. Wasn't it convenient that Joan Rivers was already scheduled to "guest host" the Friday-night show? And that Joey Bishop was in town for Monday's show and available to host the entire week? And that Tony Randall had been contacted for some guest-hosting?

The rumor was plastic surgery for the bags under Johnny's eyes. Insiders on *The Tonight Show* at the time say that Johnny was always sensitive about his eyes. Though he was sometimes characterized in the press as "skinny" and more than one found him "snub-nosed," Carson was more concerned that his eyes were too small. With the age wrinkles, his eyes seemed even smaller and his appearance may have struck him as too wizened.

But whether it was plastic surgery or hepatitis, it was clear that the strain of doing the show was heavy on Johnny. His secretary admitted that the cup on his desk was not filled with water: "When I first started with Johnny in 1969, he preferred Smirnoff vodka and tonic, but by the time I left, he was drinking J&B scotch and water."

Bob Lardine in the *Sunday News* interviewed several members of the show. One staffer hinted of

Carson's worried distractions and the discontent on *The Tonight Show:*

"In all the years that I've been on the show he has never once said hello. He maintains that attitude with most of the other fellas, too. As for his being relaxed, I think it's a great put-on. Carson is the most uptight, nervous guy you'll ever want to meet. His short temper creates tension backstage. Everyone is sniping at everyone else."

Another confirmed, "After the show Carson is often enraged. Don't ever put that —— on the show again," he'll scream. And then Carson will rant about how inept some of the other guests were. If those celebrities could only hear what Carson thinks about them, there would be some dandy street fights around town."

Truman Capote recalled what was going on at home: "I felt extremely sorry for his wife.... she was very good to him. She did a tremendous amount for Johnny. I don't think Johnny would have survived or have had remotely the career he's had if it hadn't been for her. But he was mean as hell to her. And they lived right next door. He would holler and get terribly angry and she would take refuge in my apartment. She would hide and Johnny would come pounding on my door, shouting, 'I know she's there.' And I would just maintain a dead silence."

On June 8, 1970, he changed the locks in their apartment. The terms of the settlement were reached on March 19, 1971. Joanne would receive $200,000 in cash and got a U.S. president's yearly salary: $100,000 a year.

After the divorce, Joanne said, "Johnny is a genius. I'm still his number one fan but I wasn't cut out to be married to such a high achiever. For ten years I was living on the ragged edge of his genius."

A female staffer during the *Tonight Show* years says, "I'm sure she would've liked to stay married for

Busty DAGMAR was the sidekick with the great sideview . . .

... and JERRY LESTER was top banana on *Broadway Open House,* considered the first incarnation of *The Tonight Show.*

ED SULLIVAN and STEVE ALLEN during their rrrrreally big feud.

In blameless
and blaming
poses, JACK
PAAR, 1962
and 1992.

JOHNNY CARSON, ED McMAHON and ART STARK on vacation in Florida during Johnny's early days on *The Tonight Show*. (Photos courtesy Anthony Stark)

Welcome to *The Tonight Show*. Producer ART STARK shows JOHNNY CARSON the schedule of upcoming guests. (Photo courtesy of Anthony Stark.) . . . George C. Scott becomes one of "The Mighty Carson Art Players."

Challenging the million-dollar *Tonight Show* with wooden nickels: JOEY BISHOP as host, with REGIS PHILBIN announcing and JOHNNY MANN conducting the band. . . . Who said he wasn't distinctive? JOEY BISHOP stands out from guests THE JACKSON FIVE.

DAVID FROST's fight to win in the talk show wars included a blockbuster appearance with LIZ TAYLOR and RICHARD BURTON. . . . Not quite TAYLOR and BURTON, but a tabloid favorite: the romance between DAVID FROST and singer DIAHANN CARROLL.

DICK CAVETT
tricked JACK
PAAR into hiring
him, treated
JOHNNY
CARSON to
monologue jokes,
then got his own
series. . . .
and his own
controversies.
That's LESTER
MADDOXX
walking away
from CAVETT
and TRUMAN
CAPOTE.

MERV GRIFFIN began his first talk show the same day JOHNNY CARSON took over *The Tonight Show*. Thirty years later, they ended their on-air rivalry with a memorable duel of ad-libs.

The original set: Johnny as ''Aunt Blabby'' with Ed McMahon chuckling and producer Art Startk near the camera. The wall clock is set for ''Tonight'' time, though the show's taped in the late afternoon. . . . During a commercial break, the producer tells Johnny and guest Richard Kiley that everything's going great. (*photos courtesy of Anthony Stark*).

Johnny in his party mode, shakes hands and smiles with opera star Jan Peerce during a photo opportunity. That's Ed McMahon looking grim in the background. . . . An introspective moment for Johnny as he gets ready for a show. Those are his three sons on the wall behind him. October, 1963 is the date on the calendar. (*photos courtesy of Anthony Stark*)

Early in her career, JOAN RIVERS force-feeds a banana to a rubber chicken in a literal gag photo. . . . RIVERS also hosted an afternoon talkfest called *That Show* (guest: ANTHONY NEWLEY) before she emerged as *The Tonight Show's* most popular substitute host. . .

. . . and most controversial competition.

They crawled on him and they crapped on him, but JOHNNY CARSON never got fed up with those lovable animal guests, including this baby monkey from a 1977 broadcast.

The many faces of JOHNNY CARSON, including: El Moldo, Carnak, Art Fern and Aunt Blabby.

Following *Tonight*, it's *Late Night With David Letterman*. But after he waited a decade to take over Johnny's job, NBC said, "Sorry, Dave."

Former *Tonight Show* guest host GARRY SHANDLING got revenge with a cable series making fun of the backstabbing talk show wars. . . . When prickly DENNIS MILLER took a stab at hosting a lat night show, he found himsself axed.

In the late 80's, JAY LENO was told that his face ''scared children.'' The comic's manager cautiously stocked two photos of her client. Potential bookers who might be ''frightened'' got the covered chin picture.

It's a confident JAY LENO who now autographs photos with an added "chin caricature" (visible bottom left) .... But don't expect an exchange of autographs between JAY LENO and the still steaming ARSENIO HALL.

To Ralph
Thanks!

All For One and
One For All:
When the end came,
DOC SEVERINSEN,
JOHNNY CARSON
and ED McMAHON
left *The Tonight Show*
together. . . .
Johnny — from a bit
part in "Looking for
Love" to hosting the
Academy Awards.

The last laugh: DAVID LETTERMAN became the 28 Million Dollar Man for CBS, banking on a showdown victory over JAY LENO.

The boyish
smile that lasted
thirty years.

the rest of her life. I think she probably genuinely loved him. She *was* his number one fan, but just as he outgrew his manager and producer he outgrew his wife. Hitting the big time, he may have wanted someone smoother, better educated possibly."

The talk show wars in New York were getting to Johnny, but they'd already gotten to Merv Griffin. He fled to California, leaving sidekick Arthur Treacher behind. Treacher had told Merv, "At my age, I don't want to move, especially to someplace that shakes."

Just when *The Tonight Show* staffers got ready to celebrate, they realized something about crafty Merv. His retreat was actually a strategic attack. Johnny might be King of late night, but Merv was royalty in California, and that's where all the *real* stars lived.

Carson vowed to march on Hollywood and battle Griffin. He spent a fortune on a new house, and NBC spent three times as much refurbishing the new Burbank home for *The Tonight Show*.

Oddsmakers were saying that Johnny was going to destroy Merv. But there were a few who believed Johnny's best years were behind him.

Johnny had been the host of *The Tonight Show* for ten years. Some critics claimed he was too predictable; the show was running on automatic pilot. A new generation was growing up — and they didn't want "hep" Johnny. They wanted hip comedy. In 1972 a formerly "straight" comic named George Carlin turned into a bearded hippie. And another ex-Ed Sullivan act, Richard Pryor, quit Vegas to become a raging counter-culture comic for blacks.

A new humor magazine, *The National Lampoon*, signaled a "new wave" in comedy, and in its September 1972 "Boredom" issue, attacked Carson and his *Tonight Show* formula.

Writer Michael O'Donoghue catalogued every cliche in the Carson monologue, every well-worn

device. These included the use of funny names of
actors and actresses (Sonny Tufts and Maria Ous-
penskaya were sure laugh-getters), funny profes-
sions to joke about (Avon Ladies and hairdressers
topped the list), funny animals to mention (yaks,
wombats, yellow-bellied sapsuckers and beavers)
and funny foods sure to amuse (prune juice and
kumquats).

The National Lampoon slapped at Carson for
doing gags about Jockey shorts and living bras,
about traffic on Mulholland Drive and the Slauson
cutoff, about the Fakawi Indians, 5-Day Deodorant
Pads, the San Andreas Fault and *Let's Made a Deal*,
about the Man from Glad, Ralph Williams and The
Jolly Green Giant. They even catalogued his ejacula-
tions ("Weird!" "Crazy!" "Yah-hah!" "Whoopie!") and
his catch phrases: "Can you imagine some drunk
watching the show who just tuned in?" "It's a
biggee." "If I said what I'm thinking right now this
place would be a parking lot tomorrow... "

The piece was illustrated with an allusion to the
now-tired Ed Ames clip. There was a drawing of
Johnny Carson, naked, the hatchet embedded in his
groin.

Back in the late 60's and early 70's, Johnny's
monologues still had to be safe enough to get past
the NBC censor, and he was still careful about what
his conservative audience would laugh at. They still
loved glib, Vegas-styled comedy and the vicarious
thrill of being part of "show biz." A typical monologue
from that era almost reads like a parody:

"Whoopie! (Looking off camera...) You've had
your little joke. I'm giving you girls thirty minutes to
put your tops back on! You see a guy at home: "Gee,
if I'd just gone there!" (Looking at Doc) I'll get to that
outfit in a moment! I don't know why you're in such
a good mood. I love to walk to work on a cold, rainy
Monday. That's my second favorite thing in the

world. My first is taking off my shoes and socks and trying to punt a porcupine. You know what happens on rainy days? Also happens on sunny days too. Brings out the weirdos. Happens on cold days... "

Ed: "Any day you got a joke!"

"Today it rained. A weirdo stopped me on 8th Avenue and said, 'How about ten dollars for my little old gray-haired mother?' I gave him the ten dollars. He says, 'Now, when do you want my gray-haired mother?' That's weird! That's terrible.... Saturday, you know what I did? Took a blanket, went out in the park and watched the Boston Pops perform. Until the Boston moms got embarrassed, then I went on home. The reason I brought that up, and I didn't bring that up well — "

Ed: "Oooooh! No."

"Next time I'll bring it up right, or I won't bring it up at all." (The drummer lands a quick shot.) Oh, drummer gives rim shot. Guess who played with the Boston Pops this weekend? Doc Severinsen... how did it go?"

Doc: "It was a gas... I wanna tell you, those boys in Boston can drink a little bit. They do it up!"

"Symphony orchestra musicians drink?"

Doc: "How else can they stand that longhair music!"

"... Hokay... Hear about Ed last night? Quick thinking. He was out on his hands and knees. On the sidewalk. Out of the corner of his eye he saw one of those dark blue suits with a nightstick. And without even thinking, he put his two hands together and said, 'And above all, Good Lord, grant the police better pay.' Great thinking! What happened today? When's the commissary opening?"

Ed: "Slight delay."

Doc: "They're waiting for the food to spoil!"

Ed: (as the crowd roars) "Hyoooooo!"

"And I don't have anything! That's very good. Why

didn't I think of that? I will... So the food will spoil."

Ed: "One of the biggest laughs I heard around here in a long time!"

"We have something new tonight. Auditions for orchestra leaders and announcers!"

Some of the formula gags were leading younger comics to wish for an audition to become the new host of the show. The Credibility Gap performed a complete, wickedly on-target ten-minute *Tonight Show* parody complete with rimshots and Ed McMahon periodically crying out "Yessssss!" after each Carson biggie.

The guy who had been the hip, sophisticated, sexy, iconoclastic, handsome idol of late night TV was beginning to take his lumps.

Things had gotten pretty lumpy for Merv Griffin too. The move to California still hadn't turned into the ratings bonanza CBS expected. The network executives became more and more nervous, turning the pressure screws further and further. The trip to the Coast had further shattered his marriage. His wife, Julann, "came to feel she was living in my shadow', he recalls. The ballyhoo accompanies my move to CBS, and the partner of that move, pressure, pushes me away from, rather than toward, Julann."

In his autobiography Griffin wrote about the hell of working for CBS bosses: "We dealt with a dizzying maze of executives whose titles and faces melt together in my mind. Robert Blake has a term for them: 'the suits.' I'll tell you how the suits work... They'll make a comment about a guest's "revealing" attire, an off-color line, a song you did or the importance of guests you booked, nitpicking until you want to cave in from fatigue..."

Dick Cavett recalled the same thing happening to him. After his very first show, ABC bosses complained that he had performed badly, and that he had not gotten anywhere with his guests, Gore Vidal, Angela Lansbury and Muhammad Ali. They told Cavett the show was "a loser" and told him to do better the following night. They questioned whether they should even broadcast the show, or shelve it and premiere with something else.

Cavett listened for a few moments and then said, "When are you going to stop being chickenshit?"

Ultimately, the clique of junior executives, vice presidents and programming whiz-kids at ABC plotted a move to bring in a new host.

As for Merv Griffin, the executives at CBS had a Christmas present for him in December of 1971: his freedom. They canceled his show and all his old shows, too: they destroyed every single *Merv Griffin Show* they had, re-using the tape to get some of their money back.

Griffin took back his humble syndicated desk job at Westinghouse; David Frost had already succumbed to the talk wars, too.

Johnny Carson's tried and true methods had brought him through a tumultuous decade. He told *Newsweek*, "The idea of television, as I understand it, is to reach as many people as possible. That's one measure of success. Or is it to reach a manner of critical success, to do prison reform and other relevant things? If you do that, you're not going to reach the people. David Frost did that and for some reason he doesn't seem to be on anymore.

"Look, I could do a 'controversial' show on capital punishment tonight. What new things are you going to say? One guy says he's for capital punishment... The next guy gets up [and says he's against it]... Everybody does their number and then they say, 'Thank you, and good night.' Wow. Wasn't that a wonderful show? Well, was it? I don't know. I'd rather go out and entertain."

And, entertain on *The Tonight Show* each night.

By now Johnny realized that his life would be the talk show, and he'd better direct all his energies in keeping control over it and keeping it strong. He figured that he was too well known for the public to buy him in a movie role. And a prime-time television special in December of 1969 had been savaged by the critics. *The New York Times* complained: "Everyone involved... should feel contrite this morning... Two of the sketches — one purporting to spoof contemporary sexual morality, the other a spoof of the pornography in our movie houses — were witless and tasteless. A parody of Tennessee Williams' *Cat on a Hot Tin Roof* was downright dull. A fourth sketch, on children's television, was simply silly. It all added up to wasted talent in a wasted hour."

When Dick Cavett was a staffer on *The Tonight Show* he'd asked Johnny, "Where do you go from here?" Johnny had no answer.

He did have a new life in California, though. His show was still number one, he had Joanna, shapely wife number three. His pal Don Adams cheered him by pointing out he also didn't have the problems of living in a New York City apartment. The *Get Smart* star pointed out there was no New York noise and idiot neighbors. Not to mention the crazies and the crime.

Would you believe, Don... *worse* problems with crazies and crime?

It was no joke to Johnny.

Not long after he settled into his new home, less than two weeks after he married Joanna, Johnny faced the specter of kidnap and murder.

At 7:15 on the morning of October 8, 1972, workers at Johnny's home discovered a hand grenade. Careful investigation showed that it wasn't a real one. But what about the typed sheet of paper next to it? Someone wrote out a threat and it sounded real.

The wording was garbled, the spelling poor. It

seemed like the work of foreigners:

"We have just presented you with this," the mad letter next to the grenade began, "at the cost of $250,000. We believe it is senseless to tell you not to inform any enforcement agency or to discuss this matter with anyone. It will make matters worse for you and anyone else concerned.

"We want the bills in 20 & 50 dollar denominations. The serial numbers cannot be in a consecutive order of more than eight. If the money is not paid or the bills run inconsecutive order of more than eight, or the bills are marked in any way, we will reply with more conviction.

"Do not insult your intelligence by dismissing this matter; it will only denote a lack of cooperation. This will only place your family, your parents and other relatives in a very poor position.

"You have exactly three days from today. We will contact you again with further instructions."

There were secret meetings between Johnny Carson and the police. Security was as tight as a clenched fist. The grim evidence was examined, but the highest-paid performer in all of television and one of the most sophisticated police forces in America knew that the next move was not theirs. It belonged to extortionists. Identity unknown. Method unknown.

The comedian glumly hoped that it was a joke. But to reach the porch of his Bel-Air fortress and leave a warning was not the act of jokers. It looked more like the work of well-organized commandos.

It was quiet around the house.

It stayed quiet.

Then on Wednesday afternoon, Johnny got a phone call.

"Did you get the note?"

"It's a joke... " Johnny offered, still in character as the reasonable and nice comedian.

No joke. A hang-up instead. An hour later, the man called back, and the instructions were explicit. A quarter of a million dollars. In cash.

And if not? Let's just say that Johnny Carson and his family would be in serious, serious trouble.

It was cool vs. cool. The felon calmly told Carson that he didn't want the money right away. He gave Johnny time to think about it. He said he would call again within 48 hours.

The police were on guard through the tense days and nights. Everything was on ice till Friday.

By a strange quirk of fate, it had been arranged a month earlier for Joey Bishop to be the guest host that night. Viewers asking, "Where's Johnny tonight?" could never have guessed that he was participating in something closer to *Dragnet* than *The Tonight Show*.

On Friday evening, October 13, Johnny Carson drove to Lankershim Boulevard. He pulled up slowly to a parking lot and walked mechanically to the three phones near the parking lot of the Shopping Bag market. The time was 7:30 p.m. The phone rang at 7:30 exactly.

The instructions: Do a little more driving.

This time, the destination was to be the corner of Fulton Avenue and Oxnard Street near the campus of Los Angeles Valley College.

Johnny carefully wrote down the new address. Using his skills as a card-manipulating magician, he slid a carbon-copy sheet under his paper and duplicated the address. A little more sleight-of-hand and it was hidden in the coin-return slot.

Johnny drove off. The police retrieved the paper, confident that if they lost Johnny somehow, they could reconnoiter at the new location.

As the cops pulled out to follow Johnny, they noticed that another car was following him, too.

From a laundromat conveniently close to the

market, a man and a woman, both of college age, had watched Johnny leave the phone booth and get into his Lincoln Continental.

Now, for block after block, Johnny kept driving, and the couple were tailing him in a red Camaro. The police, weaving up close and then ducking out of sight, kept up the surveillance as the cars moved through the dark, warm night.

Johnny was close to his destination. He slowed down. He was at the drop site. He unloaded the money that had been placed in a suitcase.

Then the car that was following him reached the site and began to slow down.

Instantly the cops converged, screeching their tires to a stop. They grabbed their shotguns and rushed the car, dragging the man from behind the wheel.

His female partner watched in horror as he was hauled out of the car, thumped onto the ground, and dragged to his feet, blood streaming from his face. Thoroughly beaten, he confessed that he had been following Johnny Carson.

But just then, another man appeared, racing out from a garage near the drop site. He was making a dash for the suitcase with the money in it.

The cops pounced on him too, and in the wild melee, three suspects were now in custody: two bruised and bloodied men, and one frightened wo-man.

The cops brought in the couple, and the man who had made the pickup.

The man who grabbed the suitcase was the foreigner police expected, the man who wrote the garbled threats. He was an illegal alien who had arrived in America by way of Germany: twenty-six-year-old Richard Dziabacinski.

The other two were identified as Richard and Linda Culkin. And they kept saying they were just "fans" of Johnny Carson.

Horribly enough, they were telling the truth. Like anyone else, they were shocked and delighted when they happened to see their favorite star pull into the parking lot. They had been doing their Friday-night laundry when they noticed him at the bank of pay phones. Excited, shy, they didn't know what to do. When he began to drive away, they realized they'd blown their big chance!

They couldn't let Johnny get away!

The two well-meaning fans began to follow, hoping that maybe he'd stop someplace else and they could get his autograph. At least maybe at a traffic light they could pull up and get another look at him.

But the cops got them first. Richard Culkin told columnist Marilyn Beck that he barely knew what happened. But he knew what hit him: "I was hit about 30 times in my body and face. And once [the cops] threatened they'd throw me out on the highway and I wouldn't live through the night if I didn't tell the truth. They opened the car door part way open so I could hear the road pass... they kept saying obscene things about my wife, called me a fag and kept hitting me during most of the ride."

Mr. Culkin spent the evening at the County-USC Medical Center. Mrs. Culkin was treated to accommodations at the Sybil Brand Institute for Women.

Later, the two were officially cleared.

Lieutenent Charles Higby insisted that the extortion plot was "not amateur." When they searched the Sun Valley home of Dziabacinski, who claimed to be a writer, they found a sawed-off rifle and a .38 pistol. Impressed, they treated him like a pro: he was jailed. After a two-hour hearing that guest-starred Johnny Carson, Dziabacinski was indicted on charges of extortion.

CHAPTER TWELVE

JACK PAAR COMES BACK TO HELP CAVETT, AND NBC GOES TO WAR AGAINST THEIR OWN STAR: JOHNNY CARSON

With the cancellation of *The Merv Griffin Show*, the fight to topple *Tonight* was left to Dick Cavett. Cavett's program satisfied the critics and those seeking a touch of Jack Paar-like controversy in the night. As much as he admired Carson, Cavett was stylistically closer to Jack Paar.

Cavett had grown up in Nebraska, an unusual alloy of Midwestern charm and cool urbanity. An athletic boy, he won several state championships in gymnastics. His father and stepmother were schoolteachers and young Dick grew up with an interest in literature and the arts that eventually landed him a Yale scholarship.

He came to New York in 1958 and struggled to find a career as an actor. While working as a copyboy for *Time* magazine, he visited *The Tonight Show* offices carrying an official-looking *Time* envelope. He tracked down Paar and handed him the envelope containing two pages of jokes.

Paar was not known for encouraging such antics. Yet, it worked. Ironically, years later Cavett himself did not respond by mail or phone after a comedy writer performed the same stunt on him, alluding to the Paar incident as he handed over the material.

Cavett became a gag writer for both Jack Paar and later Johnny Carson on *The Tonight Show*. Influenced by the success of Woody Allen, Cavett then tried stand-up. His persona was the Nebraska farm type who, in witty fashion, could now comment on his new, sophisticated surroundings: "My whole freshman year I wore brown and white shoes. Actually they were impractical, because the white one kept getting dirty."

He gradually became comfortable enough to come out as himself and offer thinking man's gags: "I eat at this German-Chinese restaurant and the food is delicious. The only problem is that an hour later you're hungry for power."

He was ultimately rewarded with a morning TV show that was praised by the critics. When Joey Bishop faltered, ABC brought Dick in.

Cavett made sure not to get into any war with his old boss, Johnny. He paid due respect to Johnny. One night a guest made some anti-Carson remarks to win favor with Dick. When the show was over, Cavett recalls, "I called Johnny to apologize. I told him that it was pretty tacky on the guest's part and maybe I should have deleted it. He just said, 'Forget about it.'"

Occasionally in his monologue he made a reference to the competition, but it was usually the mildest of lines. A visit to the dentist's office for a filling had him wondering, "Why didn't they name it a Carson-y?"

While Cavett couldn't challenge Carson, he did make his talk show into a respectable alternative instead of an also-ran imitation.

Cavett had a lot of Paar's unpredictability. He encouraged his guests to mix it up, and the results were nearly explosive. Norman Mailer appeared with Gore Vidal and began sparring. Macho Mailer felt that gay Gore was definitely not a writer of equal stature, and as he looked around at both Vidal and Cavett, he declared, "Everyone here is smaller than I am."

Cavett asked, "What do you mean?"

Mailer eyed the little host and said, "Smaller intellectually."

Cavett replied, "Do you want another chair to contain your giant intellect?"

Another duo of writers, Lillian Hellman and Mary McCarthy, also feuded on Cavett's show. It began when Cavett asked McCarthy if she considered any famous writers overrated. She answered, "Yes. Lillian Hellman." She went on to say that "every word she writes is a lie, including 'and' and 'the.'"

Hellman sued McCarthy for libel and battled her to the death. Hers. The suit was still pending when Lillian Hellman died.

Film critic John Simon squashed the author of *Love Story*, Erich Segal, by mordantly noting that having "a choice of either being a knave or a fool, you seem to have opted for both." Simon was less effective when he picked on Mort Sahl in August of 1970.

In Sahl's monologue, he alluded to the problems of dating an intellectual actress. When John Simon joined the panel, he tartly suggested that there were "probably as many intellectual women as there are intellectual ex-nightclub comedians."

"You fellas know each other?" Cavett asked.

"We were talking about actresses," Sahl said. "We didn't condemn Simone de Beauvoir. However, why talk about the world, and important things when we can talk about the movies?"

Sahl continued the attack: "I was going to ask him, since he's defending women, how do you feel about homosexuals in the theater... Is it possible to have a piece of modern classical music performed, if you're not established, if you're not in a homosexual community in America?"

"Well," Simon sighed, "I imagine it is possible to be a heterosexual composer and get performed, yes."

Cavett asked, "Do you have evidence of a conspiracy on the part of homosexuals to keep heterosexuals out?"

"Yes," Sahl answered.

"Look," Simon interrupted, "the whole trouble in the music world is there are not enough good composers of any sex coming around."

After the commercial break, Cavett tried to mediate between Sahl and Simon, suggesting that perhaps there had been a misunderstanding.

Simon seemed conciliatory: "If he meant that among actresses there are hardly any intellectuals, I suppose I would agree. But that goes for male actors too. Needless to say, it is not bad not to be an intellectual, and there's certainly nothing wrong with an actor not being an intellectual. You act with your emotions, with your experience in life, with your sensitivity in life, and this has nothing to do with the intellect."

Sahl answered, "I saw Robert Blake on here with you and Truman Capote, and I found that he had more to say than either one of you and you were both intellectualizing."

"Well, he quantitatively may have had more to say. It was impossible to shut him up."

"No, he said more from the firing line. That has to do with his courage. And *yours.*"

By the next commercial break, Simon was demanding that Cavett help in his defense and tell his viewers that Sahl had threatened to punch him.

Sahl sneered at Simon, "Bad manners don't work anywhere, even on television."

In the case of late night television, he was wrong.

Cavett's show became noted for the sight of supposedly clever, urbane and witty writers, politicians and actors suddenly ready to go for each other's throats.

If there was the possibility of a guest walking out or dropping dead, it would happen on Cavett's show. And it did.

Lester Maddox, finding himself on the panel with a black (sports star Jim Brown) and a gay (Truman Capote), not to mention a New York liberal host, pulled a well-timed snit and stormed off. Cavett ran after him, to no avail.

Nutrition expert and publisher of *Prevention* magazine, Jerome Irving Rodale had described the joys of a limber body, organic foods, bone meal and good health. After his segment was done, he moved to the next chair and let the new guest, reporter Pete Hamill, take over. Rodale closed his eyes and began to make strange gasping noises.

Cavett walked over to try and wake Rodale. That's when he turned and asked, "Is there a doctor in the audience?"

Taping was stopped. Cavett helped the arriving emergency team and reporter Hamill began scribbling down notes for what seemed like a great story. Rodale was rushed to a hospital, where he was pronounced dead on arrival.

Several members of the audience that evening had walked away in a daze or begun to weep. Cavett had remained tough and professional, helping the medical team as well as firmly keeping control over the bewildered crowd. A mere 5'7" 130-pounder, often fey and cutesy in conversation, sometimes prone to verbose, self-obsessed musings àla Paar, Cavett had a core of steel.

Interference from the network led to some of Cavett's better jokes: "I have terrific relations with the execs at ABC, except for one vice president who's angry at me. I once called him at 11:35 making him miss Carson's monologue... My ABC show censor is affected by his job. He goes to the zoo and tries to shame monkeys by looking at them"

Cavett did not suffer fools gladly, no matter how famous. During a conversation with LSD advocate Timothy Leary, he simply said, "I really think you're full of crap." When Norman Mailer made fun of Cavett's use of a question sheet, Dick told him to "fold it five ways and put it where the sun don't shine."

For a few years, there was relative peace during the time slot where the sun didn't shine. CBS appeared content having enough advertisers buying its late night movies. ABC had a respectable alternative with Cavett's critically acclaimed program. And *The To-night Show* was king.

Then executives at ABC began to get itchy. Cavett was too smart for them, too independent. And there was so much more money to be made if they had a host more like Johnny. They stepped up the search for a replacement.

Steve Allen had remained a powerful force in show business. He had written a library of books, produced musicals and stage revues, and had his own talk shows periodically as well as television specials. He had often pinch-hit for Merv Griffin, keeping things light and funny with his parenthetical humor:

"You're probably wondering where Merv is. I know I am. Well, Merv was in a hot poker game last night, and he lost the show... But the real story is that it's Merv's mother's birthday and so he had to go to San Quentin to see her. No, seriously, I'm filling in for Merv because he had a slight accident. I ran over him..."

There were rumors that ABC wanted to replace Cavett with Steve Allen. But when Steve guest-host-ed for Dick Cavett, he had a different surprise for viewers. He affirmed what people in the industry couldn't believe was true: Jack Paar was coming back:

"Dick's on vacation for a few days. So am I, come to think of it. So I thought I'd spend my vacation here on his show. It's a nice place to vacation. It's quiet here... Say, did you read in the paper about Jack Paar coming out of retirement? He'll host this show for one week a month. The other three weeks he'll go back into retirement. You know, Jack made an emotional plea to the network to keep Dick Cavett on the air. Then ABC said, 'Do you want Cavett's job?' Jack said, 'Yeah, sure, sure!'"

Paar was ready to get back into *The Tonight Show* wars. "I'm funnier now," he insisted. He wasn't.

A suburban recluse for so many years, he was woefully out of touch with the entertainment industry. He looked like a refugee from another era with his bowties and wet-look toupee. Viewers didn't understand why he was being a cornball and showing his home movies. He embarrassed himself with his tirades against rock music and long hair. His sidekick was Peggy Cass, and together they looked like someone's parents videotaping an evening with dull friends.

Paar's week was the weakest. Cavett had his own week. And the other two were given over to a hodge-podge of rock concerts and cheaply thrown together specials. Producer Dan Curtis was given the tough job of creating two-part made-for-TV movies and began to rework the classics, everything from *Frankenstein* to a version of *Dr. Jekyll and Mr. Hyde* starring Jack Palance.

The official title for the confusing mess was ABC's "Wide World of Entertainment." Viewers never knew what they were going to get. Fans of Dick Cavett couldn't be sure when his one week was going to come up. Most viewers didn't know *why* Paar's week was even there.

Paar was telling everyone that he was the savior

in a bad situation: he had only come out of retirement to help his old friend Cavett. He said that ABC
wanted to cancel Dick and install Jack, but that he
had modestly offered to share the schedule instead.

When it came to his own greatness, Paar was
rarely objective. In the past he laid claim to having
"invented" the talk show. Larry Kart in the *Chicago
Tribune* pointed out: "As the virtual inventor of the
television talk-show, *Steve Allen* has shaped our lives
more profoundly than Bob Hope, David Sarnoff, and
Johnny Carson put together." Many others gave
Steve the honor, as well.

Paar also liked to take credit for discovering almost every major performer of the 50's and 60's. On
an NBC special, he showed clips of Bill Cosby on the
prime time *Jack Paar Show*, neglecting to mention
that Cos got his *Tonight Show* exposure during
Johnny's reign. Paar told so many people that he
discovered Jonathan Winters that he had most everyone believing it.

In 1993 Jonathan Winters made a cable TV show
appearance with Tom Snyder and was asked, "Where
did Paar find you?"

Winters began by saying, "Well, Paar would lead
you to believe... " Then he simply said, "The guy who
really helped me get going full blast was Steve Allen."

Coming into the talk show wars after his long
hiatus, at this point Paar was not about to discover
anyone. For one thing, he couldn't simply borrow
from the guest list of Steve Allen's old *Tonight Show*.
For another, Paar didn't know who the current stars
were and really didn't care. The comics were different, the music was different and they simply were
not his cup of tea.

When they sat next to him to talk, he assumed he
was more important. He spent more time telling
anecdotes than asking questions. When he insisted
on booking the people *he* considered stars, half the

audience didn't remember them. He sniffed that he couldn't work in front of "a studio audience made up of mostly street people in T-shirts." He bickered with his writers: "The big laugh subjects were mostly pot, dope and deviant sex. I was underwhelmed!"

People were tuning out before Paar even began the monologue, unable to take gravel-voiced Peggy Cass shouting "From New York City... Jack is back!"

While Steve Allen had remained vital and current with syndicated talk shows, Paar was rusty: a poor choice, an instant failure. He couldn't even work up a good feud with anyone. He was gone quickly, dragging Cavett along with him and the entire ABC "world" of late night entertainment.

Paar was gone, Cavett gone and Merv Griffin safely tucked into his 8:30 p.m. time slot in syndication. *The Tonight Show* was now unchallenged. With his comeback over, Paar turned up on Merv Griffin's show muttering, "I guess the next event in my life will be my death."

It was a complacent Carson who began to take even more time off from his schedule. In 1975 the *New York Daily News* reported: "For the first eight months of this year, Carson had at least a week's vacation every month except May. He was off for two weeks in April, two more in June and the entire month of August."

Why should Johnny toil so hard? It was *good* to be the King. It was great to live in California. Back where Jack Paar and Dick Cavett had struggled, New York City, there was just misery: "New York has changed," Carson told writer Richard Warren Lewis. "The city is increasingly rude, hostile and unfriendly. People on the streets are unsure and insecure. They're uptight about everything. If a stranger says hello, your first reaction is that he's attacking. I don't like people coming up and grabbing at my clothes... or when I'm having dinner being confronted with somebody saying, 'Will you sign this?' That's irritating. Things are much more open in California... people have a different attitude toward you. They're not as curt. There's a greater feeling of peace."

He told another writer, Cecil Smith, "I've had it with cold and snowstorms... If you really want to see snow and ski all you have to do is drive up to the mountains here in one hour. But you can also get to the desert in one hour, or San Francisco. That's what I like about California."

TV critic Tom Shales voiced discontent with the complacent program. He wrote that the show looked "sad and worn. Severinsen suggests an aging urban cracker who buys embroidered jeans at E.J. Korvette's and should have changed to gabardine about a decade ago. Ed's jaw trembles slightly, like a grandpa's, and during interviews he sits silent on the couch, out of camera range, like a still-life from the Hollywood Wax Museum."

And Johnny? Well, the popular gag wasn't "Heeere's Johnny" but "Wheeere's Johnny?"

He wasn't around much, and when he was, he seemed to be operating on automatic pilot. He used formula jokes. His characters were all familiar, too. "Aunt Blabby" was just Jonathan Winters' "Maude Frickert." Late night pitchman "Art Fern" had Jackie Gleason's "Reggie Van Gleason" voice. "Carnak" was Steve Allen's "Question Man" in a turban. "The Mighty Carson Art Players" could be traced back to Fred Allen's "Mighty Allen Art Players."

Steve Allen defended Carson to some degree. If Johnny's characters weren't that original, there was a reason: "Some people seem to have a natural ear for other people's speech, and an ability to imitate it. Johnny Carson has this, and it is perhaps one of the reasons for the frequently mentioned imitativeness of his work. When he does an old lady character, for example, he doesn't do one somewhat similar to

Jonathan Winters' old woman's voice. He does a precise imitation of Winters' voice."

Viewers didn't seem to mind. Johnny could go on forever. The biggest controversy on the show was at contract time, when Carson would test NBC by threatening retirement. Steve Allen said that Carson "ought not to retire at all, but simply stay at his desk until one night he dropped dead before our very eyes at the age of 75."

Carson had the chance to "stretch" and try something else, but he felt it was too late. Mel Brooks had offered him the lead in *Blazing Saddles*, which was eventually played by Gene Wilder. *Blazing Saddles* could've done for Johnny what *Cat Ballou* did for Lee Marvin. (In fact, Carson was slowly beginning to resemble the snub-nosed, gray haired actor).

"Anybody could make a movie," Johnny said, "but I'm on every night playing myself, so it would be hard to make the transition."

Johnny was enjoying the relaxed tempo of a talk show without all the pressure. Some of the best gags were never seen by viewers. After a monologue, a beautiful girl strutted out to hand Johnny a sponsor's product to plug. She smiled at him. The letters "F-U-C-K" were printed on her front teeth. The audience had no idea why Johnny was laughing so hard he could barely finish the spot.

Once when he had to tape a promotional spot for a douche manufacturer, Carson moaned, "This is so embarrassing," and suggested new names for the product: "Maybe, Vagi-go. How about Cunt-away!"

One good thing about the "Who gives a damn?" atmosphere of the day was that it sometimes produced spontaneously silly comedy, like the time Ed McMahon and Johnny began to do a Laurel-and-Hardy-type routine together, snipping at each other's ties. Or the time Burt Reynolds and Johnny methodically battled each other in a whipped-cream-in-the-pants duel.

Occasionally, there was a killjoy who put a chill on Johnny. It wasn't just a griping critic. Over at *Saturday Night Live*, the new generation of hip comics began to jeer at "hep" Johnny. One night the gang parodied the Ed Ames tomahawk routine, insanely milking laughs by hacking a statue to bits.

Asked for his appraisal of that show, Johnny said, "I've seen some very clever things on the show... but basically they do a lot of drug jokes, a lot of what I would consider sophomoric humor, and a lot of stuff I find exceptionally cruel, under the guise of being hip."

Meanwhile the *Saturday Night Live* crowd pointed to the less-than-adult style of adult humor that was on *The Tonight Show*. Like this exchange between Dean Martin and Johnny Carson:

Johnny: Can I...

Dean: That's *may* I.

Johnny: Excuse me.

Dean: You were dangling a participle!

Johnny: Well, I'll wear a long coat and nobody'll notice! Ever thought of having a partner again? No?"

Dean: I tried Linda Lovelace but she said she had it up to here."

There were rumbles that Chevy Chase, the man who bore a faint resemblance to Johnny and was so clever behind the desk with his "News Update" routines, would go on to take over *Tonight*. Chase shrugged off the rumors, but in doing so gave the impression that *The Tonight Show* was beneath him. He said he found nothing very creative or challenging about doing a talk show.

Carson growled, "Chevy Chase couldn't ad-lib a fart after a baked bean dinner."

Which was just a typical formula joke, a switch on Fred Allen's line on Jack Benny: "He couldn't ad-lib a belch after a Hungarian dinner."

Still, there was nothing wrong with a light evening that mixed formula jokes, an occasional brilliant sketch and easy-laugh conversation. Especially
since Johnny was still doing it a lot more hours each
month than *Saturday Night Live* could manage with
a full cast.

The veteran Carson was a lot more hip than he
was given credit for. He was just mellowing a bit.

One night, the busty Elvira was on the show, talking about a horror film called *The Thing with Two
Heads*. Showing off her cleavage, she referred to the
film as *The Head with Two Things*.

The audience roared. Johnny grinned and cut
away for a commercial. During the break, Elvira
recalled, "I turned to Johnny and said, 'Oh, I'm so
sorry, I didn't mean that.' He said, 'Don't con a con
artist, baby.' But he said it in a very nice way."

In this mellow era, headline-making controversies
on *The Tonight Show* were few. Carson helmed a
tight ship. But, sometimes, he forgot just how powerful and influential he was. During his monologue one
night in December of 1973, he confided to viewers,
"We've got all sorts of shortages these days, but have
you heard the latest? I'm not kidding... there's a
shortage of toilet paper."

A Wisconsin Republican named Harold Froehlich
had publicly worried about the paper industry (a
mainstay of his state). He declared that without the
customary four-month storehouse of toilet paper, "a
toilet paper shortage... is a problem that will touch
every American."

Before Johnny could get the jokes out, hundreds
of viewers were out the door. Once America heard it
from Johnny, they went rushing out into the night to
hoard precious supplies. Before long, the panic
chain was pulled and the toilet paper sections of
supermarkets were completely wiped out.

As ridiculous as the whole thing was, that night

in December proved that what Johnny Carson had to say to America each night was taken far more seriously than anything government officials put in the newspapers.

And, in his power position as undisputed star of late night, through the 70's Johnny became more political. Instead of being compared to Steve Allen or Jack Paar, Johnny was now being considered another Will Rogers or Mort Sahl. Americans who never read a newspaper began to know about "flaky" Jerry Brown, nasty James Watt and power-obsessed Alexander Haig. They heard President Ford described as looking like "the guy at the Safeway who okays your checks."

Political pundits carefully watched *The Tonight Show.* When a candidate became fodder for a Carson monologue, that was a sure sign that public sentiment was changing. The question was whether Johnny was reading public opinion or actually forming it.

A few choice lines from Carson could be devastating to anyone or anything. As a lead-in for a Sara Lee ad, Johnny ad-libbed, "Who is this Sara Lee person? I'll bet she's some drunken old bat in a kitchen somewhere in Des Moines... "

Sara Lee was actually the daughter of the company president. *The Tonight Show* lost a sponsor. But the amount was chicken feed for Johnny. And if a company wasn't a sponsor, he dared them to sue over one of his gags. McDonald's was always a target. During one Christmas season, he scorned an ad that had announced, "This season give Chicken McNuggets." He stared into the camera: "All I want for Christmas are some dried lumps of processed chicken."

When he got involved with corporations, it was for big money. In 1975 he filed a $38 million civil suit against Paramount Pictures over the failure of his Carson-Paramount Productions company. In 1977 he filed suit for $3 million against Brown Realty, claiming that the real estate company had circulated rumors about Carson moving from Bel Air to a development site they owned in the San Fernando Valley. He pursued L&R Industries, for two years, after being injured while exercising on one of their slant boards, finally arriving at an out-of-court settlement in November of 76. The amount was not specified, but if it was anywhere close to the five million bucks Johnny demanded, the suit was worth it.

Carson took on his neighbors, too. Sonny Bono's yelping, mewling miniature poodles were driving Johnny crazy. Johnny filed suit against the noisy nuisance. And Sonny Bono became a favorite punch line for most any *Tonight Show* gag involving a goofy celebrity.

Throughout his tenure on the show, Johnny took the opportunity of needling those around him, from his own accountant ("The Bombastic" Henry Bushkin) to stars he didn't like either personally or professionally. Sometimes the only people who got the digs were Carson and his target. One night he mentioned old movies on the late show featuring forgotten stars: "I watched Glenn Ford and Edgar Buchanan in bed. They certainly are a lovable pair!" Only insiders knew that Glenn Ford had been dating Johnny's ex-wife Joanne.

Johnny rolled through the late 70's, his comedy playing well and paying well. In December of 1977 his contract was valued at $2.5 million a year. But *People* magazine estimated that he was making another $12 million or more from his real estate holdings and other investments. His own Carson Productions was now raking in money from *The Tonight Show* and he was part of a group buying the Garden State Bank. Someone suggested it be renamed after Johnny, but that wasn't necessary. The bank happened to be on Carson Street.

1979 saw Carson completing the decade and in absolute power. Merv Griffin was still doing a syndicated show at 8:30 p.m., but it was no competition. Carson could mildly kid Merv for his "theme shows," imitating Griffin's fawning "Oooohhh" of excitement over the often less than exciting guests he had booked.

NBC had vaguely hoped to groom a replacement for Johnny with Tom Snyder. Snyder was following at Johnny's heels with something called *The Tomorrow Show*. For modern viewers who missed him (he was replaced by *Late Night with David Letterman*), Snyder was a cross between Charlie Rose and Jim "Hey Vern!" Varney. While he could sometimes come up with an intense and provocative one-on-one interview session with an Alfred Hitchcock or John Lennon, he usually ruined it with bumbling questions and an obnoxiously goofy demeanor.

Interviewing rock star Meatloaf, the amazingly obtuse Snyder called him "Meatball" for the first fifteen minutes of the show. Even when he was trying hard to be complimentary, Snyder seemed to have that disc jockey personality of talking before he started thinking. He hadn't changed when in 1993 he got his own cable TV show. He said, in all seriousness, to Jonathan Winters: "The movie *Mad Mad Mad Mad World*, I have *not* seen that picture since it came out. It's brilliant! It's hysterical!"

Snyder was a favorite target of Dan Aykroyd on *Saturday Night Live*. Dan caught the man's oblivious bull-headedness, guffawing laugh and relentless klutziness. To top the confused Snyder package of sincerity, solemnity and stupidity, Aykroyd parodied Snyder's hairstyle which seemed a lacquered beaver pelt of browns, blacks and gray.

Richard Corliss in *New Times* gave one of the many thumbs-down critiques of Snyder: "...His personality works strangely against the medium. In McLuhan terms, his style is too 'hot,' too preeningly assertive. He thinks of himself as a comer, but he comes too soon... he comes on like a kid on his first date, masking insecurity with bravado." By contrast, Johnny was deemed "the personification of what the Average American likes to think of himself as: witty but not intellectual, cheeky but not arrogant, irreverent but not malicious, naughty but not lewd, the Golden Mean and not the Lowest Common Denominator — the very model of charm and professionalism."

About the only one who had an objection to Carson was, ironically enough, the president of NBC, Fred Silverman. The next fight for *The Tonight Show* was a battle from within.

Flashy Fred was wooed away from ABC for the impressive sum of one million dollars. He was going to turn NBC around. Aside from *The Today Show* and *The Tonight Show*, the network was losing ground.

Silverman wanted to bring NBC back to number one, and he was expecting his number one star to lead the way.

It was "The Boss" vs. "The Franchise." It wasn't enough that Johnny's show was raking in millions for NBC. Silverman wanted Johnny to become a team player. Johnny was taking Mondays off 12 weeks a year, and Silverman didn't like that 4 for 5 workday. Silverman liked Johnny's 3 for 5 workday even less. Johnny only had to show up Wednesday through Friday for 25 weeks of the year. And Silverman hated Johnny's 0-5 workdays: the 15 weeks of vacation time scattered through the year.

Even a George Steinbrenner would've thought twice about criticizing a money-making superstar who went 3 for 5 and 4 for 5 consistently; whose hot streaks saved many a ratings week, who had absolutely no competition and no replacement.

But Coach Silverman went on the attack, using shaming tactics. He went to the press and complained that Johnny was loafing: "I only hope that there will come a moment in time when he will say to himself: 'I love *The Tonight Show* and I'm going to do a little bit more.' He intimated that Johnny's ratings could be better: "He's a very competitive and professional guy. I don't think he must enjoy reading that the thing is slipping." Silverman, according to a reporter on the *New York Post*, was trying all kinds of schemes to make Carson look bad, "leaking stories to reporters relating Carson's sweetheart contract... "

On March 18, 1979, Johnny confronted Silverman about the sneaky doings and vowed to take a walk. Permanently.

"You have a contract and we expect you to honor it," the boss said.

Carson said no.

If it had been Lou Gehrig calling it quits after 2,130 games it wouldn't have had more impact. Gehrig had been a Yankee regular for 14 consecutive years. Carson was in his 17th consecutive season with NBC.

When Carson quit cold, it made the front page of the usually staid *New York Times*. The paper reported that Carson was ready to broadcast his last show on September 30, which would mark the exact end of his 17 years (which began October1, 1962).

Johnny, master of timing, would be leaving NBC at the start of the fall classic — the fall schedule of premiere programming. Without Carson anchoring the late night schedule, NBC wouldn't have a chance of being the number one network in overall ratings.

Don Rickles one night joked with Johnny and said, "Who cares if you don't do *The Tonight Show!* It's not important! You think you're a big star and you're not!"

The *Times* differed. It reported that Carson's bombshell had shaken Wall Street: "The shares of the RCA Corporation, the parent of NBC, eased 3/8, to 27, yesterday on the New York Stock Exchange after trading as low as 26 3/4. Wall Street analysts attributed the decline to reports of Mr. Carson's plans."

Wall Streeters knew that Carson's show was generating $23 million for the network. 17 percent of NBC's profits were tied to one man: Johnny Carson.

Old nemesis Mike Douglas was one of the few talk show hosts past or present to take a dig at Johnny. He boasted that a five-day work week hadn't harmed his daytime show at all: "I feel that if people tune in *The Mike Douglas Show*, they're entitled to see Mike Douglas."

One of the more unlikely celebrities to pay tribute to Johnny was Andy Warhol. He said: *The Tonight Show* is always good simply because you never have to get embarrassed for Johnny Carson: he has TV magic, is always cool, clever and American... he wants to make things easy by entertaining, and he does that night after night. When you look at him you never have to worry that he has a problem — you know he won't fall apart... "

More important, with Johnny around, it was a sign that everything was all right with the world. Through any crisis of war, assassination or natural disaster, Johnny could always be counted on to offer, with his assured manner and easy personality, the only light moment of the day. He gave America a good feeling to face the night.

Carson and Silverman's feud remained front-page news. Some ardent Carson fans prayed for Johnny to stay on. *The Christian Science Monitor* prayed for him to go. It decried Johnny's "sophomoric double meanings," and the "hours wasted" with what it called the "trivia and innuendo purveyed during those midnight hours."

Johnny pointed out that, if anything, NBC should be offering another raise in salary. He said that $2.5 million wasn't much considering what Marlon Brando was getting for a few weeks' work on *Superman*. As for Silverman's demand for a full five-day week, Johnny insisted, "If I stayed on the show and did five shows a week... it might contribute to an audience getting tired of me." And, he added, he might get awfully tired of the show, period.

He told NBC all about his feelings — on a show broadcast by ABC. Interviewed on *World News Tonight*, he reiterated his desire to quit, and added, "No one can force a performer to work if he doesn't feel he should. It isn't as if I'm threatening to walk across the street and do the same thing at another network."

Johnny didn't have to threaten to walk across the street. A remark like that was enough.

ABC loved Johnny's work when he hosted the Academy Awards show for them, and it was no secret they wanted him permanently. In an interview for CBS' *Sixty Minutes*, Carson admitted that "they had made no direct overtures, but I would assume that when somebody has you socially for dinner and — I'm not that naive — they might say, 'Hey, it would be nice if Johnny Carson worked over here...'"

How ironic that back in 1977, when Fred Silverman was over at ABC, Silverman had urged Johnny to defect.

Now, the ABC's question, 1979 was "Would you go?"

Answer: "I can't answer that."

Johnny was then asked if he had any comment for Fred Silverman, should Silverman be tuning in.

"I hope when this show is seen you're still with NBC," said Johnny.

Johnny knew NBC was quaking. Corporate headquarters at the suddenly crumbly "30 Rock" in Rockefeller Plaza was in turmoil. NBC was having a tough, tough time. The new shows were disasters. In an untimely Federal investigation into embezzlement, fourteen VPs and company big shots were fired in a scandal over nearly a million dollars in expense-account spendings. Parent company RCA had recently dumped $200 million worth of businesses that were not making enough profits.

Did Johnny realize the state NBC was in?

"That's like saying the *Titanic* had a small leak," he said.

Ratings points told the story: none of the guest hosts Johnny used in 1978 or 1979 delivered the numbers NBC needed. The bright young comics of the day – Steve Martin, Gabe Kaplan and David Brenner – barely reached a 30 percent share of the audience watching TV at that hour. Bill Cosby and Joan Rivers were not hot stars in 1979, averaging 27 percent and 25 percent. Carson's pals, Don Rickles and Bob Newhart couldn't break 30 percent. When Johnny Carson was on the air, he was snatching away nearly 40 percent of the available audience.

NBC looked to their old hosts. They didn't want Paar back. As for affable Steve Allen, Johnny had been sporting enough to let the man guest-host from time to time. But Steve only averaged the same percentage as Joan Rivers: 25 percent.

Like Israel's Six-Day war, Carson's fight with the big NBC power machine was short. Sunday night, May 6, 1979, Carson and Silverman officially ended their war. Carson would stay. Silverman would back off.

The truce came in front of more than 1500 people — a packed house at the Waldorf Astoria Grand Ballroom. The crowd had gathered to join the Friars Club in honoring Johnny Carson, "Entertainer of the Year."

Carson and Silverman were not smiling as they sat on the dais, only Johnny's wife Joanna between them. But, if this momentous event could bring out such disparate guests as Ambassador Evron of Israel and Ambassador Ghorbal of Egypt, anything was possible.

Silverman got up to announce how happy he was that Johnny was going to stay: "I was so relieved that I got down off the chair and put the rope back in the closet." Freddie completed his penance, admitting that his new shows like *Supertrain* and *Hello Larry* were instrumental in "bringing the network from third place to where it is now." Third place, of course.

Silverman said to Johnny, "You're more than the entertainer of the year. You're the entertainer of your time, you're the best friend TV ever had."

Bob Hope interrupted, "He said the same thing to me last year!" Hope added that Silverman was "the only man in America who knows what it feels like to rearrange the deck chairs on the *Titanic*."

After hearing a long, long night of tributes, not just from Silverman but from his fellow comics and friends, Johnny rose to say, "When Ruth Gordon arrived here tonight, she was jailbait."

Johnny's new deal with NBC brought radical changes to *The Tonight Show*. In return for being on four days a week, taking Mondays off, the show would be cut from ninety minutes to an hour. And the big blocks of vacation time remained.

Everything was going Johnny's way. Why, in November of 1979 even neighbor Sonny Bono moved out and took his yelping, mewling miniature poodles with him.

CHAPTER THIRTEEN

FIGHTING IN THE 80'S: JOHNNY vs. JOANNA AND JOAN

1982 marked twenty years for Johnny Carson on *The Tonight Show*. His wife, Joanna, told him, "You're only happy when you're performing."

She seemed to know. The couple separated and by the end of the year, Johnny had new fuel for his monologues: the stinging $44,600 a month maintenance he had to pay to wife number three. Johnny told viewers, "I heard from my cat's lawyer. My cat wants $12,000 a month for Tender Vittles." As for marriage, he announced, "I resolve if I ever get hit in the face again with rice, it will be because I insulted a Chinese person."

Some critics were once again mumbling about *The Tonight Show* getting a little stale. The audience didn't think so. They loved Carson's monologues and what some considered "time-worn" segments like the "cute zoo animal" spots, high-schoolers imitating birds or the "Tea Time Movie" sketches featuring Art Fern.

If there was a problem, it was in the interviews. Rising star David Letterman (now firmly in control of the 12:30 a.m. spot after Johnny) got laughs by attacking his guests. He developed the reputation for being an iconoclast and a wiseguy.

By contrast, Johnny was on defense, not offense, a "reaction" comic. His most memorable laughs were the faces he made when a talking parrot didn't talk, or the topper he ad-libbed to a Don Rickles insult. If a guest was dull, Letterman would start attacking, trying to shake out something interesting. Johnny, ever the tactful host, simply went along with the bland guest while viewers snored.

But viewers could count on the sketches during the first half-hour, and his prepared "desk routines" from reading mock-romance novels to ad-libbing answers to questions supplied on cards from the studio audience. The biggest excitement for the show was in the up-to-the-minute monologue, and the zingers he was serving up about his divorce problems.

When the divorce proceedings were finally settled in 1984, Joanna got the mansion along with five million dollars in cash. She also was given $35,000 a month to help her along during the first five years of her new life. She also won the apartment she and Johnny used in New York and three cars.

And, since Joanna was part of Johnny's life between 1972 and 1982, she obviously was instrumental in producing a big chunk of the comedy material he used on *The Tonight Show*. At least, that seemed to be court thinking when Joanna was awarded half the residuals Johnny might get for re-runs of *The Tonight Show* during that period.

Johnny moved into a new home in Malibu. He had a condo in Los Angeles, an apartment at the Beverly Hills Hotel, and a duplex at New York's Trump Tower. He was seen squiring Sally Field, Morgan Fairchild, Angie Dickinson and Dyan Cannon. There was more variety in his life off-camera than on.

The Tonight Show continued easily enough, with Johnny's tireless Carnak divining the questions kept "hermetically sealed in a mayonnaise jar on Funk and Wagnall's porch."

Sis Boom Bah: Describe the sound made when a sheep explodes.

Art Fern presided over his "Tea Time Movie" segments, referring to "Squirt the Wonder Eel" and "Screamer the Wonder Beaver." As Fern unveiled his gag map, the audience waited to hear that reference to "The Slauson Cut-off. Get out of your car, cut off your slauson!" And they loved to shout out in unison once they saw it: "The fork in the road!"

Johnny's physician, "Al Bendova," was still in practice. Carson told the crowd: "Instead of a rubber glove he used a Kermit the Frog hand puppet."

And there were questions from the audience.

"Susan? Where are you, Susan? Susan writes: would I like to go out for ice cream after the show?"

"That depends, Susan", says Johnny. "Do you have two big scoops?"

Speaking of which, there was still the easy laughter over any well-endowed guest. When Dolly Parton appeared one night, she started the giggling herself. She mentioned a joke going around: "What's worse than a giraffe with a sore throat? Dolly Parton with a chest cold."

Then she said, "People are always askin' if they're real."

Johnny broke in, "I would never —"

"You don't have to ask. I tell you what, these are mine."

"I have certain guidelines on the show," Johnny insisted. Then he said, "But I would give about a year's pay to peek under there!"

It was vintage Johnny. And vintage Johnny was perfect for late night in the 80's. Challengers those days were barely blips on the television screen.

In September of 1983 Allan Thicke offered a show called *Thicke of the Night*. It was thick with the host's singing and comedy, and critics were sick of the obnoxious comic sidekicks on the show: Richard Belzer, Fred Willard Charles Fleischer, Gilbert Gottfried and Rick Ducommun, a who's who of known irritants. Just to make matters worse, L.A.'s deliberately abrasive talk show host Wally George made frequent appearances.

Low ratings forced desperate changes (as usual, this meant a switch in bands, from the Tom Canning Band to the John Toben Band) and Thicke hired a new comic by the name of Arsenio Hall. But *Thicke of the Night* disappeared in a puff of smoke. Old nemesis Fred Silverman was the producer on that one. After Thicke's show folded, Carson mentioned seeing a familiar face toiling as a security guard: "Pops" Silverman. The audience didn't get it, but the laughter off-camera from the staff more than made up for it.

The only talk show host who seemed in any way capable of taking over *The Tonight Show* was the man right behind it: David Letterman. After NBC bounced Tom Snyder, some executives had a notion about hiring Steve Allen, but Johnny was in favor of Dave, the wiseguy comic who had been impressive in stand-up work on *The Tonight Show*. Dave's series, *Late Night with David Letterman*, premiered February 2, 1982.

As Tom Snyder admits now, "I used to say to people then, 'It's not Dave's fault, it's NBC'... what Dave did was remarkable, he didn't come in and continue *The Tomorrow Show*, he took it to the next level."

But it took a while. NBC gave Dave the time to find himself. At the beginning, a more obvious Carson-imitator did not exist. Dave had the same hands-in-pants stance and the same odd twist of Midwestern normality and slick urban hostility. Over the years he would develop his own style, but back then, he was an acolyte.

He would later tell Bob Costas that he really did idolize Johnny Carson: "I've never been able to feel comfortable with the man. He's been very gracious to me, very nice. I could spend every minute of my life with Johnny Carson and I don't think I'd get over that sense of awe."

Letterman borrowed from all the talk show hosts he had seen. Jack Paar liked it when some guests sparred with him rather than fawned over him. He found it bracing to be challenged by the neurotic Oscar Levant. Letterman had a similar obsession with Sandra Bernhard. If Steve Allen could cover himself in tea bags and get dunked in a huge cup, David could cover himself in Velcro and hurl himself at a wall. Merv Griffin baffled viewers with regular guest Brother Theodore. David re-discovered him. Johnny had a "light in the loafers" band leader in trendy clothes. David went with the effeminate, oh-so-show-biz Paul Shaffer. Everyone knew Doc was kidding, but in the early days of the show, viewers were not so sure about Paul, the bulb-headed chatterbox with his endless "nutty" interruptions. It took a while to see that Paul's love-hate reaction to show-biz glitz, hipness and insincerity was taking the form of parody as much as Letterman's love-hate reactions to doing a talk show.

Just as viewers watched *The Tonight Show* and relished the monologue, Severinsen gags, Carnak bits, commercial parodies and Carson characters, *Late Night* developed Stupid Pet Tricks, the Top Ten List, Viewer Mail, Dave's "dumb guy" character in blackout sketches, the NBC bookmobile, phone calls to Mom and some catch phrases ("What's the deal?") and favorite words ("Weasel!")

Letterman, always loyal to Johnny, insisted he would never even *think* of coming in and taking over *The Tonight Show* in the 80's.

Another friend of John's, Joan Rivers, made no such promise.

Joan made her first appearance on *The Tonight Show* in 1965. At the time, her stand-up persona was the nervous and self-deprecating loser, a female Woody Allen. She articulated neurotic jokes about herself: "I was a fat kid. Nobody got close enough to me to find out I was fun. I began to retreat very much into myselves." She offered weird Woody-esque imagery: "I have bad luck with plants. I bought a philodendron and I put it in the kitchen and it drank my soup."

Joan wrote in her autobiography, *Enter Talking*, "The empathy that... existed between Johnny Carson and me was there from the first second. He understood everything. He wanted it to work. He never cut off a punch line. When it came he broke up. It was like telling it to your father — and your father is leaning way back and laughing, and you know he is going to laugh at the next one. And he did. He made it fun and that spilled over to the audience."

Johnny said, "God, you're funny. You're going to be a star." He invited her back again and again. Ultimately, in 1983, she signed a deal to host the show nine weeks a year. As the "permanent guest host" for *The Tonight Show*, Rivers sometimes had better ratings than Carson. She fought with the producers to get guests she could relate to, hip celebrities like Pee Wee Herman, Elvis Costello and Cher. She sometimes battled over the censorship of jokes as the staid staff, especially Peter Lassally, questioned exactly how far she could go before alienating Middle America.

Though she was having trouble behind the scenes, all the audience saw was a brash woman in total control. From a neurotic comic turning her anger inward, she had become a bold insult comic roasting the biggest of stars, from Mick Jagger ("He has child-bearing lips!") to Elizabeth Taylor ("She has more chins than a Chinese phone book!"). Her celebrity put-downs were new, her kibbitzing interview questions unpredictable. Her frantic personality was a good contrast.

Johnny didn't mind. Joan was his protegée. And

there was no way her "hot" personality could work every night in his cool medium. So Joan continued insulting celebrities, pointing out that when dumb Bo Derek saw a sign that read "Wet Floor," she did. Joan, Johnny admitted, "gets a little tough sometimes. But it works for her. What some people think is funny, others find in abominable taste. I caught Eddie Murphy in concert. Wow! I've heard the language, but *he* gets away with it."

Johnny admired Joan professionally but they were not close socially. They had little to say to each other in between commercial breaks when Joan was a guest. Joan recalled that if she didn't come up with some bland comment like "Gee, the band sounds good," Johnny would lapse into silence and start drumming his pencils on his desk.

Friends knew how much it bothered her that Johnny never congratulated her for a show, or peared to even watch one. She found herself caught up in the machinery at Carson Productions. When she negotiated her contract with *The Tonight Show*, she was forced to use Carson's lawyer "Bombastic" Henry Bushkin as a consultant. It was a sure way to keep Rivers' salary down.

In 1986 Johnny was once again seriously talking of retirement, planning to walk away within a year, making it an even, solid 25. Joan Rivers saw the secret memo listing the choices for new host. She wasn't on it. She brought her complaint to the press. Johnny appeared to be only mildly annoyed.

The Boss had better things to do than worry over one employee. When columnist Kay Gardella called Carson for a reply, he said, "Joan's a pretty clever girl when it comes to publicity. I'm sure the whole thing started out as a joke and she got caught up in it." He added mildly, "NBC has never come to me and asked, 'Who do you think would be a likely candidate.'" Besides, he said, he was still the host and still enjoying the show. "I wouldn't continue if I didn't enjoy it. The show is still fun."

Barry Diller, the big man at Fox Broadcasting, knew that Joan wasn't happy. He also knew that to become a "Fourth Network," expanding on the key independent stations Fox had in six major cities, he needed a big attraction. For years Diller had played in friendly poker games with Johnny Carson. Now, he decided to cut Joan in.

"Carson's old, he's tired, he can be taken," Diller told her.

Joan was a little surprised to hear this kind of talk from Diller. Especially when Diller was socializing with Carson on a regular basis. But if the foxy Fox executive said business was business, it was ok with Joan. At *The Tonight Show*, she had come to realize the difference between business and friendship.

The secret memo had hurt her, but she had figured it was the work of the NBC executives. What was more like the last straw was discovering just how little she meant to the world of Johnny Carson. Her first book had recently appeared and she sent a copy to Johnny. Not only was the book filled with praise for him, she'd dedicated it to him as well.

The next time she guested on his show, she realized that the book meant nothing to him. When she heard producer Fred DeCordova call off-camera to Johnny, "Read the dedication," she couldn't believe he had not even opened it. She thought to herself, "I've been loyal to a stone wall."

Joan was still guest-hosting *The Tonight Show* in May 1986 as she negotiated with Fox. They offered her a three-year contract worth $10 million. She had two months left on her NBC contract when she made the switch. Disloyalty? When Johnny signed to take over *The Tonight Show* in 1962, he still had six months left on his ABC contract.

As Joan later told *Playboy* magazine: "I defy any-body in any job who's making more than $30 a week to jeopardize that job by walking away from it until the next job is secure. We couldn't tell anybody about the deal until all the i's were dotted and the t's crossed — which happened on Monday, the day before the press conference. As soon as that hap-pened, I called Johnny. I went through my hotel switchboard in Las Vegas, so I have my bill — and reached his secretary, who said, 'Hold on. I'll put him on.' And then the phone went 'Click.'"

On Tuesday morning, Joan tried again. She was surprised that Johnny picked up the phone himself. She barely got a word in before he hung up on her.

That was the quiet before the explosion.

Front-page newspaper headlines blared out the story: JOHNNY VS JOAN.

Joan told reporters she couldn't understand why Johnny wasn't happy for her. She was bewildered; in tears.

Johnny wasn't talking to the press, but those around him confided that he took this as another betrayal in the cold world of professional entertain-ment.

What bothered Johnny was not the competition from Joan. It was the sneaky secret dealings with Fox. Doc Severnsen said, "Johnny would have been very supportive of Joan. He probably would have plugged her show or even done a walk-on for her. But he and others on *The Tonight Show* were disap-pointed nothing was said to them until the last minute." Johnny had expected her to come to him like a dutiful daughter and say "John, can we talk? Fox is offering me a wonderful deal. Can I take it?"

This was pretty much what David Brenner said *he'd* done. Brenner, who got his big break on *The Tonight Show* just like Joan, and had been a fre-quent guest host, had recently been offered a syndicated talk show, too. But he didn't take it without consulting Carson.

"Think of Johnny Carson as the father," David frankly admitted. "That's what he is, a television father-figure for Joan and me. I went up to him and said, 'Hey, Dad, they're talking about giving me a job out of town and I might be leaving home,' and he wishes me good luck... Then the daughter calls up from 4,000 miles away and says, 'Dad, I'm living here now... ' that is the difference. When I left home, Dad knew all about it from the beginning."

Today, Rivers finds Brenner's logic a bit faulty. Had she done what Brenner did, she says, "I would have been out the same day — which was just what happened to David Brenner." Insiders agree with Joan: Brenner suddenly disappeared from *The Tonight Show* guest list after his defection.

Whatever had happened before or after negotiations, the fact was simple: Johnny would not forget and could not forgive.

Joan was still under contract to Johnny. He made an emphatic point of ripping up her contract and canceling the two weeks of guest-hosting she was scheduled to complete. Front-page headline for May 7, 1986: CARSON FIRES RIVERS."

That night was Johnny's first show after the big blow-up. Everyone was waiting for the monologue. One of his stock lines was "Let's see, what was in the papers today... " Today the front page was him.

He smiled easily. He told jokes on all sorts of topics. But he never mentioned THE topic. And instead of a clenched fist, there was his easy golf swing... "We'll be right back."

When the commercial was over, there was Johnny, sitting at his desk. He picked up his coffee cup and quietly raised it. "To you," he told the audience.

This would serve as his only response to the controversy in the papers that day. Among Johnny's guests that night were a pair of Bunnies from a local Playboy Club.

"What turns you on?" Johnny asked one of them.

"Big tips!" a blonde promptly shouted.

Over the laughs, Johnny said, "As MacArthur said, these proceedings are closed!"

A few moments later one of the Bunnies remarked that she hoped to go into show business one day, and maybe take a stab at hosting a talk show.

John simply asked another question. His modus operandi would be to maintain a stiff upper lip and cool, dignified silence.

For Joan, there was hell to pay. She was on the defensive, she had to explain herself, she couldn't duck the press even if she wanted to. She had been booked months in advance for interviews promoting her book *Enter Laughing*, the one with all the praise for Johnny. During the week of May 12, she found herself in the busiest days of the book tour, in the spotlight of TV cameras and local talk-show appearances. Over and over she apologized for the misunderstanding.

"If I walked out of this door right now and bumped into Johnny, I'd be delighted," she said. "I'd say, 'Isn't this funny and didn't we get a lot of press out of this?'"

She insisted, "I've had a wonderful relationship with Johnny, twenty-three years... I wanted it to end nicely. I'm a lady, my mother brought me up right. I knew I owed him a call."

Looking stressed and tired, Joan brought her book promotion to *Live at Five*, the news show on NBC's flagship New York station. She wearily confided to Liz Smith, "I've become a tabloid tootsie." As for her battle with Johnny, she groaned, "There's *no* fight. All I did was defend myself against statements that NBC put out. *Never him. Never him.*"

The Carson vs. Rivers feud continued to rage. Editorials actually appeared in newspapers taking sides. the *New York Daily News* on May 8, gave a succinct appraisal of the two talkers: "Johnny Carson is a comic; Joan Rivers is a buffoon." Disc jockeys made it the topic for call-ins. *Entertainment Tonight* polled their viewers and found support leaning toward Johnny Carson.

On *The Today Show*, Joan defended her *Tonight Show* decision: "The whole thing really comes down to one question people should be asking. If he was signed for two years in the last contract, why was I signed for only one? I think that tells you that you're not as secure as you think you are in your job, and if another job comes your way, just take it."

What about that memo that seemed to nix Joan as the next host? Who was to blame for that? Rivers said NBC, not Johnny: "I'll probably write him a letter, tell him I love him. I *do* love him. All this has nothing to do with Johnny. What NBC was saying was 'We don't want you.' All I'm saying is 'I'm a fifty-one-year-old lady. Let me go off and be my own hostess because you don't want me.'"

Strange press leaks began appearing. Newspapers reported that Joan had been calling up her friends from *The Tonight Show* and offering some of them jobs on her new show. There were furious charges and denials from both sides.

Peter Lassally was quoted as saying that Rivers propositioned him, begging him to become her producer. It was, according to the newspapers, just one of several "raids" Rivers was trying to stage on *Tonight Show* personnel.

Today Rivers is still steaming over that one: "Why would I offer a job to someone who for three years did nothing but argue with me over guests?" She adds, "It's very sad to hear a man like Peter, in his 50s with two grown children, say, 'Look, Johnny, she offered me a job, but I'm staying with you.' It's so pathetic that at his age you have to toady up to someone."

Joan insists there wasn't even real competition between her new show and *The Tonight Show*. Hers was scheduled a half hour earlier, and was not even on a real network: "It's five stations against 200. What's everybody getting so upset about?"

She insists that for years she had turned down many networks and syndicates who asked her to host a show: "I've had secret meetings in hotel rooms, in limousines, and I've had solid offers. But I didn't accept anything, out of loyalty to Johnny. I cannot begin to tell you the deals I've turned down. I just didn't want to go up against him." She repeats that she wouldn't have taken the Fox offer if she'd gotten some loyalty from NBC. And over and over, in case Johnny was ever listening, Joan said at the time, "I love you. I wouldn't do anything to hurt you. I still want to be friends."

The sob story of Johnny hanging up on Joan got so much press that Carson finally couldn't keep still. He began to sneak in a few remarks about it in the monologue. On May 15 1986, Johnny mentioned that NBC was canceling its remake of *Alfred Hitchcock Presents*, which colorized the late director's opening remarks and re-used them to introduce the newly done episodes. He mentioned that NBC president Grant Tinker "tried to call Hitchcock, but Hitchcock hung up on him."

Another night, Carson described the tense situation in the Soviet Union. Gorbachev was mad at America. "It's all my fault," Johnny said. "He called me... but I hung up on him."

Johnny's deadpan disgust and disdain surfaced again and again, and each time he got applause and support from his audience. Bob Hope came on the show May 23. Johnny asked Hope about his plans for the next year.

"I don't know," Bob shrugged. "I was supposed to be on NBC, but I don't know about it. I called Grant Tinker, but he hung up on me."

The audience snickered and Johnny's face reddened. He giggled out a spasm of laughter, wiping his eye. "There's a lot of that going around," he said.

"You don't have to worry about it," Hope added drily. "She left, but there's one you don't have to pay alimony to!"

As far as the audience was concerned, Johnny was the victim. And Johnny was once again doing those "Why me?" jokes about encroaching competition. June 17: "Justice Warren Burger retired. He wants to take on a new challenging job. He's starting his own late night talk show." June 25: "I hope Reagan runs again. If he doesn't he'll probably start his own talk show."

While Joan Rivers was about to start her show on Fox, David Brenner was telling audiences to look for his new show. Brenner said that all the stars afraid to choose sides between Joan and Johnny should appear on his show instead.

ABC signed up Dick Cavett and Jimmy Breslin for a program, hoping to establish a new block of hit talk shows. Cavett had been doing a program for the USA network. Glum and cranky comic Robert Klein got the good and bad news: he'd take over for Cavett on USA, and try and fill the hour with the rejects and leftovers from Carson, Rivers, Bren-ner, Breslin, Cavett and Letterman.

Talk show hosts past and present were asked for their predictions on the main event, Carson vs. Rivers. Alan Thicke didn't want to get into the debate, and for a good reason: "I'm the wrong guy to ask. If I had anything brilliant to say on late night, I'd still be on it."

Dick Cavett and Mike Douglas both had doubts

about Joan Rivers' ability to sustain. Cavett said Rivers was "high energy," the wrong wattage for late night. Douglas added, "I think she's going to have her hands full because Johnny wears well. As good as Joan is, I don't know if she'll wear as well. Also, Johnny will have all that network muscle behind him. It's a tremendous thing to overcome."

David Letterman suddenly made an announcement: "I just signed a lucrative contract. I'm going to be the new, permanent guest host on the new Joan Rivers show!"

Behind the scenes, Fox scrambled to work deals that would strengthen Joan's position. They stole WBFF in Baltimore, signing the affiliate to switch from Johnny to Joan. Bristol-Myers announced it would pour $1.6 million worth of ads into the Rivers show. Sponsors that had heard their products lampooned by Carson now put their bucks behind Joan. Stars that had been unable to get on *The Tonight Show* were calling up Joan to volunteer.

Buoyed by this support, Joan was no longer apologetic. At a press conference, she announced that her talk show war would feature a lot of powerful recruits: "There were certain people I couldn't get as guests [while guest-hosting *The Tonight Show*] because they felt it was not the right image for the show. I had to fight to get David Lee Roth, Boy George and Lily Tomlin." Now she'd fill her hour with rockers and movers and shakers.

In ads for her program, her show was billed as "live, unpredictable, daring and funny... late night's early alternative... more than just talk."

While Rivers was booking many stars who previously couldn't or now wouldn't do *The Tonight Show*, she was definitely not going to get any Carson loyalists, especially not Burt Reynolds. While the Elizabeth Taylor-Joan Rivers feud was in reality more a case of hurt feelings that could be – and were –

soothed, there was real bad blood between Reynolds and Rivers.

Reynolds: "I never argue with a female impersonator. I was friends with her when she was a guy. She played on the same football team. She was Ray Gichgy before surgery."

Rivers: "He hates me, and I don't even know why... I've always liked him. I like anyone with humor, and he has a great sense of humor. I just figured he had a bad day because his toupee was twisted or his caps might have fallen out or the heels on his boots could've been broken or his dildo may have been pinching. He could have just looked at himself in direct sunlight and realized how old he really is. But, look, I have nothing against him!"

Joan's show premiered on October 9, 1986. For the first night of war, Carson enlisted Richard Pryor and Sean Penn. Rivers looked to take away the under-40 crowd by booking David Lee Roth, Pee Wee Herman, Elton John and Cher. She dubbed her young house band "The Party Boys and the Tramp," the latter an allusion to the group's lone female, a hapless blond sax player.

Introduced and given a standing ovation, Joan was overcome with emotion. "I have a whole monologue — which I won't do tonight. I am just — it's been five months and so much has been said and so much has been written — I'm just — so happy to be here!"

The audience rose to give her another standing ovation. Impulsively Joan reached out to the front row of fans and began to kiss some of the ringsiders.

The premiere show was an event, a party, a glittery high that peaked when Joan stood beside the piano while Elton John belted out "The Bitch Is Back" in her honor. Joan stared into the camera, as if into the face of Johnny Carson, and shouted along with Elton, "I can bitch, I can bitch... better than YOU!"

Over at *The Tonight Show*, it was business as usual. Johnny made only one remark about the competition: "There are a lot of big-time confrontations this week: Reagan versus Gorbachev, the Mets versus the Astros: and me versus "The Honeymooners Lost Episodes."

The overnight ratings were a surprise. Joan took San Francisco, and in New York edged him with a 27 percent share to his 22 percent. In Mid-America, Johnny easily won the night, 25 percent to 19 percent. David Brenner's talk show *Nightlife* hardly registered on the ratings scale at all.

Critics were less impressed. Fred Rothenberg of the *New York Post* seemed to have the majority opinion: "Joan Rivers finally got her own talk show. The next step is to make it funny." Steve Daley of the *Chicago Tribune* wrote, "Her show is typical talk show pap." Ray Richmond of the *Los Angeles Herald-Examiner* complained, "Joan is trying to be a glitzier, younger version of *The Tonight Show*."

Gary Shandling replaced Joan Rivers as guest host. On his first night, June 2, he hushed the audience and said, "Before I can continue I have to take the guest host's oath."

A judge came through the curtain with a Bible saying, "Raise your right hand and repeat after me. 'I, Gary Shandling, will never host another show opposite *The Tonight Show*. No matter how much money they may offer me."

Gary repeated it. The judge added, "And I will not make fun of the way Doc dresses."

"Uh, gee," Shandling grimaced, "I just can't do that one, that's where I draw the line."

The Rivers-Carson war took a lull over the summer, a slow period when vacations were a priority and ratings for all TV shows were off. Then the skirmishes began anew.

On October 24, 1986, Michael Landon showed up

for a visit. Johnny praised his friend Michael and told him how envious he was of Landon's timeless Western hits *Bonanza* and *Little House on the Prairie*. Johnny expressed the gnawing self-doubt of his own place in posterity. "Fifty years from now this show will be dated," Carson said with humility, no doubt thinking of how quickly the public had forgotten Jack Paar, Jerry Lester and so many other daily talk show personalities.

Landon then suggested that it wasn't too late for Johnny to make a Western movie. Carson shrugged, and was a little surprised when Landon persisted, claiming Johnny really had the makings of an adventure-film hero.

Landon continued to expound on the idea of Johnny appearing in a Western, and then said he even had a film clip to prove it. Carson seemed momentarily confused. Landon signaled for the film clip to roll. Carson looked toward producer Fred De Cordova; he'd heard nothing about Landon running a film clip.

As Carson watched the TV monitors along with the audience, footage of a man in a canoe came onto the screen. Landon spoke over it, setting up the scene, envisioning Johnny as a rugged outdoorsman. There were more shots of the river and the canoe. Then there were the opening credits for this proposed Michael Landon film starring Johnny Carson. It was "Johnny Carson in...

Up Rivers."

The audience roared its shock and approval. A sea of applause washed over Johnny as he put his hand to his chin in embarrassment. He had a full, toothy smile as he gasped, "I had nothing to do with this!"

"Catchy title," he added. He grinned at Michael Landon. "You spent some time on this?"

Carson shook his head, still red-faced but delighted. "I'm gonna pass on that one," he said.

Looking back on the situation today, Rivers admits that the feud should not have started in the first place. "I think the way Johnny found out was a shame. He should have heard from me, and I like to think that I could have made him understand. It must have been a huge shock. Nobody had said to him, 'Rivers's contract is up. Do you want to give her one year or two?' Nobody had said, 'The Rivers people have been calling for five months, but we're stalling them.'" As far as she was concerned, the problem was that Carson was "wrapped in cotton" by his staff, kept from bad news, bad press and any potential aggravation.

Over the long months, Joan Rivers struggled to grow from the frantic gossip/comic she'd been as a guest host to a more gentle, supportive interviewer that would wear well night after night. Every night she was getting conflicting opinions from the people at Fox. She was experiencing what Dick Cavett had called the "chickenshit" and what Merv Griffin had called "the suits." She heard TV executives yammering, threatening and ordering.

She had to take most of the abuse. Unlike the other talk show hosts, she couldn't blame the producer. Her producer was her husband, Edgar. And the producer couldn't protect the star and absorb all the shocks; they lived together. They knew each other's day-to-day pressures and miseries. What was going on at work could not be turned off easily at the end of the day.

Being a guest host was incredibly different from being the actual host. Rivers went into the world of Fox unprepared. Now she was being digested in the belly of the beast. Sometimes it was little things. Joan and Mark Hudson wrote the theme song for the show. Fox demanded to own the theme outright, not having to pay the duo a royalty.

Sometimes little irritations mounted. After a show, instead of praise there would be sniping from the big shots. They looked at her interview techniques and came away questioning her questions: "Why did you ask that tough question? Don't you realize that guest won't come back?" They listened to her monologues and choked over her jokes: "That third joke bombed. Never joke about that topic again, it just doesn't work."

Meanwhile, the big muscle from *The Tonight Show* kept flexing. Veterans of the wars, the staff there knew how to fight. Rivers recalls, "The Carson people put the word out that anybody who appeared on my show would be blackballed at *The Tonight Show.* Our friend Jay Michelis, vice president of NBC, told me, "Our job is to destroy you."

Joan quickly found out who her show business friends were. They included Ted Danson, Kenny Rogers and Louie Anderson, all defying the NBC ban. Rivers made calls herself trying to get people to appear on the show.

For a woman characterized as "shrill," Joan displayed a lot of charm. Roy Orbison, who never did talk shows and was prone to anti-Semitic mumblings about who was controlling the entertainment business, got a personal call from Rivers and was delighted to say yes. Nancy Reagan, rarely seen on the talk show circuit, was another who came around. In a competitive business where star envy and paranoia is legend, Rivers was able to count on support from the women who had been her competition, the other great female comedians of the day, including Lily Tomlin and Lucille Ball.

But it was a terrible strain: "*The Tonight Show* was like going to somebody else's party in a great dress, and now at Fox I had to throw the party myself, night after night, and worry whether everybody had a good time."

The panic at Fox continued and her bosses began to come down on her with heavy hands. Ideas for sketches were killed. Guests were vetoed. Everything she did was "not funny" or "too expensive." Rivers couldn't understand what all the harassment was about. The show was making money, she insisted. The affiliates were happy to have something lively on at night instead of sitcom re-runs. But nobody seemed to pay attention to what she said, just the way she said it. "Why do you have to come on so strong?" the men asked. Everything she did was compared to the success of *The Tonight Show*.

The splashy controversy of singing "The Bitch Is Back" with Elton John was short-lived. Instead came the sticky controversy of lawsuits. Rivers was on the receiving end of a $3 million "invasion of privacy" suit after making cutting jokes about Victoria Principal and then allegedly leaking the star's private phone number. Then Jane Russell announced a lawsuit, complaining that instead of discussing her new fashion line, "Jane's Way," Rivers double-crossed her by asking about an abortion Russell supposedly had early in her career.

"I wouldn't wish this show on my worst enemy," Jane hissed to Joan after the show was over.

Amateur mistakes were hitting David Brenner too, who changed his style from suits to fluffy sweaters in an effort to look more like the Yuppies who were supposed to be key to his demographics. During one broadcast Brenner mentioned that the author of *The Mystery of Edwin Drood* was Shakespeare. When he was told that it was Charles Dickens he honked loudly to his staff, "You have just succeeded in turning me into the national dunce of all time!" Brenner was never a factor, and now he was just about through. So were the duo of Jimmy Breslin and Dick Cavett.

Breslin didn't wait to be nailed into an oversized

coffin. In his November 23rd column he expressed his disgust with his network and announced, "ABC... your services, such as they are, will no longer be required as of December 20, 1986." He added grandly, "I thus become the first person in America to fire a network." Hapless Dick Cavett watched in chagrin as he once again lost in the battle of late night.

Rivers was going down, too. By the end of 1986 *TV Guide* sounded an obituary notice. They reported Rivers was "nowhere near Carson" in the ratings, plummeting down from those first weeks of audience curiosity. *US* magazine called her a "barking seal, out of control."

As it turned out, the only person to come anywhere close to Johnny was none of the above. Not Brenner, Rivers, Cavett or Breslin. Ted Koppel's *Nightline* was getting a 6.0 share to Johnny's 7.8. CBS's re-run movies were in third place with 5.2.

As the pretenders fell away, Johnny continued onward. The only person who in any way matched him for talk show longevity was Merv Griffin, still plugging away with that 8:30 p.m. syndicated show. But now, the plug was finally being pulled on Griffin.

R.I.P. *The Merv Griffin Show*, syndicated at first, brought to CBS, then syndicated again, a show with three lives, was finally at an end: 1965-1986.

Griffin's show ended with a somber hour-long "Best of." Merv, walking through his eerily empty studio, showed film clips of his favorite moments on the show. He had many to his credit, including talks with great stars (Orson Welles) and heartfelt discussions with American politicians (Gerald Ford). He even screened silly moments where he tried to outdouble-entendre Johnny Carson:

Griffin: "Where do you feel most romantic."

Sophia Loren: "Here with you."

Griffin: "Well, I may pass away right here... Are you aware that you're 50? Does anything feel on you like it's 50 years old? Know what I mean?"

Loren: (giggling) *Nothing.*

But after the film clips, the camera came back to a clearly miserable Merv as he grimly stood around in the darkness of the studio. He walked over to the control room and introduced his director: "Has it been fifteen years, Dick? Sixteen years. Best director I could ever steal from his brother." Dick Carson turned around to acknowledge the camera.

Merv said in a strained, husky voice, "It's tough to say good-bye... I guess this is the first time on this last show I've ever said this. We will *not* be back after this message. Th-th-that's all, folks."

Merv turned up on *The Tonight Show,* talking about all those years of talk show wars and competition. Johnny admitted, "We have a lot in common strangely enough. We both worked in radio... we both did a game show."

"You did *Who Do You Trust?"*

"Who Do You Trust?" Carson admitted, wondering what Merv had in mind.

"It was originally called... "

"Do You Trust Your Wife?"

"Yes," Merv said. *"Do You Trust Your Wife?* But they changed it on account of you!"

Carson acknowledged the gag with a little grin. "And then we both did a show —"

"We started the same day, same year," Merv said. "And we would be even in years, and we probably are, if you count all your vacations."

Carson smiled broadly. "You came here to get this all out of your system!"

Griffin may have been out of the talk show system, but he did have a consolation prize. According to *Forbes* magazine, Griffin was one of America's wealthiest men, worth $235 million.

Johnny wasn't doing so badly either, but who was there to share it with?

The answer came one day in the form of a blonde named Alexis, just thirty-six-years-old. After wives Joan (aka "Jody") to Joanne to Joanna, perhaps Johnny had decided he'd find better luck starting with the A-list.

As *Newsday* put it succinctly, she "slipped into a bikini, strolled by Johnny's house on nearby Carbon Beach and got invited in." To the surprise of some, the relationship got very, very serious. But then it got sort of comical again. At least, it seemed that way to Bob Hope: "Johnny's gonna take his fourth wife. The first three took *him!* He's entitled to get married again. He still has a couple of houses left!"

Johnny's blonde was now a part of his life. The other blonde, Joan Rivers, was still a part of it, too. Joan Rivers had managed to hang on to the show, even though it was a losing proposition. It seemed that the only thing keeping Johnny from retiring with his pretty new bride was the unfinished business of seeing Joan go into the dumper. Newspaper reports confirmed this.

An agent who booked comics for both Joan's show and Johnny's admitted, "Johnny isn't going to leave till Rivers does. He's not going to let them say that Joan forced him off the air." He added that the talk show wars were wrecking Joan: "It's so relaxed at *The Tonight Show.* It's a pleasure. But the Rivers people are in chaos. It's unbelievably tense." David Brenner chimed in, "She's getting desperate... it's the old drowning person theory... She's in a state of panic."

In the midst of all this, there was a shouting match between Barry Diller, representing the power of Fox, and Edgar Rosenberg, Joan's producer/husband. It ended with Edgar crying out, "You're a tinhorn dictator!" And Barry sneering, "Go fuck yourself!"

On May 15, 1987, it was finally over. Fox announced that Joan Rivers was through. When Joan faced her audience that night, she was like a tired politician conceding defeat on election night. Her fans applauded with never-say-die enthusiasm. She shook her head, asking them to stop. She told them she couldn't talk about the miserable situation (she and Fox had yet to settle the remainder of her contract). But she did say, "It's nobody's fault." She promised that since she'd been doing television for twenty-three years, she'd somehow "be on the air for another twenty-three years." Some place.

At 11:30, the victor, Johnny Carson began his show, business as usual. He did running gags about the Scandal of the Day, which at the moment was the saga of deposed evangelists Jim and Tammy Faye Bakker. Jim had lost his ministry due to a sex scandal. "Don't worry about Tammy Bakker," said Johnny, grinning. "She just got an offer from Fox Broadcasting."

He stuffed his hands in his pockets and basked in twenty long seconds of laughs and applause.

As serene as a sunbather, he looked off at nothing in particular and added, "I've been saving that one for a long time."

Softly, over the twelve seconds of applause and laughter, he murmured, "I'm sorry... "

Joan went back to stand-up work. Her next public appearance was on stage at Caesar's Palace in Vegas. She opened by telling the crowd, "First of all, you are looking at a woman who has finally been able to make Johnny Carson happy!"

But when interviewers asked about what had happened over at Fox, Joan wasn't smiling: "I didn't ask to leave. I was fired... they raped me."

She had been physically sick during the last days of her show, but it was nothing compared to what her husband was going through. Beset by many physical ailments himself, and now broken in a power struggle with Fox, Edgar Rosenberg sank further into depression and angst. He and Joan separated as he tried to find a solution to his problems. He thought he found it with a bottle of pills in a Philadelphia hotel room.

David Brenner's syndicated *Nightlife* show was axed in June of 1987. Joan Rivers' show, technically called *The Late Show*, was still hobbling along like a turkey without a head. There was a succession of guest hosts. They ranged from the silly (Martha Quinn) to the ludicrous (Estelle Getty). Toward the end of the run, a young black comic named Arsenio Hall showed some promise.

Arsenio, the son of a Baptist preacher, had been in the business since 1979. After graduating from Kent State and working as a cosmetics salesman, he had tried the comedy clubs. One night he had fled the Comedy Cottage in Rosemont, Illinois, when his name was called. He was just too scared to perform. Four years later, he'd made it to an HBO special. After being Alan Thicke's sidekick, now he was getting his own shot at hosting.

Nobody seemed to be paying attention.

Rupert Murdoch, owner of the Fox network, recognized Hall on the street outside a restaurant. He came up to him thinking the slim black man was the fellow who valet parked his car an hour ago. "No, no, Mr. Murdoch," Hall said, "I do your show."

Hall departed at the end of 1987 and the grimacingly handsome Ross Shafer was brought in, but the show folded in October of 1988. Forlorn Fox vice president Kevin Wendle was waving a white flag. "It's crazy to try to compete with Johnny Carson in the talk area. He's the master. Joan couldn't do it, no one can."

David Brenner barely made it through one season, September 1986 to May 1987. It was an embarrassing defeat for his syndicate, King World. Brenner said, "I put more into the show than I ever put into my own life," he moaned. "It was the hardest job I've ever done — just exhausting."

But Johnny Carson continued on — no sweat.

CHAPTER FOURTEEN

WOOF! WOOF! AND THE WHEEL OF FORTUNE

Each time heavyweight champion Johnny Carson scored a knockout victory over a challenger, the press dutifully raised his hand and praised him. But somewhere, someone was saying, "He's slipping. With the right strategy, he can definitely be beaten now."

CBS got the idea that Pat Sajak was the man. An odd-looking TV personality with a dazed but intense gaze that resembled Dan Quayle on amphetamines, Pat was a glib quiz master with a big housewife following. This had been the description of Johnny Carson when he was the quick-witted game show host on *Who Do You Trust?* A younger version of Carson could easily topple an older one, right?

Sajak theorized, "As I look at Carson, as I look at Paar, as I look at Letterman even, all the men who've had success with this form have had common threads. And some of those threads run through me. I'm basically laid-back. And I've got that typical Midwestern 'I'm really no threat to you no matter what kind of despicable thing I'm saying' look."

With rehearsed humility, Sajak tried to draw sympathy for himself as he began his assault on Johnny. Pat said he was just an average guy, "not an intellectual" like Ted Koppel, not a singer like Merv Griffin, and not a brilliant monologist like Carson: "Not being able to do much of anything, I think it's a real tribute to me to have come this far."

Not clever like David Letterman, in *Rolling Stone*, February 1989, Sajak offered his own "top ten" list of why he wasn't going to do a top ten list:

10. I can't count that high.

9. I'm afraid it will detract from our stupid pet tricks.

8. CBS won't spring for the necessary equipment.

7. My lawyers are too busy with the Mighty Sajak Art Players suit.

6. It's liable to lead to a shoving match between Robert C. Wright and Laurence A. Tisch.

5. Why bother? We'd still have eighty-nine minutes to fill.

4. For the same reason that Phil Donahue doesn't dress up as a black woman.

3. It would break a bond that Dave and I made at summer camp twenty-five years ago.

2. It might mean we'd have to cut Charo's second song.

1. What if it's funnier than Dave's and he gets mad at me?

Having thus established his idea of funny, Sajak commented, "Look, the worst-case scenario is that nobody watches... There's not going to be a firing squad."

False modesty aside, Sajak was confident that he could be a late night player, and quite possibly topple Johnny Carson. After all, his *Wheel of Fortune* program was viewed by an estimated 43 million people and had become the most popular quiz show on TV. At 42, he was younger than Johnny and, to some, as attractive and charismatic. CBS thought so, having spent four million bucks to build a studio for him. CBS guaranteed him a $60,000 per week salary for two years.

Paramount had a different idea. They figured to put an end to the 80's and to Carson with Arsenio Hall.

Hall displayed a lot of potential when he took over Fox's *The Late Show*. "Overall, his ratings were stable but only slightly higher than Joan's," Jeff Yarbrough, a producer on *The Late Show* recalled. "But what was interesting was the phenomenal audience share, 60 or 70 percent, that he was pulling among black viewers in places like Atlanta."

Industry insiders had their doubts about either Pat Sajak or Arsenio Hall. One was too much a crass Carson imitation, the other an untested, unknown commodity. A few wondered if it wouldn't be better to try one of the old talk show masters instead.

Dick Cavett was back — but now relegated to CNBC cable. He had been the host of a syndicated radio series for a while and had a struggle conquering the depression that had become a serious problem during the run of his PBS series. He admitted to reporters that he had contemplated suicide at the time: "You're in a permanent state of dismal, worthless black despair that will not end no matter what everybody tells you. Everything turns sort of colorless... You find yourself not wanting to go out of the house. You lose all sense of self-esteem. Your manhood is a casualty, and that's a *nice* way of putting it."

Cavett found successful medical treatment and declared "It was as if I woke up this morning and the curtain rose and there was color in the world and I could think of at least three reasons to live."

TV Guide wrote, "While some might view Cavett's professional progress through a series of talk shows on ABC, CBS, PBS and USA to his current gig as a sign of his increasingly limited appeal, we prefer to think of it as a testament to his enduring popularity... "

Steve Allen's popularity had also endured. He too had a radio show syndicated in the mid-80's. He continued to push his list of composed songs past 4,000, and authored many more books including a murder mystery about a talk show host. He was, as always, warm, gracious and a fascinating raconteur on talk shows.

He did it without malice, which, he admitted, was not always the case with Johnny. "It is possible to detect some anger in Johnny's work," he wrote in his 1987 book, *How to Be Funny*, "and I don't simply refer to the put-down jokes he does about Ed McMahon's drinking, Doc Severinsen's clothing, Tommy Newsom's personality, the audience's not laughing at a particular joke, etc. There is a detectable cold thread running through Johnny's work, although, because he is inhibited at all points of the emotional scale, the factor probably goes unnoticed by most of his viewers... "

As for the other major host of *The Tonight Show*, Jack Paar, he had been persuaded to star in a pair of TV specials featuring clips of his old programs (mostly the post-*Tonight* prime-time *Jack Paar Show*) and had come to enjoy the spotlight again. Waking from his self-imposed hibernation had stirred his bile. He certainly considered himself more viable than some of his contemporaries.

Dick Cavett, Paar said, was just "one of my early students." These days, in Paar's opinion, Cavett was no longer worth watching: "I liked him better when he first brought his considerable intellect and charm to television." He chided Cavett for once mispronouncing "déjà vu" as "déjà vee."

Paar had thought that Merv Griffin would "probably outlast Johnny Carson... he is a decent and likeable man," and gave a left-handed compliment to David Frost: "The fact he lasted two years is amazing considering his handicap of a different speech pattern and his not really understanding the American psyche."

He had nothing but contempt for daytime talk shows, considering Phil Donahue "a disgrace" and the rest of the pack "sleazy."

Having forgotten the animosity between him and Carson, now he jokingly declared "I should never have given *The Tonight Show* to him; I should have rented it or married him."

He added that "of the newest personalities, David Letterman, will unquestionably be a big star."

Unquestionably, Paar would always be bigger. At least in his own eyes. In 1992 he attended a Museum of Radio and Television gala. But the media raced after Barbara Walters, Mary Tyler Moore, Nichols and May, ignoring Paar entirely. This seemed rather sad to one photographer, since the whole point of being in this particular reception area was for publicity. The photographer took a few pictures of Paar. With no one around Paar, the photographer ventured near and asked, "Mr. Paar, could I have your autograph?" Paar look away in disdain saying; "I don't give autographs."

Paar once noted, "I was a real pain in the ass to many people. But I really think, or wish to think, that I was interesting and one of a kind.

"Since I already have the money, it doesn't matter now."

He didn't matter much to the people in control of TV's late night world in the early 90's. They watched his TV specials but were not moved. The future King of the night, many believed, was going to be Sajak or Hall.

Soon enough, the smart money began to lean toward Hall. Sure, Sajak was cutesy, and Arsenio's hairstyle made him look like a Trivial Pursuit wedge. But Arsenio's audience was going "Woof! Woof!" and Pat's was going to sleep. There was nothing trivial about the ratings Arsenio Hall was getting. If a sponsor wanted to move sneakers, soda pop or the latest quickie flick, the demographics said: Arsenio. The momentum was building.

Oddly, for a stand-up performer, Arsenio Hall's monologue was the weakest part of his show. His real talent was the talk. As an interviewer, Hall could be more warm and ingratiating than any host since Merv Griffin. Griffin was the prince of "Oooohs," but Arsenio encouraged celebrities with a dreamy sigh of agreement: "Yeaaaahhh."

He seemed genuinely interested in his guests, and was the first since Joan Rivers to ask a personal question with enough sincerity to get an answer instead of a slap. Suzanne Somers talked about her new husband:

"I went out with him, slept with him, and been sleeping with him ever since."

Arsenio, wide-eyed and admiring, "You *didn't* sleep with him the first date, though?"

"Yeah!"

"Really?"

"Haven't you ever done that? Do you even *need* a date?"

One reason why Hall was so poised in his new job: he had dreamed of hosting a talk show ever since he was a kid. His idol? Johnny Carson.

Not only did Hall admire Johnny, he even wanted to dress like him: "When I was twelve and saw him in those Johnny Carson fashions, man, he was the guy. Even when he wasn't funny, he looked good."

Arsenio Hall always had an ambition to replace Johnny Carson. When he was a rising stand-up star, he even went down to *The Tonight Show* after hours to see what it felt like to be Johnny: "I snuck in the studio and pulled off the sheet and sat in his chair at the desk. I said to myself, 'Good stuff.' And they threw me out."

Hall was not so enthused about David Letterman. He said, "The object of *this* show is not to have Cher call me an asshole."

Or even Arse Hall.

Hall analyzed all the failures that came before, including his old boss, Alan Thicke. "What they all had in common is that they tried to out-Johnny Johnny. I'm not going after Johnny's crowd, I'm going after Johnny's crowd's kids."

As Hall took off, the tremors could be felt at both the Carson and Letterman camps. Rap had recently become a force in music, trumpeting a "fear of a black planet." Oprah Winfrey was besting Phil Donahue. And now, invading late night was Arsenio Hall with an army bellowing "Woof! Woof!"

Hall's style shocked some of the old show biz veterans. Instead of *asking* for applause, he was demanding, "Give it up!" He didn't have a band, he had a "posse." Instead of wanting a civilized audience, he revved them up to raise their fists in the air.

But after a while, it was clear that Arsenio was only slightly more hip than the kids in the mall. He was as much a child of 60's TV and Johnny Carson as most any other comic his age, and he had a great respect for his elders. He was just as keen on having Kirk Douglas on the show as having Michael Douglas.

Hall had always insisted, "It's not a black-white thing. There's a changing of the guard. Johnny has his people because they grew up with him, they've watched him all their lives, and we are creatures of habit. But in the other room they've had kids who don't have a talk show. I created the talk show for them."

Over the months, he also made it a talk show the whole family could watch. He wasn't filling each hour with only brat-pack stars in trendy new clothes and black entertainers. He was booking many mainstream guests.

Of course, for guests "out of the loop" as far as young viewers were concerned, Hall found himself having to explain all the credits of a Kirk Douglas.

And he had to ask very simple, basic questions that young viewers would like to know. There had to be some mention of Michael Douglas to get the kids really interested. And then there had to be a way of explaining to the Arsenio Hall audience what Kirk Douglas was promoting: a book. Hall ended up gently telling the crowd, "If you're *into reading*, check it out."

Most celebrities appreciated the gentle treatment and were flattered that Arsenio not only was so starry-eyed, but that he felt that young viewers would even care about them.

Arsenio had another star author promoting a book on his show: Joan Rivers. They shared a mutual disgust for Fox. But their opinions on Johnny Carson now were varied. Arsenio was still in awe. He asked:

"Do you think you and Mr. Carson will ever be friends again?"

Joan answered, "I couldn't care less. It's like a different time. He never wrote me when my husband died. I mean, who cares? It's his problem, not mine."

By November of 1989, Hall was beating Pat Sajak and, in some urban locales, Carson. He was even putting some "great moment" clips into the vaults for an anniversary show.

He made headlines when Andrew Dice Clay came on the show literally crying about how misunderstood he was. And later on, he scored a major upset by being the talk show host to feature a sax player named Bill Clinton. "It's good to see a Democrat blowing something other than an election," Arsenio cracked.

As for Pat Sajak's program, critics seemed to be most delighted with the commercial breaks. The nicest thing to be said about Pat was that he actually wasn't that much of a Carson imitator. The host he most tried to copy was Dick Cavett, hoping to present himself as tongue-in-cheek coy and witty. It came out numbingly cute and smug. His patter with sleepy, basset-faced sidekick Dan Miller was belabored. In stand-up, Sajak lacked believability. While audience members knew that Carson, Letterman and Hall didn't write their own jokes, they knew that they *could.* With Sajak, he was reading jokes the way he announced new contestants on *Wheel of Fortune.* Trying to ad-lib was not as easy as getting vowels from Vanna White. Sajak's talk show spun slowly toward "bankrupt."

Newsweek, in August of 1989, pointed out that "old conventional wisdom" labeled Sajak "The Next Carson. New conventional wisdom: the next Bob Barker." Meanwhile, the "old conventional wisdom" that had marked Arsenio Hall as "Eddie Murphy's sidekick" was replaced by the "new conventional wisdom: The next Carson."

It was Arsenio Hall who took off and it was Sajak who sputtered. *The Pat Sajak Show* had premiered in January of 1989, just as *The Arsenio Hall Show.* But Sajak was history as of April of 1990.

Arsenio Hall didn't just say "I told you so." He wanted to know: "Why were they pulling so hard for Pat Sajak to succeed instead of me? Why? Is it because I'm black? Because I'm syndicated and not network? What made them say I didn't have the guns, that America wouldn't watch me? They nailed me to the side of a wall because I wasn't like their heroes, Merv Griffin and Johnny and Dave Let-ter-man. All I heard about was how black I was. I was having people here in Hollywood tell me, 'Be careful. Don't be too black.' What the hell is too black? Let's chill with this color bull. No one told Johnny not to be too white for the brothers in Detroit. I'm gonna be me."

Newsweek was saluting Arsenio Hall as the up-and-coming late night host. *The New York Times* gushed that he was the personifcation of "late night cool." And *People* magazine wrote: "C'mon, America, he seems to be coaxing. Can you say 'Hip?' Can you say 'Bad?' Can you say 'Def?'"

The man who was supposed to be the next Carson, David Letterman, wasn't about to crown Arsenio king, or say "Def." And he wasn't having animal noises from the audience. Once when somebody let go with a few whistles, Dave stopped and jeered him: "What was that? A spotted owl? A drunken loon?"

Dave was not intimidated by what the media was dubbing "bad" and "def" and "hip." He wasn't too thrilled to see Arsenio's ratings come up against his in some of the cities where they were being matched head-to-head. But he wasn't going to dump his favorite Southern folk chicks like Edie Brickell and Nanci Griffiths and start loading up on rappers. "I think Dave hates my guts," Arsenio said.

Still, Dave remained Dave. And Johnny Carson also resisted those who urged him to try and fake an appreciation for kid movie stars over ones who'd paid their dues. If Carson had sold out, he would have looked ridiculous. The proof of that was "Carsenio," a character played by Dana Carvey in a *Tonight Show* spoof on *Saturday Night Live*.

The big laugh was imagining Carson desperately trying to keep atop the ratings heap by getting a buzz cut and calling himself "Carsenio." According to Carvey, Johnny actually appreciated the sketch. Especially since, in its own way, it saluted Carson's integrity. But Johnny was extremely displeased with other *Saturday Night Live* parodies of him. In Dana Carvey's impression, Carson was an out-of-touch old show-biz type who was almost senile, always muttering "wild, wacky stuff" and "I *did NOT* know that."

Actually when it came to cool, Arsenio was losing his, not Carson. Arsenio was quickly discovering that anyone sitting in the big seat had better check it for booby traps and poisonous snakes.

Feuds between Arsenio and other celebrities began to simmer. Madonna seemed to find his triangular hairstyle pretty ridiculous and he responded with a few insulting cracks. When Arsenio personalized some standard fat jokes by attaching Roseanne Arnold's name to them, she retaliated by spitting out a spate of insults and insinuating that he was gay.

She raged on stage, "It seems every time I turn on that shitty fuckin' suck-ass show of his, there he is again telling another Roseanne fat joke, and it just pisses me off! And they're not even funny... Woof woof woof. He does have some good stuff about him. It's not that often that we get to see a black nerd on TV... Fuck with me, ya triangle-headed Eddie Murphy kiss-ass motherfucker!"

Things got serious when Tom Arnold stormed the Paramount lot, wanting to brawl with Arsenio. It took a lot of the Arsenio Hall charm to finally get a truce with the feisty Arnolds. He also managed to avoid more fighting with Madonna, declaring "I know two sides of Madonna. There is the Madonna who supports AmFar and other AIDS-related organizations, and, of course, there is the Madonna who will bare her breasts at the drop of a hat. Personally, I'm not sick of either Madonna. There's a big heart beneath pop's perkiest nipples."

As soon as one feuded ended, another began. Hall and Spike Lee had a heated TV encounter. Lee's latest whipping boy among black celebrities "not doing enough" for blacks was Eddie Murphy. Murphy was no fan of Spike Lee, either. Jovial ladies man Eddie laughed at pebble-headed, myopic little Spike, figuring he had all the appeal of "a cricket." When Lee attacked once again, Hall defended his friend. He told Spike Lee, "The change doesn't occur any quicker if you go to the Caucasian journalist looking to stir up conflict and tell him what you think of your black brother."

Lee now added Hall to his list. He called Arsenio "an Uncle Tom Negro obsessed with hugging white women." Hall answered, "maybe a ghetto ass-whipping will teach him not to talk that stuff."

Arsenio realized that he had to start carting around bodyguards, just like Eddie Murphy, just in case there really were some ass whipping brawls.

Out at the China Club, Arsenio had a confrontation with Sam Kinison. "Your show sucks!" Kinison shouted. Hall shot back, "Get outta here before you get your ass kicked." Arsenio and his posse of bodyguards stood their ground until Kinison left.

Other stand-ups just laughed off the idea of a tough Arsenio Hall. Ellen Cleghorne, who would soon join the cast of *Saturday Night Live*, joked in her stand-up act that in Swahili Arsenio Hall's name meant "Am I gay or am I not? Only Eddie Murphy knows for sure."

While Hall tried to find his way through the frustration, backstabbing and controversy that Johnny had calmly realized "comes with the territory," the bottom line was the ratings. Johnny Carson remained on top, as he had for nearly thirty years. Arsenio's ratings began to level out. They even started to dip.

Arsenio was cool about it: "Johnny has earned respect and fought for it for 29 years. I'm happy being the Prince while he is the King."

CHAPTER FIFTEEN

THE KING ABDICATES: ANARCHY RULES

The 90's began with a new challenge in the fight to dethrone *The Tonight Show*. In July of 1990 a California disk jockey named Rick Dees launched a late night ABC show called *Into the Night*. It promised to swipe away all the young viewers at that hour.

The problem was that the baby-faced Dees looked about 12 and that was the mentality of his humor. Few 12-year-olds were up at midnight to watch the disc jockey snicker, babble and run contests and money giveaways. Even 12-year-olds would have preferred old *Andy Griffith Show* re-runs to the excruciating running gag of guest appearances by Greg Binkley impersonating "Deputy Barney Fife Jr."

The show was instantly attacked by critics. In response, changes had to be made. The house band, Billy Vera and the Beaters, was fired in favor of the Master Mix. Eventually someone at ABC realized that the man they had put on the air was an airhead. If ABC hadn't finally pulled the plug on Rick Dees, he might have turned up on a Ted Koppel news show the next time the subject was clinical imbecility.

The 90's seemed to start pretty well for Johnny Carson, but as he struggled toward his 30th year as host of *The Tonight Show*, he faced some of his most humiliating and depressing professional setbacks, along with heartbreaking tragedy in his personal life.

The first sign of trouble was a haunting from the past. First wife Joan "Jody" Wolcott Carson Buckley hired a high-profile divorce lawyer and sued Johnny for a new alimony settlement. She broke the silence she evidently agreed to years ago and spilled stories of Carson's coldness and infidelities, painting him as unfeeling then and just as mean now, forcing her to exist on a pittance.

Back in 1963 she agreed to a then-substantial settlement, getting $15,000 a year, $7,500 in child support, and 15 percent of Carson's earnings after $100,000. When she remarried in 1970, she managed to get a lump sum of $160,000, and took a slight reduction on her yearly fee, down to $13,500. Now she wanted at least $100,000 a year.

To Carson's lawyer, Stanley Arkin, this was "a baldfaced holdup." He claimed that Jody had "cash assets in excess of $388,000." The public sympathy Jody figured would go her way didn't, but the strain on Johnny was obvious to those around him in those tense weeks.

Dabney Coleman turned up on the show one night and brought along an old photo that he wanted Johnny to see. This was a Coleman habit. On a previous show he unveiled a picture of himself during his days as a magazine model. "Now go up a little," he told the cameraman. The old photo came into focus. "See that? That's my first wife. That's Ann. I have not heard from her in twenty years."

Coleman paused and asked innocently, "Have you heard from your first wife?"

Carson forced a smile. "I really — I'm really gonna let that one go."

Letting go of Johnny had become an obsession among NBC's new young executives. Networks traditionally went after the high-spending 18 to 35 group and over the years many older stars were dumped not by low ratings, but by demographics. To foster a *now, happening* network image Jack Benny was sent packing in 1965, and Red Skelton in 1971. Both were big influences in the life of Johnny Carson and he had long worried about sharing their fate.

And now, it was Johnny's turn. The success of Arsenio Hall, the ability of Ted Koppel's *Nightline* to topple him on "strong news nights" and the good numbers being turned in by stand-up comic Jay Leno as a guest host were part of the reasons for the rumblings at NBC. Another part was that the network had an influx of college whiz kids, communications majors who were being put in charge of big decisions on the theory that it took a kid to know what kids wanted. Older writers, directors and stars found themselves dictated to by bratty Yuppie know-it-alls. It didn't matter if they refused to listen to seasoned veterans and bombed miserably (NBC's fiasco series *Parenthood* was a notorious example). Youth would be forgiven and youth would be served.

At NBC, they could hardly wait to boot ancient Andy Griffith's *Matlock* and start pushing around the old man who had made millions for NBC over so many years of service: living legend Johnny Carson.

The mentality was: "Better to get rid of someone too early than too late." Besides, Johnny was syphoning off between $15 and $25 million. Jay Leno was making a fraction of that. "Hey, this is a business. It makes good business sense, right?"

Rumors of Carson being canceled were now as common as the annual "He's going to quit this time" prognostications.

Suddenly the *New York Post* headlined on February 11, 1991: "There Goes Johnny: NBC Looking to Dump Carson for Jay Leno."

Just a few months later, Johnny Carson appeared at a New York conference and announced "This is the last year I'm doing *The Tonight Show*. My final broadcast will be May 22, 1992. I hope there is always a show like *The Tonight Show* on TV. Television has to discover its own new people... "

Carson's people angrily denied that there had been any pressure for Johnny to make such an announcement. The reason, staffers insisted, that he was making the news known a year early was to assure affiliates that a smooth transition would be made.

NBC was apparently losing another beloved star. The tabloids were reporting the terminal illness of Johnny's good friend Michael Landon.

On May 9, 1991, Landon appeared on *The Tonight Show*. Johnny told the audience what they already knew: that on April 8 Landon had been diagnosed with inoperable pancreas and liver cancer. In the face of such news, Johnny said, "He has continued to face this battle with the humor and honesty that characterizes this man."

Looking strong and wearing a brave smile, Michael Landon walked out to a standing ovation. Johnny quietly mentioned he was "rather touched" that Landon had chosen his show to discuss the situation. "You're my buddy," Michael said. He didn't want any sentiment, either. He was upbeat and filled with unexpected, ironic good humor.

"One thing I want to clear up right away," Michael said. "There's a big headline in one of these incredible magazines about how I want to have another child so my wife will have something to remember me by. I have *nine* children... My wife needs something to remember me by?"

He leaned back and laughed heartily, the audiences joining in.

"You're lookin' good," Johnny said.

"I feel good... I must tell everybody, thank you for the tremendous mail response. I really want to thank everybody — a lot of great suggestions. I'm using a little bit of everything. There were *some* that I didn't try. One guy wrote and told me "The reason you got it, The Big C," is that I did not get enough sex! He thinks it was only the nine times! So he gave me the regimen. Which would kill the average 25- year-old...

"Someone said all I have to do is swim with a dolphin. The sonar from the dolphin, and ping, ping, it goes away. What can I tell ya! Here I'm going to all these hospitals; all I gotta do is go to Marineland... "

Like a Catskill comic, Landon didn't miss a beat. "Oh. I take coffee enemas. Anybody out there heard of coffee enemas?"

There was some applause. Michael looked out at the crowd and said, "Oh, *you* must be fun to have breakfast with! I invited John over. He wanted cream and sugar, and I'm not pouring!"

Johnny chuckled and added, "You better hope that somebody isn't going to secretly replace your coffee with Folger's crystals! It could be a long day..."

A good listener, the best definition of a friend, Johnny let Michael Landon talk about what was important to him. And at that moment, what was important was to share advice with anyone going through similar uncertainty. He urged families to keep a positive attitude around the house, and never to forget their sense of humor.

It was only after this pleasant, friendly advice that he brought up one thing that was his pain alone. It was the way the tabloids had exploited the news of his illness.

"It seems so totally insensitive to me," he said. "How do they know what my little kids have been told in my own home? That a tabloid would write 'Four Weeks Left' Or 'It's Over.' Can you imagine that? Can you imagine? It's unbelievable that people can be that way. *That's* a cancer. That's the cancer in our society."

The audience applauded. Having made his point, Landon changed the subject. With Johnny alongside him, Michael Landon was not asking for tears or sympathy, nor was he lashing out with righteous rage. He was a man of dignity.

Johnny tried to keep his dignity during the trying, tumultuous month, but just one week after his announced retirement, the network made an announcement of its own. They were nudging him off his 11:30 p.m. time slot.

For nearly thirty years, Johnny had fought for the good of *The Tonight Show*. He made NBC respect it. He reminded them that it was a money-maker. For years he had successfully kept NBC from scheduling sports events or long movies that would interfere with his starting time. He knew the importance of viewers remaining in the habit of tuning in at the same time each night.

But now, in May of 1991, NBC announced that Carson's show would start at the awkward time of 11:35, allowing affiliates five extra minutes of commercials for their 11 p.m. news shows or sitcom reruns. The spin, from their point of view, was that some affiliates were thinking of dropping *The Tonight Show* (which has national sponsors and less opportunities for money-making local advertising). If they were able to make up some of that money by getting a few extra minutes of commercials during a lengthened news show, then they wouldn't be tempted to simply schedule two sitcoms at 11:30.

Johnny received more irritating news. It was also in May of 1991 that Dennis Miller announced he would be competing with a new talk show. Miller, a stand-up comic from Pittsburgh, had become the biggest *Saturday Night Live* wiseguy since Chevy Chase. His version of the "Weekend Update" news was mordant and salty, influenced by past masters like Mort Sahl.

Asked what the new show would be like, Miller said, "It'll be much like the standard late night talk shows. It'll have a couch, chair, a rock band and celebrity guests. And I'll open with a monologue."

Clearly the big difference, then, would be youthful hipness.

Miller liked to spit out tough, irreverent one-liners and challenging, vitriolic observations. On Hare Krishnas: "It says in the Bible, God created us in his own image. I just know he wouldn't wear his hair like that... Daddy Warbucks with a fuckin' Slinky hanging off the side of his head." On female gymnasts: "I love this activity since the summer Olympics. Specifically the women's uneven parallel bar event. I think I'm gonna be a little skeptical the next time a woman tells me I'm being too rough in bed. I'm watchin' these girls bang their cervix off a frozen theater rope at 80 miles per hour. You don't see men in that event, ok... if I ever hit anything that hard with my dick I'm gonna spot-weld to it." And on born-again Christians: "I'm a little indignant when they tell me I'm going to hell if I haven't been born again. Pardon me for getting it right the first time!"

A self-admitted difficult personality, cynicism and arrogance were Miller's choice of weapons even in some social settings. The man with the piercing black marble eyes and nasal sneer was not known for sentiment. Yet when Johnny had Dennis on his show and wished him good luck, even Miller was melted by the Carson charm. "Who is classier than this?" Miller asked.

In June, *The New York Times* theorized on who the new King of late night might be. Their choice: Arsenio Hall. "His ratings have dipped over the past several months," it was admitted, "but the show's audience is predominantly young, and that's an invaluable plus with advertisers. Mr. Hall's on-camera persona can be endearing or grating, depending on your mood or his. Some of his established routines are already a bit tired. The woof-woof antics used to rev up the audience at the beginning of each show could use a rest. The milking of audience hysteria might be toned down, though evidently the host really does store up energy from the spectacle. And the opening monologues are embarrassingly uneven, at their worst when Mr. Hall looks at the prompter cards and clearly realizes that the material he is about to deliver is weak. That's when he generally slips into a bad case of the cutes, stammering slightly, laughing curiously to himself, and assuring the audience that "that's — heh heh – funny."

During the miseries of the affiliate and corporate meetings, Johnny Carson nostalgically dropped by his old NBC studios in Rockefeller Plaza. It was his first time back in the nearly two decades since he took the show out to California. He made a brief appearance on David Letterman's show. The last time he'd appeared live on that program was six years earlier, when Dave brought the show to Los Angeles for a week.

Carson gave Letterman a put-on view of his retirement plans: "I've always wanted to be a shepherd. It's just one of those things that appeals to me, to just go out there and sow a little grain or something... just sit there with the missus."

Johnny had not specified his replacement when he announced his retirement, and NBC had not made a decision. Letterman reiterated to interviewers that he would not mind replacing Johnny: "If it were offered to me, I would certainly take it. I'd like to at least be considered for the gig."

It seemed logical that Letterman would be up for the job. Letterman's show was co-produced by Carson Productions. While Carson had joked during an anniversary special with Garry Shandling, Jay Leno and David Letterman, bringing them out individually and assuring them that each was his favorite, it was clear that Letterman *really* was.

The question was whether at this point Johnny had any control over the situation.

Just two weeks after NBC got its way with the 11:35 time slot, the network announced its choice for the new host of *The Tonight Show:* Jay Leno.

Looking at his calendar and noticing the date, June 6, 1991, Leno quipped to reporters, "this is probably the only profession where you go in, meet your future bosses and they say, 'Great, you'll start in a year!'"

NBC was happy with the stats. Leno would get $3 million instead of Johnny's $15 million. Leno at 41 was a full 24 years younger than Carson. And they would get the workhorse Leno Monday through Friday, not Wednesday through Friday. And while Johnny was only working 37 weeks of the year, they were figuring on Jay to take a modest two-or-four week vacation.

Leno said, "When I called my mother, she said, 'Oh, I love Johnny. Why can't Johnny stay and maybe they can find something else you can do? Isn't there another time spot for you?' I said, 'Ma, whatever you do, don't talk to the press.'"

Carson wasn't talking to the press. Except to say that "they didn't ask me one way or another. NBC never discussed it with me. But he's a bright young comic and I wish him every success."

He commiserated with David Letterman on the air, joking, "How... pissed off... *are* you?"

Dave had trusted NBC to do the right thing. While Jay Leno and others were out campaigning for *The Tonight Show* job, Dave had refused to do anything so corny or blatant. He recalled, "When Johnny was still there, it would have hurt *my* feelings if he'd thought that I was politicking for his job... So what I did was take every opportunity, if asked, to go on record as saying 'Yes, I would like to be considered for the job.' I wasn't comfortable with anything more than that. Because in essence what I would be saying was 'John, the clock is ticking, it's time to go.'"

NBC added insult to Dave's injury. They sold old re-runs of his show to the Arts & Entertainment cable network. He hadn't been told, and newspaper columnist Cindy Adams reported that due to contractual fine print, "Letterman gets s... "

The thinking at NBC was that Leno had proven his ability to perform at 11:30 after so many years as a guest host. Leno, born in New Rochelle, raised in Andover, Massachusetts, had always been a company man. He had worked in a Ford dealership as a teen, and when he was fired for dropping a hubcap,Leno wrote to Henry Ford II asking for some fair-and-square treatment. He got his job back. Over the years, Leno enjoyed the reputation of being the "blue collar" comedian, a workhorse ready any time a nightclub owner needed a reliable performer. While he enjoyed political satire, he also believed in truth, justice and the sanctity of womanhood. If a woman felt one of his jokes was in poor taste, out it went. Leno idolized Mort Sahl, but did not believe in Mort's cheerful "Is there any group I haven't offended?" Jay's chiding style was to point out laughable ironies without turning off a potential ticket buyer.

NBC knew that Letterman enjoyed turning off members of the audience. While Dave seemed to have a solid Midwest upbringing (he was born and raised in Indianapolis and attended Ball State University), he was always a wiseguy. On the university's classical radio station he would make strange announcements: "That was *Clair de Lune*. You know the de Lune sisters. There was Claire and there was Mabel." While a weatherman on local TV he would declare "The hailstones today were the size of canned hams!"

As the host of *Late Night*, Letterman liked to admit, "We may have alienated as many people as we may have won over, because there are people who hate me and hate the show." In truth, his show was often best watched on tape, with the fast-forward button handy. He seemed prone toward echolalia, often seizing on a phrase and repeating it till he would declare, "I'm even beginning to annoy myself!" When he'd giddily become obsessed with flipping the pencil on his desk or making his tie move by pulling on the shoulders of his jacket, even arthritics were compelled to flip that dial.

Warren Littlefield, president of NBC's entertainment division, had been one of the executives to question Dave's "quirky" style. Now he met with Letterman in an effort to soothe him. It did a lot of good. It gave Dave a new target for laughs. Letterman placed a photo of Littlefield on the set of his show and took to making desultory wisecracks about him.

Jay Leno was conciliatory: "I don't think I would have this job if it wasn't for David. I think Dave does the brightest stuff on TV, and I'm always annoyed when I watch other talk shows and they lift, verbatim, chunks that Dave has made famous... What we don't want to do is the same shows back-to-back. Letterman is the innovator there. I think of *The Tonight Show* as a talk show that has comedy and *Late Night* as a comedy show that has guests on occasion... I'd like to do cross-promotional stuff with him, plug each other's shows, make it an NBC night."

Leno and Letterman had a mutual admiration of each other's work and had begun in stand-up around the same time. Both were so down-to-earth they did their own warm-ups, even coming into the audience to answer questions. Letterman was not about to attack Jay.

Asked by writer Tom Shales if it was true that he was fit to be tied, Dave said, "I've never been tied in my life. There's not a man alive who can tie me."

And he insisted Leno would do "a fine job."

As for the forgotten man in all of this, Johnny

Carson, May of 1991 had been hellish. There was Michael Landon's wrenching appearance on the show. There was the life crisis of retirement and the insult of the time slot cutback, his "lame duck" status and the hoopla surrounding his replacement. It didn't seem things could get worse.

On June 19, 1991, Carson's son, Ricky, celebrated his 39th birthday. Three days later, Ricky's car slid 125 feet down an embankment and he was killed instantly.

Less than two weeks after Ricky Carson was killed, the man who had appeared so vibrant on that recent *Tonight Show*, Michael Landon, passed away.

Johnny gave a statement: "This has been a devastating week for me and my family. Michael called last Monday expressing his deepest sympathy on the death of my son Ricky. The courage and sensitivity he showed in our conversation, in comforting me when he was in great pain, attests to the quality of the man and his great character."

When Johnny returned to *The Tonight Show* on July 17, he opened with his usual monologue. Nothing, absolutely nothing, would interfere with the light heart and good humor that fans expected from him every night. For nearly thirty years, it was his duty and his pride to give America a laugh and a good night's sleep no matter what the news was at eleven.

It was only in the last minutes of the show that he allowed himself to talk about his own troubles. When the newspapers headlined the tragic story of Ricky Carson, they ran the only picture available of Ricky, the little photo on his driver's license.

"These have not been the most happy several weeks," Johnny admitted, his dry mouth straining against his words. He showed the audience a photo of Ricky. "I'm not doing this to be mawkish," he said. "I don't think any of you would want to be remembered by your driver's license picture."

He kept it very brief. "He left some marvelous memories for the whole family, and that's what you hang on to." Ricky was a photographer. He had left an impressive portfolio of pictures. Asking the audience to "forgive a father's pride," the show ended with a portfolio of Ricky's photographs, including a sunset.

The Tonight Show continued. Johnny periodically joked about his lame duck status and the odd situation of dragging out his retirement for nearly a full year. Most of his jokes remained topical, and his comments, both political and social, were often as sharp as anything to be heard from Arsenio, Let-ter-man or guest host Jay.

His supposedly easy and safe Carnak routines could bounce nearly out of bounds. Answer: "French toast." Question: "What does a very lonely Pepperidge Farm baker do?"

He never hesitated when a joke was a little off color, weird, or both:

"Never trust a door-to-door condom salesman who uses his own body as a display case."

Complaining about the anti-porn antics of Ed Meese, Johnny said it was going too far to "hire construction workers to sandblast the boobs off the statue of Justice."

Even the bad boys of comedy would've thought twice about some of Carson's lines. He talked about a great way of getting a free lunch: "If you sit next to a blind man at Sizzler, you can sometimes steal his onion rings."

Carson often had wiseguy answers as hip as anything the young guys could think of. When someone asked, "What made you a star?" Johnny answered, "I started out in a gaseous state, and then I cooled."

On screen Carson remained cool, even as the "countdown" to Johnny's last show became a hot media event. Tributes came from all over. *TV Guide* interviewed the two surviving guests from Johnny's first show, Tony Bennett and Mel Brooks. Bennett recalled with irony how Carson left his desk after the first show and said, "Well, that's the first one. I hope this works." Mel added, "Johnny is the greatest audience known to man because he listens and *gets it*. You can go very far out and it won't be wasted. He will always get it. We will never again get a guy that is, in the old-fashioned sense, so fair and square — but who can also be so devilishly witty."

Guests eagerly signed up for the historic last months of the show, glad to have one more chance with Johnny. He brought out his old characters, from his beloved and perpetually failing El Moldo to Art Fern and Carnak, for their last bows.

For the last three months of Carson's reign, NBC raised its rates for commercials, until by the last week, they had gone up five times the regular rate: from $40,000 for a thirty-second spot to $200,000.

Talk show TV was at its best during those last weeks of Johnny's run on *The Tonight Show*. The magic was there every night. The guests came on just for the joy of joking and talking.

They came for the reason talk shows had first become popular: to share their humor and their personalities, not to sell things. They arrived with their best anecdotes and were attentive to both the host and the other guests. They came to entertain Johnny, not the other way around.

Steve Martin had never performed his legendary "Great Flydini" routine on TV; he practiced for weeks to perfect it and give it to Johnny as a special gift. Elizabeth Taylor made her first *Tonight Show* appearance ever, just to thank Johnny for thirty years of great entertainment. As a favor, Bill Cosby tried to perform his classic "Noah" routine. He had to quit, both men chuckling, when he confessed, "This is all I remember, John!"

It had been said often and endlessly, that Johnny's show was soothing, that he washed away a nation's troubles enough for another night's sleep. So it was ironic that the last weeks came after the tumult of the L.A. riots. The nation wanted and needed Johnny those nights. To go to bed happy, members of the studio audience had been willing to wait on line from five o'clock in the morning for the chance to get a ticket.

The atmosphere those last weeks was sparkling and spontaneous. Even Ed McMahon could get in a wisecrack. Ed asked Johnny about coming out on his yacht, something Carson had resisted for years.

"Where would we go?" Johnny wanted to know.

Ed shrugged. "Down to Redondo Beach."

"Wait a minute! You're at Marina Del Rey! You're gonna take me to Redondo Beach? What a cruise! Redondo Beach! I can *walk* there from Marina Del Rey."

Ed said, "You'd probably walk on the water."

Johnny broke up. That was the kind of thing he really wanted to hear. Irreverent comedy was a big part of the show when he first arrived on *The Tonight Show*, and he was not going to get overly sentimental even thirty years later. Some of his contemporaries recognized that. Jonathan Winters resisted any maudlin praise. He told Carson he didn't think retirement was so bad for him; "It sounds like a downer, but *you're* going straight to the bank!"

When David Letterman made his farewell appearance with Johnny, he was pragmatic: "People keep asking me, are you gonna miss Johnny... " He looked at Carson and said, "First of all, you're *not* passin' away. You're still funny. You're vibrant, you're charming, energetic, entertaining, a very nice guy. You're *not* going to prison, like many of our top Hollywood stars. You're *still* gonna be in show busi-

ness, you're gonna be on television. I have a show —
you could be on *my* show. You could be a guest."

The crowd applauded in approval. Dave was still
revved up: "You could be a guest host! Come to think
of it, you can have the damned thing!"

Johnny smiled calmly and said, "Still pissed,
huh?"

Many guests wanted to use their final appearance
to give Johnny a tribute, but he would modestly
wave it away and change the subject. But if some of
his comic colleagues couldn't do it seriously, at least
they could do it for a laugh: on three different programs, Steve Martin, Bob Newhart and Rodney
Dangerfield all pretended to burst into tears, crying
at Carson, "Don't go! Don't go!"

Buddy Hackett's face went red and his eyes
popped in mock anger as he growled, "I'm angry
about that Pat Sajak! He said he was gonna chase
you off the air and he did it!"

But after the gag, Buddy faltered, and for the first
time in all his many appearances he grasped for
words. He repeatedly tried to describe his feelings for
Johnny, giving his heartfelt appreciation for all the
times Johnny had let him come on to plug upcoming
live shows, or the times Johnny had helped out at
the last minute by making charity appearances with
him. Even more than helping out a friend, Buddy
praised the way Johnny had helped out so many
young comics. It wasn't just booking them. He pointed out to the audience the way Carson guided young
comics through their nervousness and played the
perfect straight man, feeding them lines that they
could convert into confidence-building laughs.

Johnny gently touched Buddy's hand and said,
"Don't get sentimental on me." But in a voice that
trembled with emotion, Buddy found himself unable
to hold back, saying "I can't thank you enough... I
can't thank you enough... Some people, you go on

with them and they're supposed to give you a plug. They couldn't care less if they say it clearly or if they get the date right... "

Johnny wouldn't hear of it. He said it was a two-way street. He deflected all of Buddy's warm praise. He pointed out that for a comic to appear on a show that paid scale, and to entertain with fifteen solid minutes of laughs, the least a talk show host could do was give the man a little plug for a local concert.

The tribute for many of Johnny's friends was to come out and give *The Tonight Show* one more memorable night of entertainment. When the two surviving guests from that very first show, Mel Brooks and Tony Bennett, made their final appearance that last week, they electrified the crowd with their very best.

Bennett belted out "I Left My Heart in San Francisco" as if he was singing it for the first time. He sang one of Johnny's favorite tunes, the poignant ballad "I'll Be Seeing You." Then he unveiled a pen-and-ink portrait of Johnny as a final tribute. Johnny showed a picture taken at that very first *Tonight Show*. He was mortified looking at the cheap, chintzy decorations that served as the set for Tony Bennett's songs that night. Tony looked at the picture, and then said to Johnny, "It's not where you started, it's where you finish."

The crowd applauded.

Mel Brooks, indulging Johnny, told Carson's favorite anecdote, the long and hilarious story of Mel's meeting with Cary Grant. Later Johnny played straight man to Mel's "2000 Year Old Man." Mel said simply, "In the forty years that I know you, you always *listened*. The other hosts, whether it was Merv or Les Crane, they never looked at you. They were concerned with somebody off-camera. You always were a mensch, a gentleman."

Each night brought more friends, from Richard Harris and Carl Reiner, to Clint Eastwood and Bob

Hope. Recognizing the emotional strain Johnny had to be under, they all came to praise Johnny, not to bury him. They knew Johnny would prefer a friendly handshake and a smile to a tearful hug of farewell.

Roseanne Arnold spoke for the fans when, in her most endearing little-girl voice, she groused, "Why do ya have to *do* this? Why do ya have ta quit?"

Reassuring even when it was *his* trauma, Johnny simply answered, "That's nice of you. I want to quit while I'm on top of my game." He mentioned an anecdote about opera singer Beverly Sills. She said, "I would much rather have people say to me why did you quit rather than why *didn't* you quit." He smiled and added, "You go out when everything's going great."

On the night of May 21, Johnny came out to an overwhelming tidal wave of applause. When the music for Johnny's theme stopped, it took an unbelievable one minute and thirty five seconds before Johnny could begin the monologue. The crowd would not stop, even as Johnny called out, barely audible over the din, "please... come on... please... please sit down." He gave up, looking over at Doc and at Ed, his hands upraised as if to say "What can I do?" At last he tried again. "Folks," he said, "it's getting embarrassing!"

He kept trying to speak, and finally over the roar he said, "Folks! I'll be very honest with you, I don't think I could *take* another night of this!"

When he was finally able to start his monologue, he still deflected all sentiment. "It's almost over... All we have is tonight and tomorrow." He paused. "I haven't used that line since World War II!

"Look, it's not like we're never gonna see each other again!"

Each night, before the interviews and songs, Johnny sat at the desk and showed a few vintage clips from the vault. For this, his last program with celebrity guests on the panel, he played the Ed Ames clip.

"We weren't gonna play this," he said, still sensitive about the cutting remarks made by young critics. "We haven't played it in seven years." But by popular demand, he gave in and gave it one last time. The night it happened, the errant hatchet had provided one of the longest laughs in television history: 45 seconds of roars from the moment it landed before Johnny could say a word. And when he said, "I didn't know you were Jewish," the laughs kept right on going.

The laughs kept right on going this night, too. What was so special about it now, after so many reruns? Nothing much. A sight gag and an ad-lib. Just one small example of what Johnny had done for thirty years. He gave us the unexpected, and then he topped it.

All through the last weeks he had dusted off memorable sketches, commercial parodies and even silly slapstick. Like funny faces in a family scrapbook, they produced a warm smile. Like a pair of Johnny's idols, Laurel and Hardy, the laughs came even when the audience knew the routines almost as well as the comics did.

Johnny always enjoyed the spirit of silliness behind Laurel and Hardy. He was also influenced by the slickness of Bob Hope, the devilish whimsy of Jonathan Winters, the tangy self-parody of Jackie Gleason, the wit of Groucho Marx, the good nature of Red Skelton and the beloved humanity of Jack Benny. The influences were all there. But at the finish, thirty years later, Johnny Carson had become a legend too.

The last two guests booked for *The Tonight Show* gave it a memorable finish. Robin Williams worked full tilt, putting on a final blazing show just for Johnny, putting out all of his energy for what was more a half hour's concert than an interview.

Bette Midler sang a comic version of "You Made Me Love You," now dubbed "You Made Me Watch You." There was irreverent sass to many of her lines: "I watched your hair turn slowly from dark to white. And when I can't sleep I count your wives at night."

She ended up sitting on Johnny's desk, vamping, "How am I gonna get by without you, you sexy thing!"

When she sat down, she talked of all the many great moments in her life that had come from *The Tonight Show* and Johnny, and she shared the emotions of exhilaration and anxiety that came with her very first audition and now, this very last appearance.

For weeks, for years, performers had sat opposite Johnny and in some small way tried to express their feelings for him. Some nights it was a young comic trying to say "This has always been my dream, and it's come true." Some nights it was an old pro hoping that by making an appearance for scale, and with nothing to plug, Johnny realized the unspoken words: "I respect you; you're the best."

This one night, this one moment, Bette Midler looked into Johnny's eyes and began to sing a soft chorus of the sad, haunting "Here's That Rainy Day." Along with the song Tony Bennett had sung, "I'll Be Seeing You," it was Carson's favorite.

And this one night, this one moment, Johnny's eyes reflected back all the love and emotion he felt in his heart. Silence gripped the studio. The moment belonged to Johnny and to Bette Midler. Theirs was an intimate, touching duet as they both softly sang, on this last show together, "Here's That Rainy Day."

Gazing into the earnest face of Bette Midler, Johnny sang wistfully to *all* his fans. Gazing at her sweet lips, he sang a sad goodbye to *The Tonight Show*. But gazing into her moist eyes, his voice sounded smooth and assured; there would be so much more in the future, for both Johnny and everyone who was touched by him.

She sang "One More for My Baby, and One More for the Road," while Johnny sniffed and held back a tear.

Bette kissed Johnny and wreathed his neck with a Hawaiian lei. Then she rushed backstage, overcome with emotion.

The following night, Johnny showed film clips of past shows. It moved quickly, like taking a plane ride over the Grand Canyon. Every viewer was waiting for that final emotional moment, the journey's end. But they wanted to savor the ride, too, even as all the memorable sights were slipping by.

The studio audience that night was made up-of the show's staff and their families, along with members of Johnny's own family and his friends.

They wanted him to stay. He didn't want to go.

It was out of his control, but not his final moments on *The Tonight Show*. He was still its master of ceremonies and its master.

"And so it has come to this," he said at the end. "You people watching — it has been an honor and a privilege coming into your homes and entertaining you."

His eyes were a little moist and there was an edge of sadness in his voice, but he made it quick and he got through the last, simple sentence: "I bid you a very heartfelt goodnight."

CHAPTER SIXTEEN

THEY'RE AFTER JAY'S ASS — NOT TO MENTION HIS KUSHNICK

On December 17, 1969, *The Tonight Show* had attracted over 50 million viewers for the wedding of Tiny Tim to Miss Vicki. That union did not last long.

On May 22, 1992, over 50 million viewers now paid tribute to Johnny Carson's unprecedented, undefeated, unbelievable thirty years of *The Tonight Show*.

Johnny's last show, Friday night, attracted an average 63 percent of the available viewership at that hour. In some cities it was less. In New York where nightlife is plentiful, 56 percent tuned in. In Portland, Oregon, 77 percent tuned in.

On Monday, Jay Leno's premiere received an average 38 percent share.

NBC was not too happy with Jay's numbers, but when Johnny Carson retired, many viewers simply said "goodnight" too. Like *The Ed Sullivan Show* decades earlier, *The Tonight Show* saluted excellence; only the best young comics, the best singers, the best stars were good enough. When Leno came in, the show wasn't special anymore. The Ramones, Howard Stern, the Arc Angels... anybody could get on. That is, if they paid homage to Leno's manager, Helen Kushnick.

The warm feelings of nostalgia and tribute that had flooded over *The Tonight Show* during Johnny's last weeks, were on-camera only. Behind the scenes there was a cold power struggle between the old and the new. Helen Kushnick had gotten herself appointed *The Tonight Show* producer, at a million bucks a year. Her idea of a smooth transition was to insist, "Carson should have retired ten years ago." As for the "old men" who she said were too plentiful on Johnny's staff, "They're history. Take a look around. I'm hiring women. I'm giving all the women a chance."

"I guess it was like the White House with George Bush," one staffer says. "The old leader goes, and all of his best people have to be thrown out with him. What hurt was that Jay wasn't such a new guy. He had used us for years as the guest host. But now we weren't good enough. Even the older people who would have left with Johnny anyway; they had a bitter taste in their mouths. It was like, "Come on, hurry up, clear out your desk and get the hell out.' Those last weeks were very draining, emotionally."

TV Guide wondered, what of "the host's refusal to wish *Tonight Show* successor Jay Leno good luck?"

Says a staffer, "I wouldn't offer best wishes to someone who wished me dead. Johnny knew what Helen Kushnick was all about."

When Johnny left the show, he maintained his silence. It was as if he disappeared off the face of the planet.

"Where's Johnny?" "Oh, enjoying retirement. Playing tennis. Over in Europe some place. On the beach at Malibu."

But back in downtown Burbank, Johnny's sidekicks had trouble maintaining their professional cool.

Ed McMahon pointed out that Leno would not have been *his* choice to take over the show. He would have chosen... Jerry Seinfeld.

For years the faithful mugwump, now Ed showed his independence. He pointedly refused to appear on

The Tonight Show as a guest. His mug turned up on the enemy, Arsenio Hall's, show instead, and as he wumped down into a seat next to Hall, the crowd whooped.

Ed felt a kinship with Arsenio's young audience, since his *Star Search* show was geared toward young kids fantasizing about show biz fame. He booked young performers and was viewed as a benevolent grandpa. He was looking forward to a new daily version of *Star Search*, and to getting as far away from Helen Kushnick and Jay Leno's *Tonight Show* as possible.

Doc Severinsen had more reason to loathe NBC and the new regime than Ed McMahon. Dumping Doc's big band was a high priority in re-making the show into something young and hip. The added injury was that after thirty years of service, Doc wasn't going to be allowed to make a living on the road with "The Tonight Show Band." Even though they were all being let go, the name had to stay.

Doc said that he wasn't going to be watching *The Tonight Show* with Jay Leno. For one thing, he couldn't get past the opening credits, where a plethora of multi-colored curtains kept rising or parting: "What is that?" Doc laughed. "It looks like a bunch of ladies underwear."

Why not? Helen Kushnick expected ass-kissing, so why not hang her undies up to be worshipped, too?

Juan Peron had Evita. Ronald Reagan had Nancy. Jay Leno had Helen Kushnick. For years Jay had left all the decisions and power to his trusted "right hand." And that hand had slowly become a huge fist that pounded and thrashed out in all directions. *The Tonight Show* quickly got the reputation for being a chaotic, unpleasant place to be. The firings, the arrogance and the new rules and dictums being handed down by Kushnick and her crowd were becoming the talk of the tight-knit TV industry.

"It wasn't as seamless a transition as we had hoped," NBC's entertainment president Warren Littlefield admitted. "Obviously we had a problem and that was with the executive producer."

Littlefield had been too far out of the loop to know that Kushnick had been a petty tyrant for years. It's just that with so many sharks in the water, it was difficult to tell which ones were the true killers.

In her role as Leno's manager, she was expected to be obnoxious. Many managers were. It was necessary for a manager to act as if her client was the greatest performer on earth and worth the highest salary. Kushnick prided herself as being Ms. Machiavelli, as much of a player as any other manager.

She was a tough bargainer with nightclubs seeking Jay's services. "So you don't like me?" she told one club booker. "So, do you think I care?"

Leno always looked the other way. "When I would do small comedy clubs," he recalled, "the manager or owner would say, 'Boy, your manager, what a pain in the ass. You should get someone else... ' But Jay had a different way of thinking: "It wasn't my manager overdoing her job. It was the other people not doing theirs."

Back in 1988, when Leno was still the "warhorse" doing hundreds of comedy concerts on the road, Kushnick refused to allow Jay to do an interview with the comedy club magazine *Rave*. This, even though he was in those clubs over 200 times a year. This, even though *Rave* was the acknowledged best friend of young comics, responsible for the balloting on the "Young Comedians" award for the *ABC Comedy Awards* show. "What the *Wall Street Journal* is to stockbrokers," George Carlin said, "*Rave* is to comedy."

Why in the world would a manager refuse *Rave* an interview? "I won't let you have Jay," Helen ruled.

"I'm changing his image. He's not just a comedy club comic. We don't need that kind of exposure."

The bottom line: "Don't argue with success." Jay was hawking Doritos in TV commercials. He was taking a stab at the movies with a comedy action film called *Collision Course*. His manager took the credit for guiding him up from his first appearance on *The Tonight Show* in 1977 to his reward in 1987 of being named permanent guest host.

Leno took it all lightly: "Permanent guest host? That's a triple oxymoron, three words in a row that contradict the one before." Kushnick took it seriously. As soon as he became the permanent guest host, she began setting the stage for Jay's takeover as host of *The Tonight Show*.

Helen told Jay to start toadying. Whenever he was touring, she made sure that Jay dutifully visited the city's NBC affiliate. Any way that Jay could ingratiate himself was fine with Helen, whether it was just glad-handing around the office or doing little promotions. The affiliates were all quite impressed with the nice, helpful and hard-working up-and-coming comic.

Jay learned to take pride in playing the game. He was always quick to admit, "The thing that got me *The Tonight Show* is that I would visit every NBC affiliate where I was performing and do promos for them. Then they would promote me in turn. My attitude was to go out and rig the numbers in my favor."

But each year that Johnny held off on his retirement, Helen Kushnick got more impatient. More than one NBC executive heard her grumbling about Carson, "When's he gonna die?"

Jay uttered no such remarks, though he admitted that he and Johnny were not pals. They went to dinner together a few times over the years, and that was it: "I mean, there's a social and economic barrier and, I guess, an age difference... We have a professional friendship. I don't hang out with him. He's not a car guy; he's a tennis player. Our interests are not all that similar. If he was into cars, I'd be over there every day."

Slowly members of *The Tonight Show* began to see that the permanent guest host had a manager who was a little out of control. Alarm bells didn't go off loudly yet, mostly because Johnny still seemed to hold the power position. But some of those around Johnny showed a great deal of caution in dealing with Jay.

Ed McMahon was one of them. If Helen Kushnick was trying to jockey her boy into Johnny's chair, Ed was not going to help with an endorsement. Asked who he watched, aside from Carson, he made Jay Leno a distant third choice: "I'll watch the competition — Arsenio Hall or Dennis Miller — and once in a while I'll watch Leno to see how he's doing... "

Arsenio Hall knew what Jay and Helen were doing. The war between *The Tonight Show* and Arsenio had escalated while Jay was guest-hosting.

Hall issued a challenge even before the premiere of Leno's version of *The Tonight Show*.

Back in November of 1989, Arsenio Hall and Jay Leno appeared together on the over of *Rolling Stone*. They looked like a happy couple, both grinning, Arsenio digging a finger into Jay's cheek as if trying to create a cute dimple. Arsenio said of Jay, "I love him." Then he added, "But when he got his job with Johnny, I thought that should've been me."

In the December 1990 issue of *Playboy*, Leno was saying, "I genuinely like Arsenio. He and I started together. I taught him to ride a motorcycle. We used to hang out every night... People think of us as being in competition. I suppose, to a certain extent, we are, but the shows are so different. He doesn't do a lot of political things, and I don't get in there and mix it up with the band."

A few months later, and the talk show war had heated up. Hall was no longer pulling his punches: "Leno can't replace Johnny. I think it's an insult to his legacy to say Jay is replacing him. Johnny's been too good."

Then Arsenio stopped boxing and threatened to start kicking.

Hall told one of the weekly magazines, "I always hear that Jay and I are friends... Jay Leno and I aren't friends! And you know what? I wasn't anointed, OK? No one put the late-night silver spoon in *my* mouth. I earned every drop of mine... And I'm gonna treat him like we treated the kid on the high-school basketball team who was the coach's son... We tried to kick his ass, and that's what I'm going to do — kick Jay's ass."

A Leno defender, Howard Stern, came to Jay's defense. He called Arsenio "Ass Smoochio," and claimed, "He's the guy who kisses your ass. Everything is safe on that show."

Helen Kushnick wasn't about to let anybody get into a fight with her Jay. Now that Jay wasn't the guest host, but *the star*, nobody was going to get in the way. She issued her own declaration of war: "Anybody who appears on Arsenio Hall's show will never, ever appear on *The Tonight Show.*"

It didn't matter how big that show business celebrity was. Elizabeth Taylor was shocked to get a call on her home phone from the aggressive new producer of *The Tonight Show*. Kushnick told Taylor to cancel a planned appearance with Arsenio. Liz could't believe Helen's harangue. The only reason for appearing on Arsenio's show was to raise money for her AIDS charity. When Liz pointed this out, Kushnick loudly challenged her to prove that this was a completely legitimate charity. Kushnick intimated that someone should investigate Taylor's supposed AIDS group. Elizabeth Taylor's lawyer sent a strongly worded letter in response.

Bill Cosby, long a favored guest of Johnny's, was treated with contempt by Kushnick. Cos was always the first guest of the night, and Fred De Cordova made sure that the other guests were compatible. Kushnick, having purged the staff of all Carson loyalists, wasn't about to cater to guests who were in any way close to Johnny.

Cosby was already wearing his cautious, stern face as he finalized arrangements to do the show. He had heard the veiled threats about not doing Arsenio's show and didn't like it. Then he got the final insult: Kushnick had scheduled Howard Stern to be the co-featured guest. Cos canceled.

David Brokaw, Cosby's publicist, declared, "Bill is fond of Jay Leno and he's also fond of Arsenio Hall, and is supportive of *both* shows." He went on to admit that Cosby was, at the very least, "puzzled" by Kushnick's attitude.

More "puzzled" were Jay Leno's contemporaries. Jerry Seinfeld wanted to use *The Tonight Show* set in an episode. Permission was denied. He wasn't even allowed to use a similar-looking set or the show's logo.

Stand-up comic Robert Wuhl, a friend of Jay's for over a dozen years, appeared on Howard Stern's radio show to decry the shoddy booking practices on *The Tonight Show*. He had hoped to appear on his friend Jay's show to promote a recent breakthrough movie, but was turned down.

Since he had Jay's home number, and they had been such friends, Wuhl decided to call Jay and find out what was going on. Jay professed innocence of the entire situation and told his pal to just call up the office again. When Robert Wuhl did, he was given another icy put-down. This time there was an added warning: "Don't call Jay at home."

Robert Wuhl appeared on David Letterman's

show instead.

Not that Dave was really taking sides in the dispute between Wuhl and Leno. Letterman was also staying out of the feud between Leno and Arsenio. In fact, the only talk show host Dave was attacking was a guy who had recently retired: Merv Griffin.

For some reason, Letterman enjoyed joking about some of Merv's well-known personal problems, from weight gains to the tabloid reports of a secret gay lifestyle.

One night Gene Siskel asked Dave, "If you could interview anyone who would it be?"

Letterman answered, "Merv Griffin's pool boy."

Another night, Letterman held up an unflattering old photo of himself. He looked fat in the picture, which was taken before he dieted down from 200 pounds to 180. Looking at the photo, he said, "My goal was to weigh more than Merv Griffin ever did. I wanted to be the fattest talk show host on television. Big, fat and greasy!"

While Dave took shots at Griffin, Leno and Hall continued to exchange potent fire. Mostly it was a tug-of-war over guests.

When an actor asked to change his booking so it wouldn't come before *The Tonight Show*, Hall was enraged. He left a message for the guy, and the most mild line of it was "Just do the other show and get out of my face."

"I don't want any of this second-hand crap," Arsenio told a staffer. Everyone got the message. One comic who had shown up for the program after appearing with Jay a few weeks earlier was told: "No re-runs, here. You've got other jokes? Use 'em!"

Hall made it clear that he expected his guests to bring fresh anecdotes and stories: "I don't wanna hear anything for the *second* time."

The Tonight Show continued to play tough. One way of making sure the big stars fell into line was to intimidate them by not booking their lesser-known friends. Tim Allen appeared on Arsenio's show, so Helen Kushnick not only canceled his *Tonight Show* spot, but also dumped actress Sheila Kelley, who was also a client of Allen's publicist.

Columnist Kay Gardella tried to defend Kushnick: "Of course, tact helps. That's probably why Fred De Cordova, who for years did the books for Carson, was never the cause of such an industry-wide rebellion. But, if you'd permit just a tad of feminism to enter this argument, he's also not a woman. Women in such capacities are easier prey. Too, they often develop a hard edge that rubs people the wrong way."

Somehow, it rubbed Dave Letterman the wrong way when he read a a story in *The Wall Street Journal* suggesting that Jay Leno's program be expanded to 90 minutes. The story was planted by Helen Kushnick. She was only thinking of NBC. If Letterman was so "pissed off" over losing out to Jay Leno, why keep him?

NBC executives loudly refuted the idea of a ninety- minute *Tonight Show*. They were getting a little tired of having to perform damage control every time the *Tonight Show* producer suddenly derailed.

If anyone needed more proof of the backstabbing world of the talk show wars, they could find it... on a new series created by Garry Shandling.

Shandling had been a player in *The Tonight Show* race for years. Almost as strange-looking as Jay Leno, he had a hairstyle that might be described as blow-dried muskrat. Tiny eyes blinked from his frozen face. His voice was a nasal whine, the jokes squeezing through a screen of Chiclet teeth wrapped in rubber lips. Most of his gags centered on not being able to get a date, which, considering the impression he made, was not surprising.

Bob Goldthwait said of him, "A lot of guys do

material about how they can't get a date. If that's Garry Shandling's problem, he could buy sex. I've got bigger worries."

In 1989 a *Cable Guide* Readers Poll chose Garry Shandling as the "Least Funny Comedian."

But who ever heard of *Cable Guide?* Certainly not the producers of *The Tonight Show.* They had found in Shandling an intelligent, laid-back young comic who could handle interviews well, ad-lib a clever line, and was no threat whatever to Johnny as a guest host.

Garry got his big break back in August of 1983. He was the guest host for a guest host. Albert Brooks, subbing for Carson, who couldn't make it. Garry filled in and did a smooth job. He ended the show saying, "Johnny, thank you. I can't tell you what it meant to me. I took your parking spot."

He replaced Joan Rivers for those last guest-host weeks on her contract, and then found himself battling with Jay Leno to become the number one candidate for replacing Johnny.

Shandling dropped out in favor of helming his own critically praised sitcom, but he never forgot what it was like to be caught up in the vicious talk show world. Now he was back with his revenge, pinning all the dirty linen on the line.

His *Larry Sanders Show* on HBO in 1992 skewered the idea of an informal chat show, pointing out how calculated every ad-lib could be. He cast himself as the cold and paranoid host.

The show was even more anti-talk-show than David Letterman, as one episode involving the obligatory "animal segment" proved. Johnny Carson's anniversary show almost always included his comical grimaces the night a tarantula crawled up to his neck. Letterman got the same kind of laughs when he let cockroaches crawl all over his desk or crickets careen on the floor. One of his highlights was the night he pretended to swat a rare insect that a bug expert had placed on his lapel.

For Shandling's version, host Larry Sanders lets a man place a tarantula on his arm. Larry suddenly screams, flings the spider away, breaks a bunch of glass cases and accidentally frees dozens of spiders. Bugs begin to crawl all over his special guest, Carol Burnett, who jumps onto his shoulders, screaming wildly.

What is, in reality, a moment of chaos and terror is, of course, applauded wildly. Larry is congratulated by his producer for a great show.

Shandling was aiming more at the new talk show hosts than the old one: "I really really miss Johnny," he said. "Carson was like Elvis or the Beatles. What do you do to replace them when they've gone?" Clearly, he wasn't thinking of Jay Leno.

In an interview with Howard Stern, Garry once again dismissed Leno, saying *Tonight* "is not as creative a show" as it could be.

Garry insisted that he was the number one choice of Tribune Entertainment to helm an opposing talk show, but he turned it down. Then Dennis Miller grabbed the job on the bounce. Not that he minded: "Unless you come on the air with some new approach to the talk show format, there's no reason to go on."

Shandling's parody of talk shows was something new. But it was fiction; it couldn't top the reality of what was going on at *The Tonight Show*.

TV industry insiders were beginning to realize that Helen Kushnick had not been kidding around with that "When's Carson gonna die?" stuff.

It was reported that the *New York Post* story in February – the one leaking the news of Carson being axed and Leno being chosen to replace him – had been another Kushnick trick. "What was the headline?" an ex-staffer on *The Tonight Show* asks. "It wasn't just that NBC was supposedly going to get rid of Carson. It was get rid of Carson and get Jay Leno. The big thing was mentioning Leno. OK, Johnny was heading toward his 30th year and he was fed up. Why fight it? But Arsenio Hall? He was getting this crap all the time. It's no wonder he was ready to kick Jay's ass."

The battle between *The Tonight Show* and *Arsenio* continued to rage and flare each time a celebrity came to town.

There was more competition than ever. Whoopi Goldberg's show premiered September 14, 1992. Her syndicated series was scheduled either before or after Arsenio Hall in many markets, creating a time block designed to battle Leno and Letterman. Whoopi said, "I've taken my cue from a show in England called *Face to Face* and from Dick Cavett. Those were the shows that I was interested in, that let you sit down and talk to somebody for a while... "

She lined up an impressive group of stars, from Burt Reynolds and Cher to Robert De Niro and Michael Douglas. A strong force in the film world since the success of her films *Ghost* and *Sister Act*, she and her agent had access to a lot of stars who didn't normally do talk shows.

As for that other talk show, *The Dennis Miller Show*, there was nobody left to talk to *him*.

Like Jay Leno, Dennis Miller had earned the respect of both Johnny Carson and David Letterman. Both brought him in as a guest even when it was announced that he'd be a new player in the late night game.

From the start, though, Dennis was a long shot. His syndication was weak and he was an unproven interviewer who had no experience handling the daily grind of a talk show. On *Saturday Night Live*, he could maintain a glower for five minutes, and be "outta here." Now he had to stay for a full hour.

Miller's quirks were magnified, his faults laid bare.

The show was strongly influenced by Letterman's program. But if Dave could be irritating, Dennis was sometimes doubly so as he muttered deliberately obscure non sequiturs and in-jokes in moments of crisis. Dave's snickery chuckle was nothing compared to Miller's incongruous, high-pitched mock-hysterical laugh.

Over the years, Letterman had become more flexible during interviews. At first brusque, intense and insulting, he was still the wiseguy but now much warmer, if not downright goofy and giddy at times. Miller, glowering and nasty in stand-up, a man who refused to smile for photographers because it wasn't in his image, learned that he couldn't be the same cold, sarcastic Dennis as a host. He needed time to comfortably develop a workable style.

Miller got little help from those around him. His sidekick was a pudgy non entity, excess furniture on the couch. Dennis had recruited some stand-up comics who shared his sharp sense of cynicism and misanthropy, but as writers they had barely put together enough really sharp lines for a half hour in comedy clubs. What they tossed out nightly was very thin. "There are nights," Miller admitted, "when something's not flying and I look out at my audience and say, "Wow, I can't believe I thought that was funny.'"

A lot of Miller's jokes were subtle or desultory, ending in a sarcastic remark rather than a real punch line: "The Bush administration has drawn up plans for another air strike against Saddam Hussein. This one will be called Operation Approval Rating."

There were few innovations on his show. One of his better segments, a "For and Against" look at a subject in the news, was just a variation on the ancient "Good News Bad News" routines of vaudeville. A "For and Against" argument about eating meat:

"For: Man, by nature is a hunter."

"Against: The meat department at Safeway isn't exactly the Serengeti Plain."

"For: Livestock farmers depend on red meat consumption for their livelihood."

"Against: So do colon specialists."

"For: Cattle? Come on, they're simple farm dwellers."

"Against: So are the Amish, and we don't eat them."

There weren't many memorable moments for Miller, no sax-playing Bill Clinton, insulting Cher or bumbling Ed Ames to grab headlines and instantly define the direction for future shows. One of the few guests to even show enthusiasm for the show was Carl Reiner. "You know how dogs and hyenas urinate in the corner of the yard?" he asked Miller. "I'm going to urinate in as many places as necessary to know that I'm welcome back here. I want to stake my territory!"

Nobody got into a pissing contest with Reiner. The Miller guest list often looked very blank. He angrily declared that his worst nightmare was "the talk show wars. I'm telling you the truth. As far as guests go, it's difficult to book people for a fledgling show like mine."

It got so bad Miller sought out the home phone numbers of celebrities and began dialing them up, saying, "Sorry to bother you, but I'm involved in publicist warfare here and I've got to cut through this."

Before he knew it, he was through.

The other talk show hosts were sympathetic.

Whoopi Goldberg booked Dennis after his show folded. He told her that doing his talk show was so exhausting he "passed out" at night after tapings. He had no time to play with his child, no time to savor the triumph of having his own show. Now he had the time to point out the underhanded antics he had endured.

"I know Arsenio wanted to kick my ass. That's the business. But all I can say is, he was never anything but a gentleman about it. People want their shows to work. They're seriously motivated, competitive people who want to win, but he did everything above-board and classy. *The Tonight Show,* my experience with them was cold, detached, they were more faceless about it and they leaned on people. It does exist, there was pressure from other shows not to do our show. I'm not manufacturing it."

On *Regis and Kathie Lee,* Dennis told Regis Philbin that there were more pitfalls to doing a talk show than he ever could have imagined. One basic problem was simply having the right time slot. "You realize it doesn't matter how good you are or how good the show is. It's where the show is placed, at what time and on what station if you're gonna go the syndicated route."

Dennis Miller said that the "worst repercussion of Johnny Carson leaving" was not the spate of new talk shows. It was something far more terrifying: "Ed McMahon's *Star Search* on five nights a week."

Arsenio Hall extended a hand to Dennis Miller. He invited Dennis to make a surprise appearance on *Arsenio,* doing the opening monologue.

As for Jay Leno, Dennis said, "Jay helped me find my first apartment in L.A. He was one of my best friends in the world. I doubt that we'll ever talk again."

He reiterated that *The Tonight Show* under Helen Kushnick "played hardball," if not foul ball.

Kushnick not only warred with the other talk shows, she battled with her own staff. There were times when Helen would thunder at her subordinates, "This isn't a democracy! We do it *my* way." She didn't want anybody getting in her way, not even the network's president, Robert Wright. She hinted that if she was disciplined at all, she'd file a sexual harassment suit.

Kushnick was still strong-arming, pinching and scratching stars and their managers. Country singer Travis Tritt was booked to do Arsenio's show before *The Tonight Show* and refused to change his plans.

Helen Kushnick banned Tritt from *The Tonight Show* and canceled a booking for promising new singer Trisha Yearwood. Yearwood and Tritt shared the same manager. Travis Tritt's manager told his story to the *Los Angeles Times* on September 15 and the rumbles of agreement were startling. NBC executives shook their heads in frustration. They had to face what everyone in the industry knew: the producer on *The Tonight Show* was going power-mad.

Throughout the industry, whispers of Kushnick's antics had grown to screams of protest. Kushnick fought back, giving inflammatory print interviews, going on radio to declare that the men around her "hate that a woman is in charge."

Now *The Tonight Show* and *Arsenio* were warring over guests merely *announced* for an appearance. When *TV Guide* printed a list of celebrities that Leno had lined up, an *Arsenio* staffer wrote in complaining that the list included people who had no intention of appearing on *The Tonight Show*, and one who, in fact, chose *Arsenio* instead. He added, "I only wonder which late night talk show *TV Guide* would have named the winner if we listed, as *Tonight* did, people we *hoped* to secure... "

The war between talk shows became a presidential campaign issue. A question-and-answer session for candidate Bill Clinton included this bit of byplay:

"As president, you might do *Arsenio* again?"

"Yeah, I might."

"Which would probably make Jay Leno crazy. How about equal time?"

"Well, he made his choice, didn't he? I never declined to go on his show. In fact, I was on Johnny Carson some years ago, before I ever did *Arsenio.*"

Slowly, more and more *Tonight Show* staffers began to admit that they were working in a chaotic situation. As for Jay's relationship to his manager, one unnamed source was quoted as saying it was "sick," almost like Norman "Psycho" Bates and his mother.

Jay had an interesting take on the match-up of male comedian to an aggressive woman: "Comics are odd with women. Very rarely are they the pursuers. You stand on stage and women can look at you and decide whether they like your face, whether you have nice eyes or a nice ass — whatever it is they want. If they like what they see, when you go off stage, they'll approach you. And you play the sort of hurt-fawn-lost-in-the-forest act... "

Certainly, Jay's jokes were always feminist-friendly: "Did you see the movie *Hook?* It's about a 40-year-old guy acting like a nine-year-old boy. Gee, that's something women don't get to see enough of!"

Still, there was nothing to suggest that Helen had such a deep psychological hold on Jay. What she did have was Jay's loyalty and trust.

A meeting with NBC boss Warren Littlefield turned into a battle and it didn't end until Kushnick had gotten the last curse word. Then she walked out, slamming the door.

Littlefield warned Jay that his manager would have to walk out — and never come back. He told Jay that if he wanted to walk with her, that was fine. There was always David Letterman.

The September ratings showed that Jay Leno was getting a 4.2 rating and 14 percent of the available audience while Johnny Carson, a year before, had a 5.1 rating and was taking 17 percent.

Kushnick tried one of her old strategies: the press

leak. She called up *TV Guide* and said, "I think I'm being set up." She blamed it on "the male power elite of Hollywood." She insisted, "The men surrounding Carson didn't like women" and now "people have been taking shots at me." Kushnick said, "I'm from the ghetto, so I'm used to rats!"

She insisted that it was the producer's right to choose the guests and dictate the terms. Now she blamed the managers and agents for trying to ruin her reputation. She was especially agitated about super-agent Michael Ovitz. She believed he was trying to control the *Tonight Show* bookings and at the same time syphon away the best people for his two rival talk-show clients, David Letterman and Whoopi Goldberg.

Next, Kushnick tried to create a story similar to the "Carson to be fired by NBC" ploy of a year ago. This time, she leaked a story insisting that David Letterman was "on the edge," emotionally disturbed and a definite risk. How could NBC possibly think of replacing Jay with such an unstable person?

On Friday, September 18, NBC executives once again met to discuss the problems of *The Tonight Show*. Then Warren Littlefield demanded a meeting with Leno. Kushnick wanted in on it, too.

Littlefield still held out hope for some kind of compromise. He told Helen that she simply had to stop talking to the press. He once again asked that she modify her destructive policies concerning the booking of guests.

Helen Kushnick and Jay Leno met with two of the show's co-producers. It was at that meeting that Helen finally snapped. She turned on Jay, declaring that she could have worked her magic on *any* young comic of her choice.

"I can't take this anymore," said one of the co-producers.

But what about Jay? He'd taken it for years and

years. How much more could he take? At 46, Helen was only a few years older than Jay, yet she had often treated him like a child. "Jay tells the jokes, I make the decisions," she liked to say.

Leno was bewildered. Was his manager really out of control? Did she, even by Hollywood standards, go too far? Had she really done unethical things?

Kushnick told him, "I've been serving you steak dinners for the last eighteen years. I just haven't bothered showing you how I slaughtered the cow."

It was a rough weekend for Jay. According to Sam Rubin of KTLA, "Jay really didn't know what to believe. He got on the phone and spoke with several people on *The Tonight Show* he trusted, and others in Hollywood, and these phone calls came as a real, sad revelation... He heard all the gossip was true."

Doc Severinsen commented, "I think she hopes she was doing the best for Jay, but I think she has some serious personality disorders."

On Monday, September 21, Kushnick was handed her pink slip. She refused it. She decided that she would continue her job as if nothing happened.

NBC had expected trouble. Fred De Cordova, Carson's executive producer, arrived and took over the show, standing in the wings while Jay did his monologue.

Helen Kushnick went into her office and began to pack. What she didn't pack, she broke. Stunned staffers heard her trash the office and backed off.

Bob Mazza, a Kushnick publicist, was ejected by the guards. The guards then took up positions at Kushnick's door.

When she left that day, the locks were changed and her picture was circulated to security. A copy was given to the men guarding the front gate. There was no way that Helen Kushnick would ever be allowed anywhere near *The Tonight Show*, not even if she stood on line with a ticket.

Fred De Cordova declared, "I have never been part of a system that was so offending or irritating to other people. It was not one thing that led to her downfall, it was a growing irritation with her methods and the way she operated."

Even David Letterman finally admitted, now that she was gone, that as far as *Late Night* was concerned, her antics were something "we'd rather have done without. We were closely tied to it because we're back-to-back on the same network and booking a lot of the same guests. But it was more of a nuisance in theory than in reality."

Jay told the press, "I regret the actions of NBC today... I feel NBC's actions are unwarranted in light of the success of the show to date and I continue to support Mrs. Kushnick." But privately he told staffers that he was sorry for all the recent misery.

With Helen Kushnick gone, it looked as if the feud between Jay Leno and Arsenio Hall would come to an end.

Hall said, "Look again!"

Hall had a question: If Jay Leno had set himself up as the man to comment on every political scandal, every movie star peccadillo and even every typo in newspaper headlines, how come he didn't know what was going on under his own chin?

"Any adult that's hosting a show should be aware of what's going on around them," Hall huffed. "That's a frightening thought if he's not."

As for the old "kick-ass" remark, he insisted, "I'm from the streets and when you hear someone calling guests not to do your show that's the first response. There was an attempt to eliminate me from late-night."

Arsenio rolled along, but for Jay, even without the distractions of Helen Kushnick, it remained a bumpy road. Viewers had to adjust to his style, and he had to find his own identity. The opening credits took a while to figure out. Just before the NBC logo appeared, there was a strange noise that seemed like static or a cat coughing up a fur ball. It turned out to be the rev of a motorcycle, symbolic of Leno kicking his show into high gear.

And night after night, as the opening theme ended, Leno would do a dumb air-guitar samba, playing along with the last notes.

Edd (double d for double dull) Hall announced the credits in one of the blandest voices in show business. White bread with legs, Hall was useless in sketches.

Years before, the joke was that Redd Foxx had found in Demond Wilson "the only black man in America without charisma." That joke re-surfaced with Branford Marsalis, who spent the first few months looking like Lester without Willie Tyler. As for the music being played during the breaks, the only people it could interest were upwardly mobile Afro-Cubans.

On the air Jay chided the band for playing tunes nobody in the audience had ever heard of. He had to sit at his desk and pretend to appreciate the thirty-second solos given by guest band members he didn't know. The straight, blue-collar comic had pointedly gone after a predominantly black band as an immediate and visual symbol for Arsenio Hall's audience. But it took months before he and the drummer established a "rim shot rapport." Even then, while some comics could "play to the band," here the band was clearly hipper than the comic. Leno fumbled through awkward black-white jokes at first, trying to find a comfortable way of being the boss in control and still "one of the guys." He ended up chiding them, "if I get fired, you get fired!"

Leno gave the band a lot of exposure in a dubious new feature, letting the studio audience play a game of singing lines from TV themes. Band members who couldn't sing to save their horns stumbled over the lines printed in front of them and then stopped... so the equally off-key audience member could continue the next line and win a dinner. At least on Letterman's show, they put up a sign admitting: "Network Time Killer."

Given the time to iron out some of these problems, Leno tried his best. He and Branford Marsalis began to work well together after six months, and Marsalis began to take small, comical parts in sketches, now beginning to flash a wide, coy Cosby kid grin. He loosened and began to ad-lib, and when he lost a Super Bowl bet with band member Kevin Eubanks, accepted defeat like a... woman. He had to wear a bikini for the whole show.

For some, the main problem was that Jay was too jarring on a regular basis. While most audience members were used to the face that one agent believed "would scare children," (a phrase some comical guests still used to tease Leno), it was hard to go to sleep after hearing that nasal voice wail, whine and lisp through the news. Jay's argumentative grumbles sounded like John McLaughlin on speed: "Looks like there's gonna be more cost-cutting in the airline industry. Airlines said today they may *streamline* the food service. Streamline the food service!! What does that mean?? They're gonna serve it directly in the barf bag, is that the idea???"

Leno would end his jokes with a cheerleading cry of "Boy!" or "Yeah!" Sometimes he'd squeal a sarcastic "Please!"

TV Guide complained, "Confident talk-show hosts — Johnny, Dave, Arsenio — make us comfortable; they don't beg us to make *them* comfortable. But that's what Leno is doing.... and while I'm complaining, his theme song is unhummable and his announcer sounds as if he's recordingd airport pronouncements about white zones and courtesy phones."

Leno used his bombastic delivery even on easy jokes. One night he urgently cried, "They're operating on hemorrhoids using lasers. You talk about seeing the light at the end of the tunnel!!"

Then a sheepish "I get better play if I shout them."

One night during those awkward months of trying to establish his own identity, Jay nearly attacked the memory of Johnny Carson. He brought on the off-Broadway Blue Man Group, an avant-garde trio that were more or less Mummenshanz in Smurf-drag. After their enjoyably baffling mime routines, Leno sweatily declared, "This isn't your father's old *Tonight Show!*"

Leno was joking with the slogan for a car commercial of the day, but Carson supporters choked in disbelief.

Jay had many more off-nights. His interviewing style needed work. It was one thing to be "just a guest host" and forgivably look as if he was reading questions off a card. But as "the man," he was supposed to frame a question without going off on more tangents than Pythagoras.

When he invited Roseanne Arnold on the show, he was embarrassingly inarticulate. Arnold was in the midst of one of her monthly controversies. This time, she had "outed" a TV critic who had panned her husband's new series. In print interviews she had called him a "faggot." When gays found this objectionable, she demanded TV time to point out that the critic had previously referred to her as a "bitch."

Carson would not have booked her just for controversy's sake. Letterman and Hall would have attempted, in all fairness, to voice the critic's point of view. But Leno was as flexible a tool for her as a rubber band. After he allowed her to rant on and on, he sputtered out his admiration:

"The one thing I do like about all this controversy is the fact — and I think the public senses it too — is the fact that — and a lot of people don't have this and wish they had — I have it and Tom has it — is having a spouse or a woman whether you're right or wrong — they'll scratch the eyes out of anyone that comes near me.

"I have to hide bad reviews. No, because I know my wife will go down and kill the guy that wrote the article. Like with you and Tom. I admire the fact that — with all the things that have been written — is the fact that you guys are a team and I think people sense you generally like each other. And whether people like the way you do business or don't do business — you can't say this isn't a love relationship that will — that will — fight the outside world to keep the family thing together. And that's what I like. That's what makes it fun. What are you doing for the holidays?"

Jay got tongue-tied even with a softie like Goldie Hawn.

Leno: "Now, you seem like an easy-going person. Is there anything — what type of things make you mad or upset. I — I just, I just wondered, like when you started out, obviously with the *Laugh-In* thing and all that. People see the films and think, oh, she's just like the person in the films, but I know you produced a lot of the films, and, and, take them you know from beginning to end and all that."

Goldie: "Yes, sometimes that happens."

Leno: "Is that a problem? Do you have to run up against?"

Goldie: "Not anymore."

Leno: "No, I don't imagine anymore."

Goldie: "Not anymore."

By contrast, David Letterman did not suffer fools gladly. He had a comically cranky, aggressive style for interviews. At the same time Leno was falling over Goldie, Letterman was dealing with bubbly Marilu Henner. She was promoting a new exercise video.

Marilu: "Let me tell you something.... I lost 8 pounds. That was good! I thought I had cancer! (The crowd groans, and Henner is surprised.) That was a big laugh!"

Dave: "You know what's interesting there? You said that's a big laugh. Like you thought that introducing the notion of cancer would get a huge laugh."

A few moments later, Marilu was burbling about her new video.

Dave: "Somebody gave me a VCR. I can't program it."

Marilu: "It's the worst. I thought you had to be a guy."

Dave: "What did you say? I don't even know what you're talking about!"

Marilu: "I'm talking about having to be a guy to, like, program VCRs and use electronic equipment and stuff. I thought you had to have a penis to do that stuff."

Dave: "You know, from my experience, if you really introduce that into the procedure, you're vastly increasing the possibility of electrocution."

During the first six months of his reign, Jay Leno tried hard to be the good host. Dave was often the opposite: "It frequently happens that a guest is on to plug a movie and I think that picture stinks. I'm supposed to say, 'It was a marvelous cinematic work... but I can't and I don't.'"

Leno tended to suffer politely when a guest was boring. Letterman, instead, would go on the attack. He wouldn't allow a guest to be dull. Beautiful but dull Raquel Welch was on the show and the conversation was going nowhere. Dave began joking around, pointing out that he was being a gentleman and not injecting cheap sexist laughs. He changed

subjects, tried everything to liven things up, even
using his favorite catch phrase of the day,
"Buttafuoco."

Raquel suddenly said, "Buttafuoco? What a
name, anyway. Is that the way you do it? Instead of
beauta-fucko?"

The crowd roared. Raquel put her hands up to
her face in mortification. And when the laughter
subsided, she blamed Dave for flustering her. "What
is it with you?" she asked.

He just had a way of livening up bad TV. Dennis
Miller was always a fan of Dave's: "I like uncomfortable, unpredictable TV. I like it when things go
wrong, when it gets dicey and there's that weird
energy between a talk show host and a guest. I
watch David Letterman for that reason. When somebody's blowing smoke, I love it when Letterman raises an eyebrow. I guess he gets accused of being
mean for doing that, but I think it's as it should be."

The difference between *Late Night* and *The Tonight
Show* even extended to the audience. *Late Night*
didn't cater to the corporation. Letterman's assistant, Laurie Diamond, put it succinctly, saying that
most of the tickets went to the fans, not the big
shots: "Our audience sucks when there's too many
VIPs. If the audience sucks, the show has a pretty
good chance of sucking as well."

Letterman earned his reputation for being an
iconoclast — or, to put it more simply, a wiseguy.

Jerry Hall, Mick Jagger's girlfriend, Dave interrupted for this rumination: "Sitting next to you, I get
a terrible feeling, it's kind of a nagging anxiety in the
back of my mind. I think I may have over-inflated my
tires."

He once interrupted Arnold Schwarzenegger to
ask, "The steroids don't affect your ego, do they?"

Jay was the company man who brought on Bob
Hope and allowed him to promote his latest coasting

and boring TV special. When Bob Hope was seen on Dave's show, it was only a glimpse. The *Late Night* cameras ran a candid shot of Hope waiting to be interviewed on a local NBC news show. Dave looked at the monitor and asked, "Was that Bob 'I'm a Hundred Years Old' Hope?"

Dave's antics didn't always go over so well. On November 13, 1987, Cher appeared on the show and left shortly after, declaring, "You are so full of shit!"

But she would return several more times to spar with Dave.

Finally, a few of Jay's shows began to really take off, episodes that could be re-run some night, clips that might make it to the anniversary show. He had developed enough confidence to indulge in some iconoclastic sketch material. He parodied the film *Alive* by playing a flight attendant eager to literally serve the passengers. Instead of oxygen, bottles of A-1 Sauce came down from overhead, the magazine list was only *Gourmet* and *People*, and he urged everyone to pick out their favorite passenger in case of emergency. For those wanting a "kosher meal," two passengers in yarmulkes stood up to be identified. And the special of the day was the bandleader: Veal Marsalis.

Leno had loosened up so much that by St. Patrick's Day of 1993, he was drinking on-camera, downing five shots in a minute during a sketch. He might have had some more, but Branford came over and swiped the bottle, passing it around to band members.

Over the months, the dyslexic host had learned to pace himself during the monologue. As he glanced at the cues for his next joke, he could take an extra second and be sure to get it right. A comfortable and confident Leno began to banter with audience members, coming up with quick ad-libs:

"What do you [for a living]?"

"I manage an ambulance service."

"Oh, you manage an ambulance service? What's the biggest problem, lawyers in the wheel wells, that kind of thing?"

While Leno had fumbled with minor guests, he was unintimidated by Jimmy Carter, leading the ex-President through some amusing anecdotes. Carter recalled that he nearly lost the election after telling *Playboy* magazine that he had lusted in his heart. Then he added that he found unexpected support, too. A woman sidled up to him and said, "Mr. President, if you still have lust in your heart, I'm available!"

Not just a fluff interview, Leno asked Carter how he would have handled the tough transition that Clinton endured. Clinton had waffled on his pledge to allow gays in the military, leading to a crisis the first day in office. Carter said he would've "just signed the bill and got it over with," as he did when he granted amnesty to draft dodgers.

The show marked a high point in Leno's tenure on *The Tonight Show.*

It had taken Jay a while. Ten months into Leno's reign on *The Tonight Show,* Dennis Miller pointed out that within *seven* months, his own show had been kicked off the air. "This is a country that gave Rick Dees a year... Jay and I don't get along. We are different types of human beings." And he once again repeated, "I doubt we will ever talk again."

Miller wasn't the only one still getting on Jay's case. Even when Jay did a decent interview, he was criticized. After the Super Bowl, he'd booked the game's hero, Troy Aikman.

He thought he had done a good job. Then, he brought out his next guest, TV moderator John McLaughlin.

Barely settling into his chair, McLaughlin scowled at Leno and snapped, "Your questions to him were not that great."

Then McLaughlin ignored Jay and began to interview the football star and ask the questions he felt Leno had missed.

Leno tried to make amends to the guests who had endured the wrath of Kushnick miseries. Travis Tritt was booked, and before he asked a question Jay was hastily joking, "I thought you were banned from the show!" He explained, "I came into work one day and I said 'What's going on?'" He apologized: "It all got blown out [of proportion] but I'm glad you're here. You're welcome here any time you like."

Ever the thoughtful host, Jay had even created the innovation of numbered cups for his guests so that "Guest 1" and "Guest 2" wouldn't accidentally drink each other's water. Still, there were outside distractions. The war that he thought was over between *The Tonight Show* and *Arsenio* was still simmering.

Arsenio Hall could forget the dirty tactics of Helen Kushnick. But he still could not forgive Leno.

In November of 1992, *TV Guide* tried to mediate the war between Hall and Leno, but Arsenio was not about to go along.

"...This Late-night Camp David will never happen," he wrote *TV Guide*, "It's been too painful for me. From the time Mr. Leno got NBC's green light to replace Mr. Carson, I have watched as the most vicious and unethical business behavior I've ever observed began to unfold...

"Helen Kushnick, we have been told, was solely to blame for the numerous negative situations that occurred. Yet, curiously enough, even with publicists, managers, and agents disclosing their bad experiences in dealing with the show, Leno's public comment about Kushnick's termination was that NBC's actions were "unwarranted."

"Until some of the truth started surfacing I was in

hell. My fans, as well as the general public, were confused about what was happening. Every time I opened my mouth... I was accused of being an angry, jealous liar. I was deeply pained to learn that members of the press would go to such great lengths to protect Leno's golden-boy reputation. Now I am trying to close this chapter of my life, though it will never be forgotten. From Tom Selleck being told he couldn't do Letterman, to the unscrupulous acts constantly waged on Dennis Miller, to the way Travis Tritt, Liz Taylor, Mr. Carson, Mr. McMahon and Maria Shriver were treated, the list of improprieties that have transpired goes on and on... In the words of Dennis Miller, "I am outta here."

Leno was, as usual, wide-eyed and perplexed:

"I went up to Arsenio at the Carousel Ball and said, 'C'mere a sec. A lot of crazy stuff has gone on. Clean slate, OK? We were friends; there's no reason we can't be again.' I think he said, 'Thanks,' or something to that effect. I also said to let me know about any booking problems.

"I called all the guests who'd had problems and said, 'Do *Arsenio* and you'll still be welcome here." Paul Reiser, a friend, called me to say he'd also like to promote his NBC show on *Arsenio* — did I care? I said, 'Paul, that stuff is over.'"

And now it was Leno deciding that if Arsenio and the media couldn't forget it, *he* could:

"As to public sit-down with Arsenio, I don't tell people my problems. I'm not known for being a rabble-rouser or a troublemaker. The more you're on the cover of magazines talking about this, you start to get famous for doing something you don't really do... I'm not going to put the blame on somebody else. But I've straightened things out and called everyone personally... I've called Arsenio several times and didn't get a call back. That's OK. But I'm upset that this continues. If I stop to help somebody who's had an accident, that doesn't mean I caused it."

Still, the Arsenio barbs had produced a lasting sting. In his broadcast for March 30, 1983, so long after the feud had cooled, Jay was still hoping to smooth things over. In his monologue he mentioned the embarrassing news item that a restaurant chain, known for promising "free birthday meals," had denied several blacks the offer, even though they'd brought all the required documentation. "The lawsuit had an affect," he said, "Now the restaurant will no longer be serving their Grand Klan Breakfast... " Leno grinned and added, "I think this thing is great. It's finally got Arsenio and me agreeing on something. I think that's terrific! Sure!" The crowded applauded.

The ratings gave Jay some reason to breath easier. Arsenio had not kicked his ass after all. And there had been nothing to fear from Whoopi Goldberg.

Critics found her show to be more imitative than innovative. She was doing a version of Bob Costas' program *Later*. Costas would sit down with one guest for a laid-back, if not at times fan-like and fawning half hour. Goldberg did the same.

The plus for both shows was that viewers could see what stars were like in a "human setting." Whoopi worked especially well with comedians. A Robin Williams or George Carlin, accustomed to being "on" with Letterman or Leno, could rap naturally with Whoopi and not feel compelled to concentrate on schtick or gags from their stage acts. Unfortunately most listeners seemed to want the schtick, and were disappointed that the show wasn't "zany."

Like Costas, the strength was in the guest, not the host, and few TV listings bothered to regularly clue viewers on who was Whooping it up on the irregularly scheduled syndicated show.

Goldberg's coy style drew derisive laughter from

Saturday Night Live. A parody offered Ellen Cleghorne as a gleeful interviewer: "I got a new show and
a new set... I feel like Arsenio!" Guest: "You look like
Arsenio in drag!" "Oh no, I've seen Arsenio in drag
and he can't get to this!"

David Letterman even tossed a wry comment at
her. He mentioned on his show, "They have that little
hook. I noticed it the other night. Her and Ted
Danson, they sit on their own legs. Whoopi sits on
one of her legs, and Ted Danson sits on one of his
legs, and at the end of the half hour, obviously both
legs are asleep. Then a stagehand comes out [and
tries to smack the legs awake]. It's not my cup of
tea."

Joan Rivers was a fan. She praised her dreadlock
hairstyle and the unusual outfits she wore. Whoopi
said, "If somebody's really interested, they'll look
beyond the first layers... If they're lucky enough to
last till I get out of my clothes, they'll get a big surprise."

"Is your underwear sexy?"

"Yes! And tasty, too."

Others were a bit nauseous. *Esquire* magazine
called her a "sanctimonious comedienne." *Spy* magazine called her a "humorless comedienne." the *New
York Daily News* commented, "Another season of
Whoopi Goldberg's half-baked attempt to make it as
a talk show host would put Sominex out of business." *Variety* complained the show was "treacly,
reverent, safe," with Goldberg "stiff, underresearched
and deferential."

After her first year, Whoopi got up in front of the
National Association of Theater Owners in Las Vegas
and said, "My show is probably going to die." This
was no idle threat. When her sitcom with Jean
Stapleton, Bagdad Cafe, had gotten low ratings, she
suddenly walked out.

In the fight for *Tonight*, Whoopi had been content

to interview her favorite stars and do it without a lot of fanfare, publicity or competition. Whoopi had her movies to concentrate on, anyway. She stockpiled her shows by doing as many in a day as possible.

As for Bob Costas, he pointedly denied that he would ever be up for replacing Leno or Letterman. He was happy with his two million a year, to be 40 and not gray from worries and to live comfortably with his wife and kids in St. Louis.

He said his only real ambition now was to someday announce baseball games: "David Letterman wanted to be Johnny Carson and I wanted to be Red Barber."

As Whoopi's ratings drifted down and Arsenio's began to taper off as well, Jay Leno had to feel that the worst was behind him. The Kushnick fiasco was over and those first months of trying to find himself were gone, too. Hey, the drummer was even getting the rimshots right!

It was then that the mightiest talk show battle of all time erupted.

No *Tonight Show* wannabe had ever publicly demanded that NBC bump Steve Allen, Jack Paar or Johnny Carson. But now, NBC's resident anarchist, David Letterman, was saying just that: Impeach Jay Leno. Or else!

CHAPTER SEVENTEEN

JAY vs. DAVE, AND CHEVY JOINING THE CHASE

Jay Leno was hearing it: "Nice guys finish last."

Nobody likes a nice guy.

And some nasty guys were very vocal about this. Like Andrew Dice Clay:

"He always had a head the size of a chandelier. Lemme tell ya something, that guy's head is so fuckin' big he looks at the floor, his chin hits himself in the balls. He's the only guy I know a chick could sit on his face, it's like a bicycle seat. Scumbag motherfucker is what he is. He used to work in a hospital giving chin enemas. Fuckin' prick. Now his head's fat, man. He put on 80 pounds in the last month. Great, I love to see him like that. It's from eating all those fuckin' chips he sells. His head's bigger than his fuckin' pillow already."

Dave didn't wait for Dice to curse at him. The iconoclastic host had a staffer do it for him! One of the new favorite segments on the show was the appearance of Peggy, the Foul-Mouthed Chambermaid. One night the old lady came out and hissed at Dave, "You're so full of shit! I just hope your dick falls off. You miserable motherfucking son of a bitch. You bite my ass!"

A few words here and there were erased from the tape, but it didn't take an expert lip-reader to know exactly what she said.

Nice Jay Leno vs. that wiseguy Dave Letterman? The wiseguys sided with Dave.

Arsenio Hall: "If Leno and Letterman go head to

head... give Dave the decision. Dave is an original and I think you have to fear the original. In other words, that's a strong vote for Letterman."

Pat Sajak was quoted as saying that Leno was "history... dead meat." He tried to undo some of the damage by appearing on Leno's show and apologizing. Then he whipped out some prepared comedy material and started to read it. After a few moments of silence, Sajak had further reason for apology.

Garry Shandling: "David Letterman's is my favorite show. It goes far beyond just a host sitting behind a desk. I wouldn't want to be in the position of being opposite the Letterman show... As Jay goes on, he will make it more of his own show, but at the moment Jay is holding on tightly to a lot of the *Tonight Show* elements."

Leno was just trying to hold onto *The Tonight Show*. Leno had gone through the fire of replacing a living legend and then replacing his manager of 17 years. He was "the new guy" trying to make friends with five million skeptical viewers. He protected his ass from Arsenio Hall, and now his respected pal and fellow NBC host Dave Letterman was taking shots at him.

Leno and Letterman had admired each other for over a decade.

Letterman on Leno: "After I saw Jay work for the first time in 1975, I said, "Oh, *that's* the way it's supposed to be done."

When Dave got his own show, he brought on Jay Leno time and time again. Leno was grateful. Jay admitted, "I hadn't really been having a lot of success with *The Tonight Show*. I did it eight or nine times, but really, they had forgotten about me until I started doing *Late Night*. "

Jay loved working with Dave: "I come out with ten minutes of "Nice tie, Dave," bing, bing, bing, hit hard, eat sandwiches, stuff your face, make a mess, knock something over, tell a joke, screw around, boom, and leave. You come out like a tornado, wreck everything and leave."

By comparison, *The Tonight Show* was a lot more responsibility: "You can't wreck everything five days a week for an hour; it just gets frantic. This is the mistake networks make when they hire deejays as hosts. 'It's gonna be the wackiest hour!' After about twenty minutes of this frantic energy, you've had it. So when you host *The Tonight Show*, you do your monologue — boom — slow the whole thing right down, let the guests be funny, let them be entertaining, back off."

Now he was being backed into a corner.

The year 1992 was going to end soon, David Letterman's contract would be up soon, and NBC was going to give Jay an answer about his future... sooner or later.

Jay went to NBC's president, Robert C. Wright. As Jay recalls it, this was the dialogue:

"What's going on?"

"Dave has been here 10 years and we don't want to lose him. We are trying to do everything to keep him."

"I assume that means losing my spot as well?"

"That is what the Letterman camp wants."

"Are you going to give it to him?"

"Jay, we honestly don't know."

Nobody knew what was going on. This had to please Letterman, who was finally in a position to dictate to the big shots and step on the corporate weasels.

Letterman was exacting his revenge for losing out to Leno. He was making them sweat. Not only did he want a huge raise, he wanted to be moved into the 11:30 time slot. NBC was trying to figure out how pissed off he was and how serious he was about leaving the network if he didn't get his way.

Various drones got out their slide rules and calculators and tried to analyze the strengths of Leno and Letterman. Dave was getting 3 million viewers at 12:30 a.m., and Jay 4.3 million an hour earlier. Did that mean Jay was the better host, or that a million people went to sleep an hour early?

Letterman had better demographics, with a strong 38 percent of his audience among the important 18-to-34 age group and 24 percent over 50.

The over-50 crowd were more prone toward watching *The Tonight Show* (38 percent of the viewership) with only 27 percent are in the 18-34 category.

NBC thought they had trouble with the Machiavellian schemes of Helen Kushnick. Now they had to tangle with not only a very angry, very clever David Letterman, but Dave's new super-agent, Michael Ovitz. They were caught up in so many smoke screens and news leaks they couldn't tell who was smoking and who was leaking.

NBC discovered they weren't even the only ones dealing with Dave. The other networks and syndicates were seriously bidding for him, too. But which offers were real and which were rumor? Somehow the auction for Dave kept escalating, and they were told that millions and millions of bucks were being offered, and the 11:30 time slot.

There were rumors that ABC was hoping to create its own block of David Letterman and Ted Koppel. Fox had been courting Chevy Chase, but a proven winner in Letterman seemed to be worth pursuing. Stories were circulating that Paramount was ready to drop Arsenio in favor of Dave.

Many insiders believed that Paramount was going to get Dave. Despite the frenzied "woof woofs," Arsenio was dogging it in the ratings, slipping an embarrassing 20 percent. Analysts insisted that Paramount needed to make a change.

178 syndicated stations were carrying Hall, but a

huge chunk — 72 — were Fox affiliates that would be pressured to defect when Chevy Chase launched his new show. Pressure would be less if they abandoned the sinking Arsenio and made the splashy move of signing Dave. Paramount had been trying to secure Arsenio by refusing to sign new contracts with the Fox affiliates and moving to other independent channels, but this wasn't easy.

And how could Paramount let Letterman move to CBS? There were 44 CBS affiliates currently carrying Arsenio Hall. No doubt most would drop him to stand behind the network's new hope. Wasn't it wiser to stand up and take Dave right now?

Another worry at Paramount was that Arsenio's trendy audience was moving on to the next craze. They had "woofed" long enough. Like his pal Eddie Murphy, who was having a hard time at the movie houses, the thinking was that Arsenio's brand of hipness was no longer so hip. There actually seemed to be a limit on the number of times even the youngest members of the audience could wave their fists in the air before they began wondering, "What are we *doing?*"

Insiders felt that Arsenio had also damaged himself by a series of no-win feuds that were in conflict with his warm, likable image.

It was one thing to defend himself against Jay Leno, it was another to provoke near-fights with people who should've been allies. Paramount hadn't forgotten the days when an angry, tank-like Tom Arnold had been intent on storming the lot and squashing Arsenio into a pulp for those Roseanne fat jokes.

More recently, Wesley Snipes had made headlines trying to brawl with Hall. Snipes, promoting his film *Passenger 57*, was annoyed with the clip Hall chose to show. "It figures you would show that clip," he muttered. Hall told him, "This is my show. I run it the way I want to."

When they met a few nights later at the Roxbury nightclub in Los Angeles, Snipes sought out Arsenio and blasted him verbally. Not only was he angry about the way he was treated on the show, he was also steaming that his friend, actor Larry Fishburne (a star of *Boyz N The Hood)* didn't even get a booking.

"The brothers think you're a sellout," Snipes said. The best solution to the problem? "Kick ass!"

Hall managed to extricate himself before Snipes could warm up for the first punt.

Instead of fighting with Snipes, Hall began sniping at the newspapers. He insisted that Paramount was still making big money from his show, and loudly declared that there was no way he'd give up his territory.

"I'm here and I'm going to stay here," he said. "I heard somebody say the party's over. Man, the party ain't over till the people who made me what I am say it's over, and that wasn't journalists in the first place."

Paramount dropped out of the running. The Fox network was still ready to go ahead with Chevy Chase. Tribune Entertainment was still smarting after the Dennis Miller debacle. That left NBC to worry about CBS and ABC.

While Dave and Jay's fight for ownership of *The Tonight Show* continued, Arsenio and Dave's relationship warmed up considerably. Back in 1989, when Arsenio was first making a splash, he told *Rolling Stone* that he figured Dave hated his guts. Now, Arsenio was pronouncing Dave "a cool guy." Arsenio said that Dave had sent him "a really nice letter." Just what was in it, Arsenio didn't say. Arsenio did repeat that in the battle between Letterman and Leno, Dave would win.

Hall loyalists pointed out that if Letterman and Leno faced off against each other, it could only benefit Arsenio. "Leno and Letterman are really the same," a staffer insisted. "Arsenio is the one who's different. Leno and Letterman book the same guests. They both had Penelope Ann Miller last week. Does anybody really care?"

What? Jay and Dave similar?

One night, Jay sat at his desk looking at newspaper ads:

"Join us for Midnight Madness. Tonight only open until 11:00 p.m."

"Indoor Fogger $1.98. New and improved. Kills household pets."

"Shop Vise with Anvil. The perfect thing for your New Year's Eve party."

The same night, Dave looked at newspaper ads:

"Memory telephone, $12.99. Not $12.99."

"Wanted, person interested in used car lot. No knowledge, lots of money required."

"Girl scout uniforms on sale at Dads & Lads."

Maybe Arsenio's people had a point. And if one went to roving reporter Paula Poundstone, and the other to roving reporter Larry "Bud" Melman, why shouldn't everyone rove over to Arsenio's show instead?

Still, Arsenio wasn't about to utter a "kick ass" comment about Letterman. He insisted that he and Letterman would never feud: "I honestly believe that Letterman has his core audience and I have mine. They are not the same audience."

ABC seemed to emerge as NBC's big rival in snaring Dave. Ted Koppel seemed to be more willing to give up his 11:30 time slot than Jay Leno. Or was Koppel just helping Dave bedevil NBC? On September 9, Ted Koppel was a guest with Dave. "They keep telling me you want the 11:30 slot," Koppel said.

Dave answered, "You have to be very careful there, there's a big difference between WANT and OFFERED." Then Dave came up with an idea: "What about this? *Nightline* stays just exactly where it is... and when you do that little thing, 'We have to notify the affiliates we may be running over,' you just do that every night and that'll be MY time."

Koppel reiterated, "I'm a great fan of your show and please, come over to ABC when your contract runs out!"

Soon after, another ABC star, Sam Donaldson, came on the show to unveil his "Top Five Reasons Why David Letterman Should Come to ABC." Said Sam:

1. You wouldn't have the funniest haircut at ABC!

2. It's the only network that Dan Quayle can spell.

3. The weasels at ABC are better than the weasels at NBC.

4. Three words: No Bryant Gumbel.

5. Double dates with Doogie Howser.

The toying and the teasing continued until November 24 when ABC's executive, Robert Iger, formally made an announcement: "We are committed to Ted Koppel and *ABC News*. We were not in a position to offer 11:30 to Letterman, and we were told it was essential that Letterman be on at 11:30. We'd love to have David follow *Nightline*. We've heard loud and clear that David does not want to do that."

Soon the people at *Nightline* were huddling to figure out a strategy for keeping their affiliates happy. Some were very annoyed that they weren't going to get a fun guy like Dave, just the same old news with Koppel. ABC decided that, as of April 1993, *Nightline* would be shunted back to 11:35 p.m. That would match the *Tonight Show* starting time and give the affiliates more local commercials.

Then ABC sweetened the pot. An extra thirty-second commercial break would be inserted into *Nightline*, plus an additional thirty seconds in ABC's prime-time *20-20* show to all affiliates showing

Koppel's program at 11:35.

Dave respected ABC's decision, and he respected Ted Koppel. As he put it, "If it wasn't for Ted Koppel I'd have the silliest hair on TV."

NBC had no more to fear from ABC, but there was one network left.

CBS sent shock waves through the entertainment world by making a two-year $28 million offer to Dave.

Like a major league ball player, Letterman seemed to be negotiating for an astronomical amount of money, far more than he could possibly be worth.

After all, three million people were watching Dave nightly, actually down from his best year, 1988, when an estimated four million were dialing him up. In New York ("Try our street fajitas!") he was reaching 280,000 people.

CBS executives wanted him anyway. His fans were loyal. His demographics delighted advertisers. If Arsenio had the young black kids who were out partying all night and spending a hundred bucks on sneakers, Dave had a good hunk of the Yuppie crowd who were out partying all night and spending a hundred bucks on tasseled shoes.

Dave had proved he could get ratings during a "normal" time of the night. About 14 million watched his last prime-time anniversary special.

For years, CBS endured the embarrassment of not being a "player" in the late night world. Aside from the prestige of having a Carson or a Koppel, CBS had been losing out on big bucks. *Late Night With David Letterman* cost NBC about $25 million to produce. The commercial revenue it brought in was $70 million. CBS reasoned, even with Dave's raise in salary, what's wrong with a profit of over $50 million?

CBS was also counting on Letterman to lead key comedy talent their way. His pals would certainly look more favorably on working for Dave's new network than his old one. CBS also was eager for Dave and his talented staff to contribute to their prime-time line up, developing and producing new shows. Dave himself was very interested in becoming a producer and getting some of his own sitcom ideas on the air.

Could NBC affore to match CBS's offer? Could they afford *not* to? If Dave left, who would take his place? Dana Carvey? Hell, Carvey was playing it cool, too! Depending on what rumors one listened to, Carvey either was going to leave *Saturday Night Live* for the movies, or join Dave at CBS and take the low-pressure 12:30 slot there, creating a powerful block.

And if Carvey wasn't going to back Dave, maybe Pat Sajak would. Pat and Dave were friends. Why, they had spent quite some time huddled together during one of Dave's annual insiders-only anniversary parties.

Hyper Howard Stern appeared on Letterman's show and began to bludgeon Dave about the talk show war situation. He demanded to know, "Do you think Dana Carvey could take your place?"

Dave looked at Howard and said, "Maybe *tonight.*"

In *The New York Times,* Hal Katz, of the Katz Marketing & Media company, offered expert analysis. He declared that it would be foolish for Dave to leave NBC: "The Letterman audience isn't used to watching CBS." Dave was banking on his audience being smart enough to turn a dial.

NBC had to go to the bank and make a counter-offer. Grant Tinker, the former head of NBC, was quoted as saying that Dave was worth the money: "I have a feeling the answer is much more yes than no, if not one-hundred-percent yes."

NBC had the money, but that was only part of the problem. Dave still wanted the *Tonight Show* time slot.

It was "Keep me — and bounce Jay Leno."

In Boca Raton, Florida, NBC executives from both coasts met at the offices of General Electric.

"For a long time," an insider reports, "it was a deadlock. The guys in California wanted Jay, and the guys in New York wanted Dave.

NBC desperately wanted a compromise idea, and they got one from NBC executive Jim Waterbury. Recalling the days when Jack Paar and Steve Allen moved from late night to prime time, he urged that one of the hosts, either Jay or Dave, become a prime-time player. He advocated that NBC slim down its schedule, weed out all the losers and free the 10p.m. Monday through Friday time slot. In essence, he wanted to begin "late night" at 10 p.m., have a news break at 11 p.m., then resume the fun. The audience could get a good night's sleep with Bob Costas winding down at 1 p.m.

Dave wanted 11:30, Johnny's time spot, the one he had dreamed about for decades and waited ten years to get. Getting *The Tonight Show* was also Jay's dream come true. He wasn't going to be humiliated into giving it up.

Stung by NBC's waffling, wounded by the insult of being challenged as the heir to Johnny, Jay Leno, "America's hardest-working entertainer," "the blue collar comedian," decided he had only one option: take his case to the people.

They had to recognize Jay as "the people's champion."

Why not? Jay was a regular guy. Hadn't he spent nearly 15 years working his way up from his first guest spot on *The Tonight Show* to the boss's chair? Wasn't he the first host to actually accept monologue jokes faxed in by ordinary people? Didn't he do more common audience routines by playing "Name the TV theme" and showing their faces when he read their questions to him?

Jeez. Jay once mentioned to an interviewer, "When you see that guy [himself] on TV you think he's the nicest guy in the world. A fan sat down at my table in a restaurant and ate the French fries off my plate!"

Jay began using the *Tonight Show* monologue to rally support. He began cautiously. One night he opened with "Thank you for that lackluster support. Believe me, I know all about it."

The audience didn't laugh. They didn't know what he was talking about. Jay tried a stronger approach.

Jay opened another show by crying out, "Let me guess! You're all quitting unless you get my job!"

Soon he was making himself the symbol of the nation's unemployment crisis:

"The biggest fear Americans have going into 1993 is job security. *Tell me about it!*"

On December 9 1992, David Letterman finally announced that he would accept CBS's offer. NBC got more bad news. Their only Top Ten success, *Cheers*, was going off the air. They were smarting from the sting of being the not-too-smart network that couldn't keep any of its popular shows.

There was a clause in Dave's contract. If NBC was willing to match the CBS offer, they could *still* keep Letterman. Instead of quieting the talk show wars, Dave's decision to join CBS set off new explosions.

The December 23 issue of *Newsday* splashed the front page with a big color photo of Letterman and the headline: "$28 million. Is Letterman Worth it? NBC Execs Debate Whether to Match CBS' 2-Year Offer."

Leno went to the people, presenting himself as the hapless victim, Dave the sulky troublemaker:

"I don't know if you heard. Santa Claus is pretty upset. Yeah. Says he's tired of waiting till the middle of the night to deliver his Christmas presents. He says if he doesn't get an earlier time slot he's gonna take his whole workshop and move to the South Pole. I don't know what we're gonna do. The network will have to decide."

The audience began rooting for the underdog, Jay. His confidence returned as he put up his brave fight.

He did another Christmas routine. This one contrasted Christmas in 1992 with Christmas in the distant future. Leno revealed some bad news. In the future Santa Claus would be... "dead from high cholesterol diet." But the good news: "Jay Leno, STILL host of *The Tonight Show*, wishes you a merry Christmas."

As he once said, "I represent all those people who have been around the business, paid their dues, done it the right way, and finally get the brass ring."

Leno utilized another tactic. If he couldn't win the support of the president, he'd rally all the president's men. In the case of NBC, this meant the affiliates, the little people who ran the individual stations that formed the network.

Leno used his L.B.J. theory: "L.B.J. claimed that every handshake was worth 250 votes, because each person then goes and tells someone else you're a good guy and then they go and tell more people."

Leno worked fast. He called up and spoke to 100 stations in 10 days: "I asked them how we were doing in their market, would you like to see a change. I gathered the facts, the research, the projected ratings. G.E. is a bottom-line company and I gave them the bottom line... "

The executives were impressed once again with exactly how hard-working Jay Leno was. Leno said, "Everybody has a sword hanging over their head in the 90's. This is the kind of situation all Americans are finding themselves in on a day-to-day basis. They are going to work, doing their jobs, they are working hard. So why am I being fired? Why am I being laid off?"

The affiliate toadying was not appreciated by some of Jay's colleagues. *Saturday Night Live* ran a mock-promo for a terrible new NBC series. The only person to praise it? Jay Leno: "NBC has done it again. Boy, am I proud to be on this network Anything else you want me to say, 'Cause I don't mind!"

Arsenio Hall said that Leno's toadying proved he was more of a kiss ass than a kick ass: "What he's good at doesn't take place on the air."

While Jay was getting support from the people and the affiliates, he was getting teased by his guests.

Robin Williams appeared with Leno and cheerfully said, "Good to see you — you're still here!" Then he lowered his voice and added, "If something happens don't be that afraid. ABC isn't so bad!"

Guest Rob Lowe mentioned how intimidating it was when he "met Paul Newman in the men's room."

Leno neatly shot back, "If you hang around there long enough, *someone's* gonna come in."

Lowe said he was so surprised to see Paul Newman and was momentarily awed, unable to finish doing what he was doing. Leno pleasantly agreed that it might be a startling experience to discover a big star standing next to him in the men's room.

Lowe then asked, "What about David Letterman?"

In the silence, Leno lightly pointed out that he and Dave were not enemies. Their friendship, however, would not stand too much more strain.

Meanwhile Dave, the 28-million-dollar man, took a few jabs from *his* guests. Susan Sarandon was introduced to great applause and Dave wondered if she enjoyed it. After all, when she made films, she didn't get a live response.

"Absolutely," she said. "The difference between theater and film is the difference between making love and masturbating."

Dave grinned. Sarandon said, "You're pretty cocky... You have that kind of mid-negotiations multi-million-dollar glow about you."

Letterman answered, "Well, I guess that's the difference between negotiating and masturbating."

CBS wasn't jerking around. One of its own reporters, Carol Iovanna, revealed that not only would David get "28 million over 2 years, but it could amount to 42 million when you add incentives that include control over a second late night program."

Another CBS reporter, Bill Lagattuta, frankly admitted, "CBS pursued Letterman like a tiger because the network has never had a late night hit."

NBC gave it one more shot, telling Dave that it was crazy to jump to CBS. For CBS to break even, they'd need a 3 rating, and currently Dave was only getting 2.7. Not only did NBC have more affiliates, at least 40 percent of the CBS affiliates were currently running *Cheers* or *Entertainment Tonight* at 11:30. There was no guarantee these affiliates would move Dave to 11:30 instead of starting him at midnight.

CBS president Howard Stringer agreed with NBC. "That's probably accurate," he said. "And so what? Letterman already knows that."

Letterman's pal Howard Stern sounded a note of caution: "11:30 is a whole different ball game. There's real competition, not *The Love Phone*. Mid-America wants hijinks, Uncle Miltie. Dave'll have to wear a dress. He won't let Paul Shaffer drone on. He'll have to fix his teeth."

Odds were still leaning toward Dave taking over.

Leno kept waiting for the ax. In the December 19 issue of *TV Guide*, Jay got some sympathy: "Cheers to Jay Leno, who's had a lot of tough press lately, for keeping his composure — and his ratings — as the host of *The Tonight Show* on NBC. Through a blitz of bad publicity, mixed reviews and kicks from rivals, Leno has kept his, uh, chin up.... "

TV Guide's January 2 issue was full of the guessing game:

"Rumor: NBC's already decided not to match CBS's $28 million two-year bid. Fact: 'It's not a done deal,' says a senior NBC executive."

"Rumor: Dana Carvey may bolt to CBS after January. Fact: NBC insists its deal with Carvey is ironclad."

"Rumor: Chevy Chase has cold feet about his upcoming late-night show on Fox. Fact: Chase is 'already looking for an executive producer,' says a Fox insider.

The New York Times called the Jay-Dave situation "one of the highest-stakes games of television poker ever played. And nobody yet knows who's bluffing... Two weeks ago (in early December) when CBS pushed that huge pile of chips on the table... NBC seemed certain to fold its hand quietly and conserve its money to fight another day. But the pressure on NBC to stay in the game... seems to be increasing every day." Another *Times* article quoted an executive as asking "After everything else that's happened to them, how can they [NBC] afford to lose Letterman?"

While Leno sweated it, a lot of people had a good laugh. Garry Shandling brought in Dana Carvey for an episode of his *Larry Sanders Show.* Larry Sanders and his producer (played by Rip Torn) corner Carvey and grill him:

Larry: We need to know if you're gonna take that talk show offer.

Producer: Just answer the question, ya little asshole!

Dana: I don't know.

Larry: I know you know!

Dana: I'm taking the deal at NBC.

Larry: I hate this fuckin' business!!!

Jay hated the way NBC was dragging its feet. He

reminded the media that if he was let go, he'd be set for life. His contract included a severance pay clause that was worth about ten million bucks.

On the air, Leno pointed to a news item: President Bush had pardoned Casper Weinberger. Jay said he admired Bush for "being loyal to employees who were loyal to him. *I hope NBC's listening.*"

Jay even demonstrated some loyalty to his old boss, Johnny Carson. He showed a news clip of the retired legend getting the Medal of Freedom: "Johnny Carson left the Nebraska plains to preside over late night TV for almost 30 years. With a quick wit and a sure golf swing Johnny's good natured humor kept the pulse of the nation and assured us that even in the most difficult times it was still OK to laugh. The United States honors Johnny Carson who personifies the heart and humor of America."

Warren Littlefield was firmly in Jay's corner. Having Dave constantly running a beady-eyed photo of Warren and intimating he was a little pissant certainly hadn't helped. Of Letterman, Littlefield muttered, "A very tough guy to read. David is a complex man and it's hard to know what he's thinking."

As far as Dave was concerned, it was easy to know what an NBC exec was thinking. Just hold his head up to the light.

All through the negotiations, Dave continued to insult G.E. and NBC. One night he told a joke about the Pope. When it got a laugh, Dave said "Thank you!" and let his audience in on a secret. Two programming wizards and a psychologist had spent three hours with him discussing whether or not to do the Pope joke.

He imitated them breathlessly asking, "Are we pressing any hot buttons?"

He looked into the camera and told them, "Hey, press this!"

The audience roared. Dave groused, "How would

you like to spend three hours at a meeting with NBC nitwits!"

Leno was beginning to feel the same way. He told *his* audience about the CBS deal and NBC's reaction:

"Everybody knows this: After taking baseball away from NBC, CBS made David Letterman a big offer. CBS reportedly wants to steal away Dana Carvey, too. But NBC is fighting back at CBS. They're not takin' it lying down. In fact today, they made an offer to woo *The Hat Squad* over to NBC... You got to get up pret-ty early in the morning to put one over on NBC... "

Letterman always disdained "people who, without show business, would have no skills that warrant a paycheck."

Leno was disdaining the way NBC was leaving him hanging for so long. Now that the affiliates and the audience were on his side, Jay was saying on the air: "One out of every three men is afraid of long-term commitment. If you ask me, one out of every three TV networks is afraid of long-term commitment!"

Letterman didn't want all the super-agent money talk and big-time negotiations to confuse his fans: "I don't mind being accused of being a bad comedian and I don't even mind being accused of being a bad talk-show host. But I never want to be accused of being an arrogant, pompous showbiz asshole."

January 15 was the last day NBC could make a deal. They had kept squirming for months, but finally, a few days before the 15th, they gave up. CBS announced Dave was officially theirs.

Dave broke the news to his audience by coming out and saying: "I'm David Letterman. Don't mind me, I'm just a temp."

Jay Leno told his audience, "I don't care if you laugh. I GOT THE JOB!"

And over at ABC, Ted Koppel said, "I am delighted

that David is now making enough money to buy slacks to match his jackets."

On January 14 Dave unveiled the "Top 10 Reasons I'm Leaving NBC:

10. Heads CBS, tails CBS.

9. It just makes sense since I'm already commuting with Andy Rooney.

8. At last minute, CBS kicked in a new set of Michelins.

7. I've stolen as many G.E. bulbs as I can fit in the garage.

6. In order to grow as an artist, I feel it's important to do the same crap over at CBS.

5. Tired of being sexually harassed by Bryant.

4. Can't convince them to do another Triplecast.

3. Finally realized not only were they never going to make me an anchorman, but that technically speaking, this isn't even a news show.

2. CBS had the best Amy Fisher movie.

1. They insist I wear pants.

Jay breathed a public sigh of relief. He told the *Tonight Show* audience, "This whole thing has been so stupid. It was a strange position to be in: to be told you're either gonna be fired or you're gonna be our hope to bring *The Tonight Show* into the 21st century. I didn't know who was more nervous yesterday, me or the guy at the NBC concession stand with the ten thousand *Tonight Show with Jay Leno* T-shirts."

He intimated that revenge would be sweet. Eventually *his* contract would be up for negotiation, and he'd narrow the gap between his yearly $3 million and Dave's estimated $14 million.

The New York Times actually wrote an editorial about Letterman's move. After pointing out that Dave would now earn millions: "Mr. Letterman departs angry that NBC gave *Tonight* to the comedian Jay Leno and kept Mr. Letterman in a later slot. Thus ends months of power plays and poisoned leaks that would have done Machiavelli proud... The lesson for the week: in show business, petulance pays."

TV Guide congratulated Jay: "Beneath the quips was another Jay Leno. Shrewd. Tough. Relentless. A man who mapped out a strategy that brought him victory in the most nerve-racking soap opera in recent TV history."

Anxious to patch up the negotiation war with Dave, Jay Leno made a little speech to the *Tonight Show* audience. He said, "Before I introduce my first guest maybe I should address this whole Letterman thing with Dave and I. Just so people know, I read some articles and some things, and maybe some people perceived Dave to be the bad guy or something. And it's not really the case.

"This is sort of a job that everybody wants and I've been in here and it wasn't a matter of both of us auditioning for the job. It was a matter of, well, do we hire Jay or keep David or what do we do? And they chose to keep us on, which I'm glad. David will be going to CBS, but all through it Dave has been nothing but a gentleman, never anything sleazy or underhanded. And quite the contrary, we've both had quite a few laughs watching NBC attempt to weasel around these two situations. So we wish him the best of luck at CBS. I'm sure he will be a formidable competitor that will certainly keep us on our toes here. God bless him and his staff and good luck."

And then, a week later, as Bill Clinton took the oath of office, Jay staged his own ceremony. With Judge Rheinhold (who said Jay couldn't be subtle with his humor?) doing the honors, Leno put his hand on a *TV Guide* and heard the oath:

"Do you, Jay Leno, solemnly swear to uphold the fine traditions of NBC, former home of *Cosby*, former home of *Cheers*, former home of *Golden Girls*, former home of *Matlock?*"

"I do."

"Do you swear to make substantially less money than any other late night talk show host?"

"I do."

"Do you swear to do everything in your power to keep *The Tonight Show* number one even though the network is number three?"

"I do."

"Do you swear to remain host of *The Tonight Show* as long as you are able, or until NBC decides to replace you with the next pretty face that comes along? Then by the power vested in me by the General Electric corporation, defense contractor and maker of the 3-way bulb, I now pronounce you *still* host of *The Tonight Show!*"

As for Dave, the announcement that he was moving from the 12:30 time slot was cause for some relief: "The woman who used to break into my house... is now breaking into Dana Carvey's house!"

David Letterman's move to CBS ended one drama. But Dave hadn't decided *where* he'd do the show for CBS.

This was good for several more weeks of hijinks. He had made the networks sweat. Now he'd get some revenge on New York City. It was more fun than having announcer Bill Wendell growl, "From New York! Borderline psychotic? Come on down! It's *Late Night with David Letterman!*"

The depressed-looking mayor of New York City, David Dinkins, wearily led the pleas for Letterman to stay. One Dave to another, Dinkins declared, "We will not permit him to leave New York.... we love him here." Dinkins pointed out that thousands of jobs and millions of tourist dollars were at stake.

Everybody had a "Top Ten" list of reasons why Letterman shouldn't move to California. *The New York Times* reasoned:

10. Earthquakes.

9. Cher Lives There.

8. New York Has More Stupid Pets.

7. No Skyscraper Backdrops.

6. I Love New York (Really).

5. What Speed Limits?

4. No Leggy Rockettes

3. Ocean on Wrong Side.

2. Paul Would Burn, Not Tan.

1. One Word: Buttafuoco.

A Brooklyn councilman, Stephen DiBrienza, gave his Top Ten at a City Hall rally. His reasons why Dave shouldn't move to Los Angeles:

10. Right on red — just too complicated.

9. "La La Land" even dumber slogan than "Big Apple."

8. Not easy being funny in the middle of a riot.

7. L.A.'s idea of mass transit: the San Andreas fault.

6. Pacific Time Zone could really throw off Dave's delivery.

5. Buttafuoco! Buttafuoco! Buttafuoco!

4. Cigar would put L.A. on permanent smog alert.

3. Dinkins vs. Stein vs. Giuliani — grab the popcorn.

2. Lead poisoning? Hey, at least we have water.

1. Our roads and bridges take years to collapse — not seconds.

The *New York Daily News* unveiled its list of Top "Ten Reasons David Letterman Should Not Move His Show to California"

10. Connecticut State troopers won't meet their ticket quotas.

9. The World's Most Dangerous Band belongs in a dangerous city.

8. Unlike N.Y.C., L.A. is not a city that makes its own gravy.

7. "Let's Look for Swedes" would be boring.

Everyone in California looks like a Swede.

    6. No more John Gotti jokes.

    5. No more radioactive-steam-explosion jokes.

    4. No more pedestrian races. California has no pedestrians.

    3. Meg.

    2. Studio audiences would no longer include interesting people with police records.

    1. Earthquakes! Earthquakes! Earthquakes!

And then there was the *Newsday* version:

    10. Dan Quayle won't visit.

    9. Only fault line is under unfinished Second Avenue subway.

    8. Won't have to entertain guests in hot tub.

    7. New York sewage has more cachet.

    6. California's governor can't play stick ball and *Hamlet* at the same time.

    5. Dogs here don't wear Ray Bans.

    4. Wouldn't miss Donald Trump's comeback.

    3. New York studio pages better at gang control than Los Angeles Police Department.

    2. Can still get car fixed at Joey Buttafuoco's garage.

    1. Al Sharpton won't relocate.

If anything would produce a quick decision from Letterman, it was the prospect of reading any more Top Ten lists.

CBS agreed to spend over four million bucks to renovate the Ed Sullivan Theater on Broadway at 53rd Street and give him office space in the adjoining 12-story building. Seating capacity: 300 seats, nearly double the number available at Rockefeller Center.

Dan Rather, the CBS news anchorman, came on Dave's show to congratulate him on the move. He said Dave was lucky to be getting the new theater instead of having to work at the CBS building: "There's rats in that building the size of armadillos."

Dave answered, "You know the rats in this building are programming the place!"

Dave gave his own Top Ten reasons why he decided to stay:

10. Didn't want to give up my table at Blimpies.

9. I'd miss driving through Lincoln Tunnel with my eyes closed.

8. After 11 years away from L.A. I finally manage to lose my Chicano accent.

7. Would rather be shot at on subways than freeways.

6. Couldn't get cheap applause by saying New York audiences are best-looking in all of television.

5. I have a biological need to stay close to Tom Brokaw.

4. East Coast girls are hip, we really dig those styles they wear.

3. L.A. phone book doesn't contain one Buttafuoco.

2. Woman who keeps breaking into my house didn't feel like moving to L.A.

1. Three words: Times Square Sushi.

Actually, Dave insisted, the main reason he had to stay in New York was simple: "I promised Amy Fisher I'd wait for her."

And so the stages in New York and California were set. But what about Jay and Dave?

At a press conference announcing that he would continue on *The Tonight Show*, Jay Leno was more critical of NBC than of Letterman. "There was never an ego problem with David," Leno said. "Never anything cutthroat." Compare that to NBC: "NBC stands for Never Believe your Contract."

It didn't take long for the competition-panic to hit execs at *The Tonight Show*. Some were already comparing Jay and Dave and not liking what they saw. Jay's director insisted that Leno should go on a diet, complaining that Dave was looking a lot slimmer.

Jay said he was hoping for a friendly rivalry with

Dave. Bitterness over all the feuding? "No," said Jay. "Not for this kind of dough."

Letterman also played down the possibility of yet another talk show war. He had kind words for Jay Leno and even for NBC: "I have nothing but great thoughts about eleven years at NBC. What I'll miss most are the back rubs from Irving R. Levine."

Then came word from Cher: "I like talk shows a lot — and I've been offered a lot of money to do a talk show." The only drawback: "I'd want to talk all the time. I don't think that's a good quality in a talk-show host. Even though it hasn't hurt David Letterman."

Dave was asked by *Rolling Stone* to select his own replacement. He went right back to the talk show wars: "You know, I started watching *The Dennis Miller Show* before it was canceled, and I thought, if you're looking for a guy to do a talk show at 12:30, Dennis would be a pretty good choice." Letterman booked Dennis for an appearance, eager to give him some extra exposure.

The fight to take Dave's job heated up in February and March of 1993. Miller, Garry Shandling, the perpetually hyped Rick Reynolds, and Comedy Central's late night host Allan Havey were all contenders, with Martin Short and Dana Carvey opting to pursue film careers. Producer Lorne Michaels even held an "audition night" to screen a bunch of young stand-up performers. Shandling emerged as the favorite, but turned down $20 million to end his HBO contract and move to NBC.

Michaels shocked insiders by going with an unknown, 30 year-old Conan O'Brien, a co-producer of *The Simpsons* and ex-writer for *Saturday Night Live* and *Not Necessarily The News*. This was especially shocking to Leno and Letterman, who'd paid a lot of dues before hostile comedy club audiences and glaring TV cameras before getting their host jobs.

Jay Leno dutifully brought Conan the Unknown out for a bow on April 26th, the night he was annointed. Then he said, "You know, Dave Letterman is a legend here at NBC, and if anything's *fun* to do, it's replacing *legends* at NBC!" The following night he chided the wisdom of hiring a tyro by doing a mock interview with an average guy hired to host a showing following O'Brien. "How did you get the job?" he asked Jim Brogan. "I was just walking in the hallway here at NBC and they said they were looking for unknowns!"

Letterman was equally unenthused. The night the news broke, he told his audience, "I don't know the man, I've never met the man, but we certainly wish him success and happiness...seems like a nice fella." Then came a Top 10 list of tips for Conan, including these:

"A drugged guest is a well behaved guest." "Willard's insane." "GE executives are pinheads; NBC executives are boneheads." "Don't panic if you find a strange woman in your house." "When all else fails, just say 'Buttafuoco.'"

The battle to take the prime 11:30 and 12:30 jobs was over, temporarily. The battle to keep them would begin in August, when the three hosts would start up against each other. And waiting in the wings: Cher? Chevy Chase? Dennis Miller? How about those old CNBC cable talk show hosts back in circulation: Dick Cavett and Tom Snyder?

And what about Johnny Carson? He broke his talk show silence and finally decided between Jay and Dave. He appeared on Dave's show, but chose to do it via an offbeat "cameo." He took a phone call from Dave to answer the question: "Tell us about your lunch!"

Johnny told Dave he had pancakes and bacon.

He told everyone else that he had more than his fill of talk shows, in war and in peace.

As Letterman put it, "The last time I saw him, at the Emmy dinner, he just seemed great and happy. He's really getting a kick out of everybody else's troubles."